Media and Society

The Production of Culture in the Mass Media

John Ryan
Clemson University

William M. Wentworth
Clemson University

Allyn and Bacon
Boston • London • Toronto • Sydney • Tokyo • Singapore

Series Editor: Sarah L. Kelbaugh
Editor-in-Chief, Social Sciences: Karen Hanson
Editorial Assistant: Jennifer Muroff
Marketing Manager: Brooke Stoner
Editorial Production Service: Chestnut Hill Enterprises, Inc.
Manufacturing Buyer: Megan Cochran
Cover Administrator: Jennifer Hart

Internet: www.abacon.com

Between the time Website information is gathered and published, some sites may have closed. Also, the transcription of URLs can result in typographical errors. The publisher would appreciate notification where these occur so that they may be corrected. Thank You.

Library of Congress Cataloging-in-Publication Data

Ryan, John
   Media and society : the production of culture in the mass media /
John Ryan, William M. Wentworth.
     p. cm
   Includes bibliographical references and index.
   ISBN 0-205-17400-0
   1. Mass media and culture. 2. Mass media–Social aspects.
I. Wentworth, William M. II. Title.
P94.6.R93   1998
302.23–dc21   98-25986
                                   CIP

Printed in the United States of America
10 9 8 7 6 5 4 3 2 1   03 02 01 00 99 98

Photo Credits: Photo credits can be found on page 256, which should be considered an extension of the copyright page.

For our families,
Deb and Mollison Ryan
Carlene, Adam, Gracie, and Will Wentworth

Contents

Preface

The other morning, just before dawn, I put on my headphones, turned my personal sound system to public radio, and went for a run. I was in my neighborhood, but barely part of it. I confess that I know few of my neighbors and those whom I do know I know only superficially. Splendid suburban isolation. But I wasn't totally alone. As I circled through the dark streets, I carried National Public Radio's news program *Morning Edition* with me. Through my headphones voices seeped into my brain from Washington, D.C., Jerusalem, and Jakarta. In one sense, because of this ongoing stream of mass-mediated communication, I may know more about what is happening in the Middle East than I do in my neighborhood. However, this is a special kind of "knowing." I am not engaged in conversation with these voices. They bring to my attention and attempt to interpret *for* me selected "events" from the ongoing stream of life around the world. This is not a knowing that arises out of direct experience or social interaction; it is not conversation. It is a form of storytelling.

On this morning, the commentators and reporters are especially excited. The Paula Jones case has been thrown out of court by U.S. Judge Susan Weber Wright. It's a big story, but one senses that the media are disappointed that an even bigger one has, at least for now, slipped away. You can hear the sound of the hotel reservations in Little Rock being canceled. But, NPR correspondent Cokie Roberts seems happy to say (am I reading into this? I can't see her expression, I can't *ask* her how she feels), "Look, the political damage to the president has been done. We have now seen, read all of those stories (about the President's sex life)." Right. But she forgot to say "reported" or, even better, "constructed" those stories. (Incidentally, I know exactly the content of this story because I was later able to go to the National Public Radio Web Page (http://www.npr.org/), locate the story in the archives, and play it back on my computer using RealAudio® Player software. Broadcast news is no longer as ephemeral as it once was.) It occurs to me that the media seem to continually suffer from something akin to "out-of-body" experience in which the person on the operating table has the sensation of floating up to the ceiling and observing his or her body being worked on by the medical staff below. But when the media float up to the ceiling, they don't recognize the body as their own. (Look! Someone's being operated on down there! What a story!"). The media create stories and then report on those stories as if they had nothing to do with them in the first place.

I like this idea so much that when I get home, I go to the *Morning Edition* home page, find the E-mail address and send my insight directly to NPR. Now, this is something a bit more like interaction! I immediately get an automated "thank you" with an apology for its being automated. Over the next few days, I wait to hear my comment on the air. It never happens. Obviously, my brilliance is wasted on the program's producers. This is not interaction after all.

The mass media entertain us and teach us. They comfort us when we're feeling sad or ill. They are present during our most private moments. We embrace mass-media personalities and characters as if they were our friends, and use them as a basis for interacting with our real friends. They are an important form of communication. The mass media have their own constraints and their own agendas. They are our virtual companions. But they are something very different from the kind of companions human beings have had through most of their history. That's what this book is about.

Learning and writing about the mass media at the end of the twentieth century is a bit like watching a bicycle race. I've always thought that, as a live spectator sport, bicycle racing is a little strange. Take the Tour de France, for example. At most you can see one small segment of the entire course. The cyclists flash by in formation—a blaze of color, a whir of gears, and they're gone. At most one gets a snapshot (or better, a video clip) of a few small moments in time. Around the next bend, things may change. Someone may surge out of the pack. But it's harder to ride outside the shelter of the other cyclists. The pack may choose to pursue or hang back, hoping the leader will expend too much energy and burn out. Meanwhile, shifting alliances are made among teams and team members as they choose to draft for each other or block other riders. There are periods of relative rest, attacks, and counterattacks. The configuration is constantly changing.

Studying the mass media is like that too. Some of this book is a snapshot of the mass media during a single period of time. We have tried to place that snapshot in historical context. But the exact technological and organizational configuration of the mass media, like the shifting dynamics of a bicycle race, can't be pinned down. To cite just one example, in the last two years alone, 3,100 radio stations have changed owners. And picking up the paper this morning I learned that Time Warner and U.S. West Media Services are teaming up in the race to control the emerging high speed cable Internet access business, that Multimedia Cablevision (a subsidiary of the newspaper giant Gannett) is trading some cable systems in Kansas with another company (TCI) for a cable system in Chicago, and that our local cable system will soon begin offering 130 channels. I also learned that MTV is planning on spinning off seven more music channels, Disney is launching Toon City (an all-cartoon network to compete with the Cartoon Network), and Nickelodeon is developing four more children's channels. All of this in one day! The pack is shifting and changing shape once again.

Fortunately for you, and for the authors, most of this book is not about creating some definitive portrait of media configurations. This book is mainly about processes. And although the end products may change, the processes remain largely the same. After you read this book, you will have a good idea of those processes through which the mass media have become integral to social life in a large-scale industrial society. We hope that you will understand the processes through which the mass media are enabled and constrained by such factors as technology, law, industry structure, organizational structure, occupational careers, and market. In recent years there have been major changes in each one of these factors and these changes have had important consequences for you and us as media consumers. Hopefully, this book will give you a better understanding of why you have the media choices available to you that you have, making you a better informed consumer. Some of you may want to work in media industries. This book should give you insights into how the industry operates and an unfair advantage over those other applicants who don't have such insights. This is an exciting time to be studying the mass media.

Organization of the Book

This book is divided into two parts. Part I looks at what mass communication is and the place of the mass media in social life. The first chapter highlights the role of communication in human behavior and the evolution toward a system of mass communication. Chapter 2 examines the role of the media in society in the context of insights from classical sociological theorists about how society operates. This is, after all, a book written by and for sociologists. It turns out that Marx, Weber, and Durkheim, as well as Mead, can tell us a lot about how the mass media fit into larger social processes. Chapter 3 looks at the research on individual effects of the mass media, for example, the idea that the mass media can cause aggressive or even violent behavior. We take issue with those (mainly politicians and interest groups) who pose clear and powerful effects. Part of this chapter focuses on the methodological problems inherent in attempting to uncover such effects. Chapter 4 is about broader social effects of the mass media.

Having, in Part I, described what the "machine" (to use another metaphor) does, in Part II, we describe how the machine works. Using the production-of-culture perspective, in separate chapters, we look at the influence of technology, law, industry structure, organizational structure/occupational careers, advertising, and ideas about audience. In practice, these factors all act in concert to influence media content. We separate them here to highlight the special impacts of each.

That is where we are going. But, at the risk of offending the metaphor police, (apologies to Dilbert creator Scott Adams), here's one more metaphor for the road. I have this friend Scott who, in addition to being a renowned historian, songwriter, and Reiki healer, is known for creating great metaphors. I asked him what he thought about studying the mass media. This is the response he E-mailed back:

> *Media is notoriously labyrinthine. We feel our way along its edges during almost every waking moment, yet seldom pierce the center. Analyzing the media, looking beyond the fingerprints, wordsmiths, voices, and electronic corporate entrails, too easily devolves into totalizing metaphors, generating new myths or reanimating old ones.*

In this book we hope we have not succumbed to either of those extremes. We have tried neither to promote old stereotypes nor to generate new myths about the mass media. We want you to appreciate the complexities of both media production and media consumption. We hope we have been successful.

—John Ryan

Acknowledgments

We would like to thank the people who helped make this book possible. We are grateful to Donna Sedgewick, Gabrielle Chapman, Scott Brown, and Wenping Bo for their research assistance. Thanks to Pam Hawthorne and Jen Fries for their administrative assistance. Thanks also to Karen Hanson, Sarah Kelbaugh, and all of the staff at Allyn & Bacon. We are grateful for the insights into mass media issues given us by Michael Hughes, James Hawdon, Michelle Farmer, Rick Shields, Deborah Sim, Scott Bills, Tom Styron, Jeannie Styron, and the late Larry DeBord. A very special debt is owed to Richard Peterson for his mentoring, friendship, and terrific sociological mind.

The following reviewers gave us valuable feedback: Donald Warren, Oakland University; David Croteau, Virginia Commonwealth University; Chet Ballard, Valdosta State University; Roger Salerno, Pace University; Deborah Petersen Perlman, University of Minnesota, Duluth; and Beverly Merrick, New Mexico State University.

We would also like to thank the students who have taken our mass media and social theory courses, especially those at the World Leisure & Recreation Association International Center for Excellence (WICE) in Holland. The chance to discuss media issues with students from as many as twelve different countries in the same class has proven to be an invaluable experience. Thanks to Dr. T. J. Kamphorst for that opportunity.

Part I

The Mass Media and Society

1

Human Communication and the Mass Media

She remembers the "olden" days, before color television. Her 20-year-old remembers the "olden" days, before the VCR. Her 10-year-old remembers the "olden" days, before the CD-ROM. Her four-year-old will remember the "olden" days, too. But before what?
—PRINT ADVERTISEMENT FOR SONY COMPUTERS AND DIGITAL CAMERAS

In 1968 a Michigan family was sitting together watching the nightly news. They were regularly able to see actual footage, in their living room, of that day's war in Vietnam. This was new then, no other war had been televised as it happened. They were especially interested in the war because their son was fighting in it as a Marine Lance Corporal. Suddenly, they recognized their son on the screen, and the next moment he was shot. They were horrified as only parents could be. Although they immediately tried to discover how seriously he was wounded, it took several ago-nized days for the military authorities to confirm their worst fears. Their son was dead and they had watched it happen.

This actually happened to a family known to one of the authors. This family went from supporting the war to being against a war their son had willingly gone to fight. It is believed that many people had this reaction, even if the sons of others were the ones they saw on their TV sets. The impact of media coverage of Vietnam and of war protests at home is believed to have been a factor in turning the tide of public opinion against that U.S. military action.

While the experience of this family was unusual, it was, in a sense, an example of what Charles Perrow (1984) calls a "normal accident"—an almost inevitable result of the capabilities and uses of a particular technology. What happened to this family was made possible by the technology of modern mass communication. The news of their son's death was brought to these parents by technology that transcends boundaries of space and time, by a medium of communication that is well suited to presenting graphic images, by a legal and cultural system that allows for relatively open exchange of information, and by organizational decision makers attempting to grab and hold the attention of the viewing public in order to attract sponsors and make a profit. But such communication is never totally free and unrestricted. Twenty years after the Vietnam incident, despite advances in technology that would make pictures from the battle front easier to obtain and deliver, no such images of human carnage were shown from The Gulf War of 1991. Instead, television showed images of "smart missiles" hitting military targets with precise accuracy, accompanied by play-by-play explanations from Pentagon officials. Journalists were kept away from the front, obtaining their information from carefully orchestrated briefings. A lesson had been learned from the Vietnam experience.

We live in a world that is saturated with mass-mediated communication. We can awaken to recorded music, switch to a weather station, and read the newspaper—all before breakfast. TV can be used to relax, to arouse, to inform, and to prepare ourselves with content for tomorrow's conversations at school or work. And the "entertainment center" where our TV resides is simultaneously a piece of furniture, a complex symbol of status, a demonstration of particular aesthetic tastes, and a structure that allows us to organize and control our use of several media types, perhaps with the aid of a "universal remote."

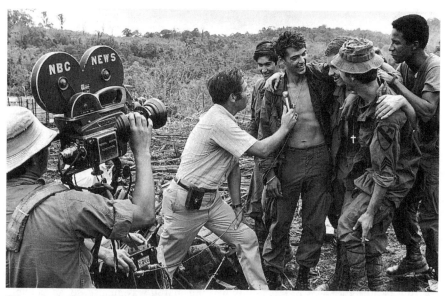

The mass media carried visual images of the Viet Nam War directly into the living rooms of America. Some have argued that these images helped erode public support for the war.

The lessons of Viet Nam resulted in carefully orchestrated media briefings during the Gulf War.

While the exact effects of the mass media are not yet clear, we know that the mass media attempt to influence what we consume, what we talk about, what humor we like, how we dress our bodies and furnish our homes, how we spend our time and money, and what themes enter into the private quarters of our life. Some would argue that even our basic beliefs, attitudes, and values are influenced by the mass media. Mass media images can provide information about our place in society. Are we: rich or poor, behind the times or fashionable, eating right or digging our graves with our teeth, informed or ignorant, conservative or liberal? The mass media may play a part in constructing our sense of who we are and our relative standing in society.

Thus the mass media penetrate deeply into the most private and personal areas of our lives while appealing to huge audiences. It is ironic that the various media for carrying the messages of our public institutions are now themselves a public institution (see McLuhan 1964). The meaning of the mass media goes beyond the content of the messages sent. Society as we know it cannot exist without the mass media. Just try to imagine how the removal of all media would change your day. Think further about how the absence of mass media would ripple through society. Education, conversation, sports, politics, shopping, attitudes, even your drive to school or work and religion (no televangelists, published lists of churches or Religion Sections in the local paper, religious videos, tapes and books, and there would be a few, but very expensive, Bibles) would all be different.

In this book we will examine what the mass media are, the processes through which they create and disseminate their messages, factors that influence those messages, and the impact of all this on individuals and society. Before we can begin to understand the role of the mass media in human life, we need some understanding of the basic dynamics of human behavior, and, especially, of the dynamics of human communication.

Understanding Human Behavior

Because human beings are so vulnerable at birth, and for years after, some sort of cooperation is necessary for human life to survive. Human beings, therefore, form groups in an attempt to meet needs and desires. Compared to many other creatures on this planet, even in adulthood we are relatively weak, so the survival of humans is dependent on cooperation. Of course, many animals and insects cooperate as well. For example, ants have something like a social system. There are a status hierarchy, cooperative roles, and so on. Ants seem to do this naturally as the result of genetic programming. However, this does not appear to be true for human beings. Just by tuning into an evening newscast or by reading the morning paper we can find evidence that human beings do not naturally cooperate. Crime, wars, legal battles—all indicate that considerable effort must be expended to bring about cooperation.

Not only do human beings not appear to be genetically programmed to cooperate, evidence suggests that *no* complex behaviors are genetically preprogrammed. Imagine that, on reaching puberty, you suddenly felt the urge to go to a building supply store and purchase building materials. Imagine also, that with virtually no training, you found yourself constructing a home almost exactly like the one that your parents live in. This certainly would be a built-in, complex behavior, but no such genetic instructions exist in human beings. However, in the animal world, analogous behavior does exist. Young birds, even if raised in isolation, are still capable of building nests almost exactly like those of other members of their species. Genes certainly do influence behavior, but only in a complex interaction with learning. As one biologist (Hubbard and Wald 1993:10) has written:

> *...genetic explanations are as confining as they are liberating. Genes participate in all the ways we function, but they do not determine who we are. They must affect our development, but so do a host of personal and social circumstances.*

Genes clearly determine sex, skin color and eye color. Genes, in interaction with in utero conditions and socialization, affect such things as height, weight, intelligence, activity level, and so on. These traits then lead to different socialization experiences. Once an infant is labeled a male or a female, an elaborate socialization process kicks in to make sure that the infants develop what are considered appropriate gender identities and behaviors. We also know that people are responded to differently because of their height, weight, and other physical factors. Returning to behavior, genes are most important when we are very young, before genetic impulses are overlaid with learning. The most important point here is that, in human beings, control by genes has been replaced by social rules. This allows for much greater flexibility and adaptability. Because of this flexibility, human beings can live in many different physical and social environments.

When sociologists look at the world, they see the stated and unstated rules that are present, and how these rules make social life possible. It is also possible to examine the degree to which social rules are understood, agreed with or disagreed with, and differentially applied. What is key for our discussion of communication is the transmission of those cultural rules.

Transmission of Cultural Rules

Because human beings are not preprogrammed to follow social rules, each generation must be taught the basic practices of its culture. The term for this is **socialization** and individuals and groups that perform this function are known as **socialization agents.** Socialization agents in our culture include: family, peers, schools, churches, and the mass media.

No matter which agents are involved, the socialization process involves the use of symbolic communication. This is because, as far as we know, no human being is directly able to experience the consciousness of another. We are each trapped inside our own biology and awareness, and it is through signs and symbols that we reach out to others. These signs and symbols include language, gestures, body language, and facial expressions.

A **sign** is something that stands for something else. For example, in the classic example of conditioning, Pavlov's dogs learned to associate the sound of a bell with the fact that food would soon be available. When the dogs heard the bell, they began to salivate in anticipation of the food they expected would follow. Of course, the dogs did not create the sign; their brains automatically associated the two events and they had no control over it. Human beings can be conditioned to respond to signs as well. But, unlike Pavlov's dogs, human beings have the capacity to *create* signs. **Language** is a system of signs that is actually created by, and given significance to, by human beings. Signs are arbitrary. That is, there is no inherent connection between the signified (an object for example) and the signifier (a word). For example, a table (the signified) can be represented by such signifiers as the words *table* in English and *mesa* in Spanish. Both of these words refer to the same object, but in different languages. The sound is arbitrary. What is important is that we agree on the object the sound stands for.

Signs are also fundamentally social. We do not call a table a *table* because that sound was accidently associated with the object. We call it a *table* by social agreement. Gestures, body language, and objects can also be agreed-on signs. If someone cuts you off in traffic, you may use a gesture to communicate your feelings. That gesture can be as loaded with meaning as any word. Like other social agreements, signs tend to be taken very seriously, despite their relative arbitrariness. In general, if you go around thinking up new words for objects for which there is already agreement, you would be, at best, considered a little eccentric. However, some friendship groups and subcultures do exactly that in order to distinguish themselves from other groups.

The ability to communicate symbolically has powerful implications for social life. This ability allows for the shifting of the very boundaries of space and time. Not only are we able to express our experiences, point of view, hopes, beliefs and values, and to understand those of others more fully, various media allow us to accomplish this without even being in the presence of the other. The written word, for example, allows us to know the thoughts of someone we have never met, or who may have died hundreds of years ago.

Communicating through signs and symbols is a complicated process. For example, in a two-person communication, the sender (person A) must select signs that come close to accurately representing what he or she is trying to convey. The fact that this is often a struggle is represented by the number of times we "can't find the words" or find ourselves explaining, "what I *meant* to say was…" While person "A" may be struggling to send the right information, person "B" may be having problems *receiving* the message. Perhaps the meaning of the words is not clear, perhaps the receiver is attending to something else internally or externally. Or, perhaps, because of past experiences, the receiver is reading into the signs meanings that were not intended. Suppose, for example, that persons "A" and "B" are involved in a romantic relationship. Person "A" is interested in continuing the relationship but feels that she should limit her contact with person "B" to once a day in order to better complete her school work. Person "B" is just recovering from a relationship in which he was rejected by his partner. Because of this biographical experience, he may read the communication from person "A" as yet another rejection, even though it was not intended as such. Because of such misunderstandings, human communication is always subjective. It is further complicated by our ability to manipulate communication— for example, not to tell the truth or to bend the truth to our needs. Person "B" is aware that person "A" may, in fact, just be using the pressures of school work as an excuse to distance herself from him.

The point is that we can never directly know the inner thoughts, beliefs, and values of another. We must rely on signs to reach out to others. Thus signs are not only created in a social context, they make social life possible. Communication is at the heart of social life. Yet communication is open to interpretation and misunderstanding. As we shall see, this problem of interpretation can be intensified as we move from face-to-face to mass-mediated communication.

The Media of Communication

Signs are not always communicated in direct interaction with another person. For communication to take place, a medium or mechanism for carrying signs from one person to another is required. In face-to-face interaction in which individuals are using words as signs, the medium of communication is sound waves created by the speaker's vocal cords and mouth. When the signs created by a person's voice need to be carried great distances, the original sound waves may be converted into radio waves or television signals, encoded in compact disks, and so on. Written signs can be dispersed through books and magazines, and pictures through television or film. Thus radio, recordings, television, and books are media of communication. Typically, media are classified into print, electronic, and photographic media. However, as we shall see, these boundaries are becoming increasingly blurred.

The media discussed in this book are called **mass media.** This is because the messages carried over these media are capable of reaching very large audiences. The term *mass* refers to the audience of the media. During the latter nineteenth century and on into the first several decades of this century, the term *mass* was used disparagingly by societal elites. This idea had its roots in the French Revolution when the social position and culture of the aristocracy were challenged by the larger population. As the populace gained more rights, the upper classes used cultural choices as a way of distinguishing themselves from the masses. The "masses" were the lower classes ("the Great Unwashed"), later, the millions of workers who flooded into the newly industrializing cities seeking jobs. Folk culture was seen as inferior to elite culture and the emerging mass media (e.g., the penny press) were accused of lowering cultural standards generally and provoking unrest by producing material appealing to lower-class tastes. The term *mass* is no longer used in this way, but the media are still blamed for various social ills.

Critiques of the value of cultural symbols are not limited to popular culture and the mass media, as is shown by persistent controversies surrounding the activities of the National Endowment for the Arts. Later on in this book we will examine some of the criticisms of the products of mass media and the evidence for and against those criticisms.

The Mass Audience

Without making the value judgments inherent in the critique of mass culture, we can say that the **"mass" audience** is *one that lives in no particular place, is not viewed in terms of individual members, and is large.* The boundaries of race, class, region (e.g., "southerner," "east European"), gender, and nationality that we typically live within do not apply to the mass audience. Usually, members of a mass audience do not and cannot interact with other segments of the audience. The characteristic audience member would not know if the people of France or Japan—or those in the next traffic lane—were a part of the audience. A mass audience generally is made up of many different types of people, and has no internal organization, no self-awareness, and does not act on its own behalf. Certainly the producers of mass media content "target" people with certain demographic properties, but the actual audience is not predictable. No one could easily know in advance that Sylvester Stallone's *First Blood* would be popular in Beirut, Lebanon, or that *The X-Files* would be a hit in Taiwan.

The makers of the original *Star Trek* had no clue as to how vast and enduring its audience would become. Nor could they predict that *Star Trek* would successfully spill over into film, print, software, and video game media, and into all the audiences these affect. When such a spillover occurs, look at its surprising consequence for the term *mass audience,* and for the scale of media effects on their audiences: other media and industries (e.g., toy and garment) became part of the audience, as well as components of the technological and cultural means to expand and diversify the audience. A mass audience is composed of a variety of actors, some flesh and blood, others corporate. Later in this book we shall see how organizations and industries become the audience for cultural products. For those surprised by the inclusion of organizations and industries ("corporate actors"), including the media industry, within the concept of "media audience," think about fan clubs. The fan club is like a corporation, an organization of durable relationships among persons who recognize their mutual connections and purpose. The parallels and similarities between the two, as well as their differences, could be explored at length. But the heart of the matter is that they are both organizations influenced by connection to the media. No one would deny a fan club's status as an audience, even as it profits from the sale of memorabilia.

In some sense, we all know what the mass media are. They are the press, radio, television—all the means of spreading information rapidly to large segments of large societies. This most narrow view of the mass media refers precisely to the technological apparatus that literally carries or transmits information. That is the strictest sense of the word *medium:* a means of communicating information. The **media** most often referred to as mass media are *television, radio, motion pictures, newspapers, books, magazines, and sound recordings.* We will primarily focus on these seven media in this text. However, this notion of mass media, while standard, is something of an oversimplification.

The Mass Media as a Concept

Admittedly, the term *mass media* is not one that can be defined with exact clarity. Some media are clearly "mass media." Here we could include radio, recordings, cinema, and television. Other media may be included—billboards or public education—only to raise the eyebrows of many media scholars. Still other media would never be called *mass media*. The bulletin board in the school hallway, graffiti on the bathroom wall, and Barbie dolls will never make the accepted list of mass media.

Other Media

As noted above, the term *mass media* typically refers to television, print, radio, and recording media. However, let us briefly explore some media on the conceptual fringes. We will examine billboards, greeting cards, public education, and Barbie Dolls for their status as mass media. In relation to the criteria listed in the previous section, we will see that there is no firm reason to exclude these under that concept—except, historically, analysts have not included them.

Compare a college radio station to two manifestations of billboard technology. Many college radio stations are low-wattage broadcasts whose signals carry only a few miles. Perhaps a given station would potentially reach 30,000 listeners, if all their radios were on and tuned to that station. Mostly just a few hundred people are listening. Is this station really a member of the mass media? It is, after all, radio.

On great occasions of state, 1,000,000 people gather in Tiananmen Square in the capitol city of Bejing to witness cultural symbols of Chinese unity and leadership. There they see giant "billboard" portrayals of their leaders, of military prowess, and of economic progress. And think of a billboard soft drink advertisement visible from an interstate highway leading into New York City. Five million people a year pass by that billboard, and versions of that same ad are on billboards around the world. For example, in 1965, one of the authors was several miles from any village in the African nation of Chad. The area was desertlike and the "road" was a nearly invisible foot trail in the dry soil. In the distance some artificial structure loomed. As he approached the intersection of two such trails "in the middle of nowhere," he was able to see that this structure was a billboard showing the same soft drink that was on the billboard outside New York. If a uniform message from a single source is indiscriminately available to millions of people, perhaps around the world, can you not claim that billboards are a technology of the mass media?

The next potential member of the mass media is very interesting indeed. Imagine a medium so cunning that we let it have our thoughts and then express them for us. Even though we may add a few of our own words, our innermost feelings for loved ones are translated into the categories and phrases of this medium. Intimate life is thus reduced to the level of icons. But, as the Hallmark slogan says, "when you care enough to send the very best," what could be wrong? Probably nothing is wrong with sending greeting cards, yet it is somehow odd to have distant strangers—artists, writers, and executives—trying to guess what I might want to say to my aunt when her husband, my uncle, dies. If I can't find my own words for sincerity, I'll buy those published by an impersonal corporation. If I want to be cute, or clever, on the occasion of my brother's birthday, I buy cute or clever. While it is true that I shop for the card that best suits me, I am limited by what someone else has decided to offer the public. Were I to take the time to be creative on my own, at least the limits and the message are mine. That is not the issue, however. The greeting card business has not always been big business. Individually and culturally, we have been converted by ads and persuaded by the product to accept greeting cards as the language centerpiece for so many of our social exchanges. The rise of the greeting card consumer demonstrates how manufactured images and messages are sold as commodities and penetrate into and mingle with our private lives.

What about public education as a medium of mass communication? Currently the United States has about 50,000,000 children in grades K–12, and 14,000,000 young adults in college. The curriculum is sufficiently uniform that, for example, a Missouri child in fourth grade or a ninth grader from Oregon can transfer to any other state, staying in the same grade with no gain or loss of credit. College courses routinely transfer between institutions with very little slippage. Every day massive amounts of information are being transmitted to millions of students of every heritage, region, and social class in the United States This information demonstrates sufficient equivalency and simultaneity for states and colleges to guarantee transfer students reciprocity. Admittedly, schools could be considered a multimedia event (from teachers talking, to books, to educational programs via satellite), but the "school" or the "school system" is a medium with an elaborate social technology for passing sharply delimited educational "programming" to a mass audience.

Somehow the "school" seems a less plausible example of a mass medium than billboards. But why? Is it the educational function? Many countries use their electronic media for educational purposes. Is the school system too decentralized in its organizational structure? Some traditional mass media appear decentralized as well. For example, the United States has approximately 10,000 separate radio stations, although, admittedly, many are grouped under relatively centralized administrations. At the same time, the school systems of several countries are run with highly centralized administration and use standardized curricular content. Is the school system too empty of political themes? Many mass media do broadcast messages replete with political content (e.g., Rush Limbaugh). In some Communist countries schools have been used to focus particular messages of political and cultural "propaganda," just as the governments have used radio and television broadcasts. Fairly or not, U.S. schools have been criticized from the left and from the right for doing the same, and for creating a climate of cultural imperialism. While school curricula do not reach the audience in the same standardized ways that traditional media do, the point is that the modern school system at least approaches such standardization. If the functions of the two forms can be similar and interchangeable with respect to messages and to audience, is it merely a matter of tradition to say that radio is part of the mass media and schools are not? Where do you draw the lines that exclude schools from this concept?

Can the Barbie Doll reasonably be examined as an example of the mass media? Let us set a context for comparison. Suppose a public radio station broadcasts a show discussing the social and political messages hidden in *Gulliver's Travels*. Suppose further that public TV aires a series on the social landscape that spawned modern art and then discusses how that genre attempted to express the conditions from which it emerged. *Gulliver's Travels* was produced for the mass print medium of its time; modern art is a medium in its own right, just not a mass medium. These programs bring to the attention of their audiences cultural products that served one function (entertainment, aesthetic experience) yet symbolized, or unobtrusively carried, another message. Here we arrive at the Barbie Doll phenomenon.

Barbie was introduced in 1959 as a teenage fashion model by the Mattel corporation. It is the world's all-time, best-selling doll: Millions have been sold and played with by the little girls of several generations. Can Barbie function as a toy and be a medium of mass communication (carrying the symbols of a cultural message to large numbers of people)? Some people have criticized her as if this were true. (See, for example, Norton et al. 1996).

Barbie, it seems, has been criticized at various times in terms of sexism, racism, and elitism. It is said that she gives little girls several not so subtle cultural messages. Barbie idealizes a particular female form that is unattainable for most women. This popular toy elevates the superiority of being like such a woman. And, while her accessories are lavish (e.g., Barbie drives a Corvette), she usually has no visible means of support, Barbie tells little girls that being rich without an occupation is the fitting life for a woman. These criticisms have been leveled at the Barbie Doll only because it is so successfully mass-produced and has the potential for very widespread "audience" contact. Perhaps Barbie is so popular with so many little girls because she does

Barbie is a widely popular, mass-produced item that carries several cultural messages to the children who play with her.

symbolize desirable, if politically incorrect, ideals. The "action figures" that excite little boys carry the symbols of unattainable powers, unlikely physiques, the battle of good against evil, and the routine use of violence. A toy is not only a toy, it is a cultural product bearing the messages of that culture. When that toy is mass-produced, and when the messages it carries are sufficiently shared among consumers, it becomes a medium of mass communication. From this perspective, Barbie is "the media."

The conversion of "toy" into "symbolic medium" is not where this line of reasoning stops. In the human world things are never exclusively as they first appear. Barbie Dolls and The Wolverine (or G. I. Joe, etc.) action figures are also examples of the mass-produced output of capitalism. They are market commodities subject to all the forces that act on the market. Yet each and every such product carries a message, although the message is not as explicit as in more narrative forms of communication.

Marshall McLuhan, a highly influential but scientifically marginal analyst of the mass media back in the 1960s and 1970s, was among the first to study this natural conversion among social forms as it applied to the media. Within one of his larger works he did a case study of the light bulb (a mass-produced technological object) as a message-bearing cultural object. He noted the "meaning" of the light bulb and the specific ways in which that meaning has changed our lives. From such thinking he derived his famous equations: (1) the medium is the massage (McLuhan 1962); (2) the medium is the message (McLuhan 1967).

Above, drawing on McLuhan's work, we discussed briefly how the mass media have changed our lives apart from any specific messages they might transmit. Here we are going a little farther. McLuhan's equations can be translated into less cryptic language: Every human act and artifact is meaningful as a cultural product (Equation 1); every human act and artifact "acts back on" (or influences) its creators (like a "massage," Equation 2); all our cultural products both reflect and embody social power—"the pen is mightier than the sword" (combining Equations 1 and 2).

Systematically reading these messages and appreciating the extent of their power is a method for unveiling and studying the underlying political, economic, moral, and social structures of society. Ryan states:

> *The notion that culture reflects social structure, and that cultural symbols can, therefore, be used as tools for uncovering the characteristics of social structure, has long been a dominant formulation of the culture/society relationship…[Accordingly], we need to determine the influence of culture producing organizations on the nature and availability of cultural products (1985: 2).*

In this section we have tried to expand our thinking about what the mass media really are. These examples suggest that the mass media, as usually considered, form only a portion of the media that act on us every day. Sociologically these media are not simply the means toward the end of expressing our cultural outpourings of dance, music, ideas, sculpture, values, and, yes, advertisements. The media are themselves cultural and structural institutions embedded in society and subject to all the complex social forces that influence any institution. Economic, moral, political, aesthetic, and normative constraints—cooperative and competitive, internal and external—shape their latent and intentional messages. At the same time these messages act back on their source. This media "massage" of society effects change and stability in the behaviors, thoughts, and feelings of individuals, and in the course of history.

We can easily understand that each type of informational medium has its limitations. For example, the popular press is not the best medium for transmitting music. Although the lyrics and the musical score can be printed, the performance is lost. By comparison, the media technologies suited to musical performance today can actually enhance the performance. Some even complain that the new technological means of conveying music are *too* good. Flat notes can be fixed, extra noises can be removed, tempos can be made mechanically precise; in short, the humanity of the performance is modified by a technology that favors precision. Radio and television are good transmitters of performance. But they are linear and are therefore not convenient ("user friendly") for conveying words that need to be referenced. Unlike books, magazines, and newspapers, the performance media cannot be skimmed, reversed to review material, indexed, or short-cut in any way. The point is that *media cannot be neutral, each has its technological biases and imperatives.* The messages each carries, then, are shaped by or shaped for the particular technology of the carrier.

There is a distinct advantage to the lack of precision in the definition of *mass media.* That advantage is flexibility. As new media, such as the Internet, emerge, they can be brought into consideration by scholars who already have expertise in studying mass media. Also, media types that fall into the gray conceptual areas encourage scholars to refine their ideas as they explore and compare the various means whereby populations disperse cultural knowledge. Lastly, as we will see over the next several pages, this lack of precision allows us to discover important linkages between culture and structure through the examination of the cultural products of social structure.

As noted earlier, the term *media* is the plural of *medium,* but *medium* is not much used. *The media* is commonly used to denote *the mass media.* Collectively, in the context of (mass) information transmission, the term *media* refers to all the means of spreading cultural knowledge to the media "audience," just described above. Such media provide a new window on collective life. Below we highlight some of the basic characteristics of the mass media that will be developed in this book.

Basic Characteristics of the Mass Media

From Face-to-Face to Mass-Mediated Communication

As noted earlier, the primary medium of communication in premodern societies was face-to-face conversation. That is, whether gossip, news, farming techniques, or traditional poetry was being passed, the involved parties directly interacted with each other. Modern media separate the participating parties in a number of ways. For example, mass media conversation has historically been distinctively one-sided. This is because not everyone has equal access to the mass media and because, until very recently, mass media communication was noninteractive. In mass media communication messages are sent across great distances, produced by anonymous senders unconnected to the audience in space, time, or community. Today the bulk of public communication derives from the "staged show," not the spontaneous conversations or the ritualized meetings of preindustrial society, and much of it occurs between a carefully crafted media "personality" and an anonymous, voiceless audience.

Speed of Communication

Current media provide continuous and rapid dissemination of information. Royal weddings, royal deaths, political speeches, faraway wars, natural disasters, all can be viewed "live" by millions, heard again on our car radios, and called up on our PC in the form of an online newspaper. We have more information than ever before and sorting information becomes as important as gathering it in the first place.

Meta-Information

Mass media offer **meta-information.** Meta-information is information that transcends the local and the particular knowledge of individuals about their immediate lives. Direct, face-to-face encounters with others allow us to discover who they are and what they do, but only as particular individuals. The media, by contrast, continually dispense information to their audiences that depicts and creates the trends, fashions, movements, fads, and statistics that characterize entire populations. At the same time, such information is often provided without regard to the historical context that might help the audience make sense of these events.

On a given day, it would not be startling to learn that Americans have increased the amount of turkey they eat (at the expense of red meat), that their rates of violent crime have gone down, that they are driving more miles per person per year, but that drunk driving and accidents generally are decreasing, that nearly 40 million went without health insurance some time last year, and that there is now a Family Leave Act. And the media also allow us to "be there when it happens" to see the "trendy" products (that we might otherwise never hear of) and see trendsetting people (who can set trends only because the media display them to the world). That is, through the media, we can take part in the birth of fashion, see and hear the debut of what will be the next "hit," or the newest dance or the latest danger (e.g., carjacking). We may not want to know these things, but that is not the point. The point is twofold. We could not know them from our daily conversations with the hometown folks in Utica, Indiana, and we are deluged by them in our everyday contacts with the media.

Audience Involvement

The media allow us to view the public world in the privacy level of our choosing, from solitude, to family, to business associates, to a crowded public place filled with anonymous others. When the physical and social environments are controlled by individual audience members, each member is freer to impose personal meanings on the content of media messages actively. We are not passive creatures who respond with narrow and fixed attitudinal and behavioral patterns to the stimuli of the media. Audience members judge, use, or resist the urgings of media according to their own purposes. How successfully they do so is a matter of some debate.

Audience Participation

Participation as an audience member of a given medium or of a given message is somewhat voluntary. We choose if we will read the newspaper today, when we like to use our CD player (and what CDs we buy), what stations and channels we will tune to, and which of the media we will ignore. The voluntary nature of media participation creates the conditions of an economic market for the products of media. And yet, our behavior is not totally voluntary. Choice is limited, by the "tyranny of the marketplace," to what producers make available. As customers, we can only choose from whatever items are available on the media menu.

A market-based media economy turns the audience member into a "consumer," and not merely an informed citizen or a partner in media-shared culture. On the basis of assessments of audience participation, as measured by subscriptions sold, Nielsen ratings, and other market surveys, individuals become stars, shows become "hits," stations and newspapers can attract advertising revenue, and media products (shows) are selected. With the exception of the occasional "human interest story," the media are frequently faulted for increasingly presenting only attention-catching, emotion-arousing themes of sex and violence, alongside uses of realistic language, and a side-show offering of the truly bizarre. (For example, a Jerry Springer show about mothers having affairs with the boyfriends of their teenage daughters.) The marital distress of England's Prince Charles and Princess Diana was a longstanding favorite of nearly every form of mass communication, as was the story of circumstances surrounding Diana's tragic death. And who was able to escape the painful stories of Nicole Brown and Ronald Goldman in the O. J. Simpson murder case?

The various news media are accused of not airing the good news. In the name of the market and by processes of corporate editorial choice, cultural items are "buried" in the back sections of the newspaper, and many good songs and ideas for shows never make it to the public. Much of the discussion in this book will be devoted to illuminating these processes.

Other Factors Determining Content

Although a strong factor, the market is not the only limit to the content of media information. The media are selective in their carrier functions. Time constraints alone would prevent bringing everything that happens everywhere to their audiences. In addition there are technological and economic impediments to doing so. Media personnel must choose what they transmit from the ongoing stream of daily activity and then shape the resulting information further for technological, economic, cultural, and political environments that form the context of the transmission (Ryan 1985).

Mass versus Specialized Audiences

The reception of media-borne information is nonexclusive and requires little cost and few qualifications (McQuail 1994). That is, almost by definition, much of media fare is intended for consumption by the largest possible audience. Often this leads to a strategy of focusing more on not offending and alienating rather than attracting. But, with the proliferation of media forms, greater specialization is becoming more possible. This specialization sometimes results in the need for greater qualifications on the part of the audience. So, for example, the qualifications for fully appreciating jazz or rap music or cruising the Internet may be greater than for watching a network sitcom.

Assumed Effects

Societies support their media for the reason of assumed media effects on the public. Whether it is businesses buying advertisements in the hope of causing increased sales volume, or governments subsidizing media for the purposes of education and the support of high culture, the sponsor believes in the power of the media. In a narrower consideration, demagogues who have the skills necessary for creating emotional impact in audiences use the mass media to amplify their carrying power. The Nazis may have been the first political party to use the media systematically to propagandize an audience, but they were not the last. All dictators and totalitarian governments use mass media for political control. Nowadays all election campaigns in free societies depend on sophisticated use of the media. Giddens (1989) has argued that public communication is one of the most important components of the nation–state. It is probably true that complex societies on the scale of the United States would probably not be possible without the mass media.

Media Synergy

For reasons of expense, technological requirements, and market, media once tended to exist independently of one another. These features of mass media are being superseded by new forms of mass media. New computer-based technologies are rapidly decentralizing information dissemination processes. These digital technologies include desk-top publishing, E-mail, the Internet, high-speed, programmable FAX machines, virtual "bulletin boards," and the many easily accessible databases (e.g., CD-ROM-based reverse phone books and nine-digit zip code directories with census tracts and other market-relevant data). With these networks and data individuals can get on the "information superhighway" from their homes and not only retrieve information at their own convenience, but also interact and add to available information. Scholarly publication has already started to turn toward electronic publishing, and away from the very slow paper-based media. Meanwhile, however, mass media companies producing different types of products are combining in new and interesting ways.

Perspectives on the Mass Media

The Humanistic Approach

There are a number of ways of studying the mass media, depending on the questions one wants to ask. For example, the humanistic approach treats mass media messages, primarily those intended for entertainment, as texts to be analyzed in order to uncover something about the author, the culture within which the author lives, or to gain perspectives on the human condition. Under this approach, mass media products are judged and critiqued using traditional literary standards. The humanistic method does concern itself with the effects of mass media messages, but this concern is largely confined to speculation about whether or not individuals are intellectually enriched or impoverished by consuming such fare. Examples of titles that suggest this approach are: "A Comparative Analysis of Narrative Structure in the Prime-Time Television Situation Comedy" (Moeder 1996) or "Hero with Two Faces: The Lone Ranger as Treaty Discourse" (Allan 1996).

The Social Problems Approach

Within the social sciences there are three basic approaches to studying the mass media. Two of these approaches, the **social problems approach** and the **mass communications approach,** deal with the content of the mass media and its effects, although in different ways. As noted earlier in our discussion of the mass culture debate, both the medium and the message of mass communications, to use McLuhan's terms, have been viewed with alarm. The medium is viewed with alarm because of its ability to bring together large numbers of people to participate in a common cultural experience. Concern about the message tends to cycle between (1) how messages reflect the interests of powerful groups in society who control the media and (2) what mass media messages say about important issues such as sex-role stereotyping, race relations, and violence. These messages are seen as either influencing or reflecting public opinion about these issues.

The social problems approach relies on content analysis techniques to produce an inventory of the content of mass media messages and on survey research to determine effects. There are drawbacks to this approach, however. Content analysis often looks at messages out of their original context and the categories of content analysis may be subject to the personal biases of the researcher. For example, events such as a murder on a television drama and a cartoon character pushing another character over a cliff may both be categorized as indications of violence. However, not everyone would agree that these events are comparable. Most importantly, since the researcher doesn't know how the messages are interpreted by the audience, effects can only be inferred or studied in non-controlled situations.

The Mass Communications Approach

The mass communications approach attempts to avoid these problems by examining issues that can be studied with experimental and survey research techniques in semi-controlled situations. This approach examines the impact of *particular* programs, advertisements, political campaigns and so on, on particular attitudes, beliefs and behaviors. By using these techniques and by looking for specific effects, the mass communications approach avoids some of the subjectivity of the social problems approach. However, difficulties arise in that the mass communications approach has problems answering the kinds of questions the social problems approach raises—for example, the long-term effects of repeated exposures to the media. It may be that the social problems approach is better suited to drawing inferences about long-term effects and the mass communications approach is better suited for short-term, empirical studies of limited effects. We will examine studies from both of these approaches in Chapters 3 and 4.

The Production of Culture

There is a third social-science approach which is relevant to both of the above perspectives. Known as the **production of culture** perspective (Peterson 1976), researchers using this perspective ask the question, "How is the content of media messages affected by the circumstances of its production?" It is this perspective which informs much of this book. Peterson (1985) has suggested six factors which influence the production of culture: technology, law, industry structure (the number and size of firms within an industry), organizational structure, market, and occupational careers. The basic idea is that these factors act together and separately to shape the cultural products, including mass media messages, that we consume. The production of culture perspective takes issue with the idea that there is any simple resemblance between cultural products and the larger society or even the personality and motivations of the creator. This is due to the fact that mass media messages are typically produced and distributed by large-scale organizations. As we shall see in the coming chapters, these organizations must respond to such factors as the legal/regulatory environment, advertisers, audiences, and the creators themselves. We will see that the technologies of production and dissemination have effects as well. Consequently, the messages may reflect these requirements as much or more than any particular creator's vision. Because of these constraints, it is impossible for mass media messages to reflect the full range of ideas, opinions and perspectives in a given society.

Normally, the production-of-culture perspective does not deal with effects of the mass media. However, effects are important to our discussion for two reasons. First, if the mass media do not have effects, then they are probably not worth studying. From our discussion in this chapter alone, it should be fairly clear that mass media have effects, they just may not necessarily be the effects that are expected or that seem obvious. Second, the belief that the mass media have powerful effects has important consequences for how media organizations do business. The debates over violence on television and "V-chip" legislation are examples of how mass media organizations must deal with effects issues. Because the belief in effects is an important part of the context within which culture-producing organizations work, it is necessary to understand the evidence for and against effects and the methodological issues involved.

Summary

In this chapter we have examined the role of communication in human life. We have seen that symbolic communication is the basis for social interaction. We have also examined some of the consequences of moving communication out of the realm of face-to-face interaction and into the mass media. We defined the characteristics of the mass media and the mass audience and suggested some of the impressive ways that the mass media have become interwoven with modern life. Finally, we examined the various approaches to studying the mass media.

2

Classical Sociological Theory and the Mass Media

Between consciousness and existence stand
communications, which influence such
consciousness as men have of their existence.
—C. WRIGHT MILLS, SOCIOLOGIST

The mass media do not exist separately from the other institutions in society. The mass media are a necessary part of the processes of societal change and maintenance. As it turns out, modern society is constantly changing and has to be functionally supported in this state of "creative destruction." Change or die; that appears to be the rule in post-traditional societies. The meta-information produced by the mass media is a significant source of society's capacity to adapt. This is so because *unlearning* (the old) has become just as important as learning (the new attitudes, perspectives, skills, and technologies). Also, the various media and media-related industries are a large and productive part of the economies of all contemporary societies. Whereas we tend to think of the mass media in terms of their products—books, sitcoms, newscasts, newspapers, hit songs—they are better understood as institutional elements basic to modern society. For these reasons, we should be able to grasp the mass media with the same conceptual tools used to analyze other areas of society.

In this chapter we will apply the classical tradition in sociology to the understanding of the mass media. This will not be the typical analysis of the conflict, functionalist, and symbolic interactionist perspectives familiar to users of most sociology textbooks. These perspectives are usually presented as contrary positions. By contrast, we combine insights from the core sociology in Karl Marx, Emile Durkheim, and Max Weber. As these insights are gathered, we also represent George Herbert Mead because he directly addressed communication between the individual and society. The above listed thinkers are the classical theorists of sociology. They wrote, roughly, between the mid-19th and early 20th century.

Newspapers were penetrating society by the time of the classical theorists, but to a more limited degree than today. (Marx actually worked as a correspondent for European Affairs on the *New York Daily Tribune,* then one of the world's three largest newspapers.) Further, their work came before the explosive growth of the electronic media. Not surprisingly, they had nothing specific to say about the mass media. Early sociologists were engaged in discovering the basic social processes and the effects of social structure. As a whole, their writings did include the discussion of *culture* (the term was not employed as it is today so the theorists used concepts that implied "culture") and communication, but not **mass** communication.

Partly as a result of their silence on the mass media, and mostly because of the rise of behaviorism, sociological theorists were bypassed by early (between the years 1940–1959) mass media researchers. In those years, most media investigation was oriented by the very individualistic perspective of psychological behaviorism. Unlike this early research, sociological theory provides the big picture within which it is easier to unite and interpret the parts. Now, the classical sociological theorists are the foundation for the "culture-production" approach that underlies this entire book. Let us see what we can learn about potential media effects and the place of media in society by extrapolating from the work of classical sociological theorists.

Lessons from the Classics

When their works are taken together, Karl Marx, Emile Durkheim, and Max Weber are an important trio in forming our current conception of "society." They ranged from the strongly "materialist" Marx to the strongly "idealist" Weber, with Durkheim in between. **Materialist** here means the influence of how we organize actual social relationships to produce the necessities of survival. **Idealist** refers to the influence of our understandings about relationships and the uses of resources. Such understandings include moral standards, authority, rationality, and a person's grasp of what is important. Their differing emphases allow them to complement each other.

Despite separate explanatory interests, they all agreed that *there is a robust element of history present in all human interactions.* This was so because whenever people interact an external "thing" forms and becomes a part of all their subsequent, mutually oriented actions, thoughts, and feelings. That external thing is their relationship. A relationship carries the microhistory of the interacting persons. Further, an ongoing relationship with its own specific history is influenced by the past relationships of the separate individuals. This means several individual microhistories fold into the one microhistory of a relationship.

Our relationships tend to stabilize around habits developed under conditions of mutual contact and influence. These habits come to be expected and even demanded by the parties in the relationship. These habits thus have two interesting characteristics: (1) They were developed in the past yet influence the present, and (2) they tend to slip out of the full control of the person who performs them and into the normative expectations of the group.

But there is more of an historical element to these relationships than is implied when we consider just the lives of particular people who develop particular social ties. Our relations have names and expectations that derive from the past: we have *types* of relations, not merely "relations." We engage in marital, sibling, and collegial relations and friendships. We have memberships in voluntary groups, organizations, clans, and societies. No one person fully invents what friendship means or what is expected of friends. How to be a juror in the court system is not a matter of individual whim. Every particular relationship among people has qualities and expectations inherited from the macrohistory of society.

Once you begin to think in this way, you see "history" all around you, and "history" integrated into every aspect of every relation with others. Our general ideas and practices about clothing, hygiene, physical attractiveness, religion, politics, science, architecture, sexuality, common sense, food preferences, values, aspirations— all these, and more, arrive out of macrohistory for our individual use. The bulk of our personal attitudes and practices were created by past generations, even as our groups modify them to pass on to the future. Every piece of technology, from ballpoint pens, to stoves, shovels, and shoes, to radio, television, and books, has a developmental history. The anonymous relations we have with others as an automobile driver (do not try to decide, on your own, the side of the road on which you will drive or that a red light at an intersection means "go"), as a supermarket shopper, as a student, and as a citizen, taxpayer, or voter are similarly derived from long histories.

If the past were not a part of all that we do, each of us and each generation would have to reinvent every aspect of life from scratch. Instead, we "stand on the shoulders of past generations" and, influenced by relations with living others, start our individual climbs through life from there. *Each of our lives is given fundamental direction, form, and content by history.* But society penetrates us even more deeply: (1) The qualities of our impersonal, personal, private, and intimate relationships are forged on the anvil of society; (2) anonymous and external social forces lend shape to each person's private actions, thoughts, and feelings. This is the startling discovery made by the classical sociologists. This is the basic structural effect: An individual's life is not fully his or her own; each life is ordered at another level, even as we each choose how to live in society.

We now call this discovery **social structure**. Social structures are where media effects accumulate, because structures represent the history of people's thoughts, actions, and feelings. Social structures act on media effects just as they act on every other aspect of the person's environment. Structures, through their patterned application of norms and values, help the individual interpret, amplify, dissipate, or oppose media messages.

Karl Marx (1818–1883)

Karl Marx was interested in the internal qualities of structure that created historical change. History was for him a history of struggles between the parts of structure called social classes. In modern society, each class was defined by the ownership or the lack of ownership of property, and particularly property related to the current means of industrial production. Ownership systematically deprived most people (nonowners or laborers) of what they needed. The **historical structure** of ownership took away the free and creative use of resources from both owners and laborers. This was not the owners' choice. "History" constrained owners (capitalists) to behave in terms of ruthless competition, or else lose property and sink to the laboring class.

Marx saw capitalism as the most materially productive and humanly destructive form of structure in all of history. Marx understood that capitalism had the dual capacities to produce the greatest sustained surpluses ever and, simultaneously, to deprive the masses of people of material well-being, fundamental control, and dignity. His ideas were very popular in an era filled with democratic uprisings against the ruling classes, labor strikes, and vast imbalances of wealth, none of which had yet trickled from higher to lower classes.

Although ownership of the means of production was the fulcrum on which this capitalist structure turned, Marx also believed that the philosophical and religious ideas of the time tended to derive from and reinforce the structure. Contemporary ideas led toward understanding the competitive struggles of capitalism as undeniably good: They were the source of evolutionary progress for the species, because only the fittest could survive. Religious belief tended to see wealth as an earthly sign of predestined salvation. Centuries of law strictly upheld the inalienable rights of property. And most of the people were supposed to render unto Caesar the things of Caesar, knowing that the meek would inherit the earth, and reach heavenly salvation. *The communication of cultural ideals helped make the structure of ownership and oppression legitimate.* Perhaps the assertion made by Marx and Engels in *The German Ideology* (1970) was correct: "...the ideas of the ruling classes are in every epoch the ruling ideas." But for the capitalist era, Marx found a chink in the armor of this self-augmenting system.

The structure of capitalist production brought the workers together into the factories and into the slums of the city. Marx wrote that this physical concentration and interaction would allow them to see that what seemed like their personal troubles really belonged to an entire class of similarly distressed people who were all at the mercy of the capitalist system. In other words, emerging *working class substructures encouraged* intraclass *communication.* Such communication reveals the shared experience of plight and a common foe. As a result, a subculture of ideas would develop that would ignite the working classes to act on their own behalf and rise against the existing structure of oppression. Marx believed that cultural ideals had material force when they reflected actual, underlying historical relationships. Intraclass communication ignited people toward action in their own interests, as a class. Intraclass communications made the abstract notion of "class" real, by providing meta-information. As we saw in Chapter 1, this is information that takes us beyond what we know locally through personal discovery and interaction. Mass media communications come from outside the immediate structures of our everyday lives, and tend to make real and relevant the abstract notion of "society" (at the level of the nation–state or beyond). Just as the workers were lifted to another level of awareness by intraclass communications, the mass media raise their audiences toward concerns and attachments beyond the level of community.

Summary of Marx

Marx did not refer to any one medium of communication, but to its circumstances. Intraclass communication stimulated by worker substructures produced meta-information. Meta-information allowed workers to become aware of the larger-than-life, historical social structures that separated them from their needs. They gained new perspective from the lens of meta-information. They understood that their individual plight was really a shared one, derived from a common structural cause. As a result, they could unite on behalf of their anonymous mutual ties to social class. It was intraclass communications that made the abstract ties of class important enough for people to grasp the idea of a unity with unknown others. The mass media of today similarly tell us of our connections to anonymous others. Marx realized that the communication of ideas grounded in real life was an exercise in and the broadcast of *social power:* Cultural communications could bind people together in action and split classes apart. Thus, Marx demonstrated the relativity of cultural communication to the specific organization of society.

Communication mediated by the masses (and not the ruling classes) was revolutionary. According to Marx, "revolution" meant, first and foremost, breaking ties ("yokes and fetters") to the past and to existing authority. Merely engaging in rebellious and resentful armed conflict was not enough to constitute revolution for Marx. Today, the mass media produce an enormous flow of cultural symbols that show no respect for any particular community boundaries or traditions. These symbols are simply "out there": at the newsstand, on the car radio, or with the mere touch of the TV remote control. The meta-information produced by the mass media is, in the truest Marxist sense, revolutionary. It gives society information about itself that creates the opportunity for change. Even if we do not unite for purposeful action, the cultural landscape is constantly redefined by the mass media.

Once communications escape the control of the ruling classes, things will never be the same. That was Marx's promise. That is the promise inherent in the mass media. Of course, not everyone would agree that this escape has been completely successful. As we shall see in Chapter 7, some observers (see, for example, Bagdikian 1997) point out that the mass media are increasingly owned by a few large companies where decisions are controlled by a relatively small elite. However, the proliferation of media technologies and the need to satisfy market demands make impossible the type of overt control the ruling classes once enjoyed.

Emile Durkheim (1858–1917)

Unlike Marx, Emile Durkheim did not judge the goodness of a society and he was not at all interested in social classes as such. Durkheim saw the structure of modern society as characterized by a particular form of change. Modern society had a rapidly increasing number of distinct parts (e.g., jobs, roles, new institutions, and organizations), each with a separate function. As new institutions appeared alongside old, and as functional distinctions grew, modern society entered into a period of cultural uncertainty, what he called "chronic anomie."

Durkheim's theory described how modern structural differentiation produced people with different perspectives, because of their different functional place in the structure of society. With no common perspective and only these functional linkages as a binding force, Durkheim believed that society would fly apart because people felt no enthusiastic sense of unity. He asked, what then was the glue that held society together?

In essence that glue was symbolic and cultural. Durkheim said that "society is above all else the idea it has of itself." For this "idea"—an enthusiastic sense of unity—to remain alive it must be somehow physically and materially represented. *It is by cultural and symbolic means that we remind ourselves of our membership in society.* These means include shared language and everyday interactional forms (such as standard greetings and handshakes). More than these, however, we use **emblems** (flags, badges, uniforms, school colors and mascots, fashion, logos, secret or ethnically unique handshakes, national anthems, etc.), and **rituals** (worship services, family reunions, parades and fireworks on the Fourth of July, pep rallies, the morning Pledge of Allegiance in schools, etc.).

These representations of the collective help remind us of our group membership. For Durkheim, there is a necessary emotional base to our membership that is stirred by engaging in ritualized bodily movement with others (e.g., the "wave" and our right hands placed across our hearts as the "Star-Spangled Banner" is sung at a sporting event). The impact of these shared rituals is enhanced by a period of common focus (e.g., on the team, the flag, in mutual conversation). Even duty and obligation are spurred by emotion. Various positive emotions (interest, joy, love) encourage us to perform as expected and negative ones deter deviance and failure (e.g., guilt, shame). Durkheim was concerned with how clearly the authoritative rules of society could be *felt* by its members.

Like any feeling, the enthusiasms of membership wax and wane. As our community enthusiasms weaken, we may drift apart. Our real underlying differences then come to matter more. Because of these inevitable tides in the emotional base of social life, Durkheim reminded us that society must be "made and remade." We carry away from moments of renewal an invigorated feeling of belonging, familiarity, and connection. Underlying differences in interest and function seem to disappear. We can learn several specifics about culture, communications, and structure from Durkheim. Durkheim tells us that our connections to others are mediated by particular cultural symbols, but that the influence of such symbols is grounded in specific forms of interaction. This interaction, in turn, renews the emotional and moral significance of the symbols. Durkheim's findings indicate selectivity and preference based on life experience in social interaction. Not just any symbol or symbol system can stir us. There must be a relevance and meaning to it that is born of experience in actual associations with others.

Durkheim understood that the relevance of cultural symbols came from participation in society. Relevance was learned. The school system of France was the most centralized, widespread, and interactive medium of his time. As a result, Durkheim chose it to disseminate and stabilize the new cultural emblems and rituals then evolving as symbols of modern France. Once a person internalizes "the nourishing milieu of society," he or she gains what Durkheim called "autonomy": a **socially acquired self-discipline** accompanied by the capacity for **judgmental sensitivity** to the potentially influential elements of social life. The person is not characterized by "blind and slavish submission" to the "sentiments, ideas and practices" that otherwise "feed" our "mental organism."

Summary of Durkheim

The influence of cultural symbols is dependent on group structures and individual judgment. Typically group and individual factors work together through the process of interaction to produce interpretations of cultural symbols. For example, as a person discusses a new movie with friends, the discussion helps the person decide whether or how much they like the movie and what that movie means in their everyday lives. In addition, because we each have a particular perspective (biases, preferences, dislikes, etc.) some symbols may have no influence—in other words, some symbols just do not connect in any way with our lives. Overall, Durkheim would argue that there is no necessary resemblance between the meaning and purpose of a symbol at its source and its meaning and purpose to a particular audience.

Now let us consider the effect of anomie on the interpretation of broadcast symbols. Anomie represents weak social ties and conflicting sources of authority. Thus, anomie increases the chance that the individual will think, act, and feel on their own and without the unquestionable influence of others. Because, for Durkheim, modern society is in a state of chronic anomie, it is a highly individualistic society. More than at any time in our history, today individual people are left on their own to cobble together a set of cultural symbols that, to them, best represents life.

What Durkheim tells us about the power of the mass media is this. The degree of influence and the specific meaning of mass media messages is regulated by two *primary* factors: the strength of attachment of individuals to their social groups, and the internal strength and coherence of those group structures. In the absence of strong membership ties to some structures or when those structures are weakened by anomie, then individuals must act on their own to interpret available symbols. If Durkheim is right, as social structures weaken the power of the media should grow. This is because the media become an important *direct* source of information for individuals (rather than the group or social institutions). But individual autonomy is also increased as structures weaken, therefore autonomy itself becomes a *secondary* regulating factor of media influence. Thus, the media become more powerful, but their effects become less fundamentally predictable because they are acting on and being interpreted in a less organized, stable, and coherent environment. It would be Durkheim's view that individuals are not the mere dupes of the symbol makers.

Max Weber (1864–1920)

Like Marx and Durkheim, Weber understood the relativity of meaning. Unlike them, meaning was not so tied to concrete relations among people. Rather, meaning was relative to the individual and to typical uses by individuals of a society's distinctive culture. Societal structure was the unintended consequence of past and present socially oriented actions by individuals. That is, people produced actions appropriate to their position in society primarily because of a sense of the legitimacy of society. Without this continued sense of legitimacy, the individual was said to be alienated from society. However, society reinforced the continued assent of individuals with its quality of authority and, when necessary, by force. For Weber, the glue that held society together was composed of a shifting mixture of legitimacy and force. Legitimacy was the primary form of social glue. Legitimacy was maintained by both deriving actions from ideal values and by the communication of ideas about values. Values are cultural ideas about worth, morality, ethics, and priority.

We exist in a sea of ideas and idea systems.

1. Some ideas, the "master symbols of legitimation," seem to define the boundaries of the culture. Weber considered the "work ethic," "deferred gratification," and "rationality" to be the defining ideas of modern society.
2. Other ideas, drawing on the master symbols, appear less central and powerful generally, but fit in with the others. The philosophies behind capitalism and science are examples here. Idea systems within the cultural ethos continually borrow from one another, and mutually incorporate ideas and metaphors. This is illustrated in the way social philosophers took the idea of evolution from the realm of biology and applied it to society.
3. Still other ideas are borrowed from outside cultures when there is an apparent fit with existing ideas: Here as an example we might remember how the important Catholic theologian St. Augustine relied on the ideas of Aristotle.
4. Some ideas leave derivative offspring as their system grows and develops. One important instance of descendance among idea systems concerns the Protestant Reformation. It has spawned a multitude of separate Christian churches and sects.

5. Sometimes idea systems provoke the development of opposing idea systems. Here we may consider the way that Western religious fundamentalism was generated in antagonism to the ethos of modern society. Or regard how "Creation Science," particularly, came to be. Creation Science is part of a religious resistance to science, first to biological evolution theory and the scientific dating of the age of the earth at over 4 billion years. But second, some Creationists are now resisting Galileo's idea that the sun is the center of our system of planets (they believe in an earth-centered system on Biblical grounds).

We must remember that ideas cannot exist in a fully disembodied way. They exist insofar as they are being used by people. They are formulated into doctrines, political strategies, pastoral exhortations from the pulpit, common sense, and expectations within groups. Drawing on this communications rhetoric, ideas also become a part of the psychological dispositions of individuals. Weber's point is that the cultural sea of ideas forms an unintended "atmosphere" that people must take into account. They use it and their actions communicate it. They borrow, redefine, and recombine ideas from within and without their cultural system. Even if they defy it, the climate of ideas is woven into the "dynamic assessment" each individual makes in order to create the practical actions of everyday life.

For Durkheim ideas and symbols of ideas defined our relations with others at the same time that ideas grew from our interpersonal relationships. For Weber ideas suggest how individuals seek their own practical interests, which might well include relations with others. This does not contradict Durkheim, it adds a new dimension. Unlike Durkheim, for Weber ideas in human society had qualities that were not fully tied to patterns of interpersonal relations (if they could be traced to their historical roots). The autonomous dynamic of individual choice produced an affinity among ideas that was not fully predictable from either social structure or the ethos itself.

Summary of Weber

Weber did not concern himself with any medium of communication, much less the mass media. We may still glean some important communications principles from his writings. Communications within modern society creates an ethos, an overall climate of ideas. As individuals use ideas to instill their actions with direction and meaning, these ideas become fused with practical purpose and given power. More than that, the ideas become detached from their original purposes and sources.

As ideas are communicated and attached to personal uses, more than simple culture production happens. Culture and borrowed cultures are being combined and then recombined as bits and pieces are reconnected (cf., Hay 1989) in the twin processes of communication and use.

The recombination of culture tends to remove the local or provincial quality of culture; culture becomes more a "mass" culture (or more a "cosmopolitan" and less "provincial" culture, depending on your biases). The recombination of culture in modern society has an extended effect. Because the source of ideas, and even their purity, becomes lost as they are recombined, we in society lose our ties to physical places and particular institutions (cf., Meyrowitz 1985). The special hold that our hometown or our church or our political party might once have had is weakened as their messages are mixed with many others, with each claiming the privilege of interest. Consequently, the exceptional grip of authority once commanded by these places and institutions is diluted. As Durkheim suggested, this creates a leveling of authority, a virtual marketplace of authority he characterized as the "chronic anomie" of the modern society. Logically and inevitably in such an environment, authority itself loses its "appeal" (to use a Weberian word).

In Chapter 1, some qualities of the mass media were discussed. The main characteristic was that the media provide a new window on collective life. Weber's theory would suggest that this new window supports and amplifies the effects of the recombination of culture(s) and its detachment from any originating structures. Chapter 1 additionally refers to three characteristics of the mass media that amplify the merging and uncoupling operations of cultural elements. The mass media provide *rapid and continuous dissemination of information,* they are *nonexclusive* sources of knowledge, and the media offer *meta-information.* These three media qualities act effectively to remove the barriers of volume and speed, class and ethnic group, and geography. Potentially, immense quantities of symbols of enormous variety are available to everybody. Thus the ability of individuals and groups to assimilate is increased over time, their sampling range of information is huge, and their contexts of awareness are enlarged. Simply put, the more "ideas" that are available to individuals, the greater are the possibilities of recombination. For example, the New Age philosophy of health, interconnectedness, well-being, and spirituality is a combination of a large number of traditional beliefs and practices from around the globe and across time. It is highly doubtful that the New Age synthesis of these idea systems could have occurred so rapidly in an age without mass media.

Transitions to a Modern Social Psychology of Communication

George Herbert Mead (1863–1931)

As with Durkheim, for Mead the mind and the self arose within organized society. Human society and the mind were both structured social processes, and both were constituted by acts of communication. For this reason Mead's approach has been labeled "symbolic interactionism." Mead himself described his work simply as social psychology:

> In social psychology we get at the social process from the inside as well as from the outside...[by] starting off with observable activity (Mead 1962: 7).

How does one get at the "inside," at consciousness? This was a problem that the science of the time had dismissed as always leading to subjective (nonscientific) solutions. Durkheim's notion of "representations" gave a solid but incomplete start to the objective exploration of the mind. It is known that Mead was aware of Durkheim's work, but the degree of influence is not known. Mead's solution to the problem of scientifically exploring the "inside" was parallel with the more social psychological portions of Durkheim's work. Mead, however, went beyond his French counterpart. Durkheim did not inquire how external "representations" could cross the boundary to the inner life of the mind, and, there, become a part of it.

Mead's approach was brilliant for his time: Language acts are outer acts of communication, but language acts are also a medium of thought. Language was both an outer and an inner activity. Language was the conduit that joined the inner and the outer worlds, made the inner one social (not purely subjective), and opened the "mind" to a level of scientific analysis not before possible. Mead's goal was to understand how mind and self formed and how they were sustained. More than that, Mead inquired after the reciprocal relationships of mind, self, and society. He was remarkably successful. He also succeeds in an area that is significant to this text. Mead's work yields insight into the connection between the individual and the messages of the mass media, and how these messages may influence the individual by their effects on society. Before we discuss the insights gained from Mead's work, however, we need to understand better the "mind" and the "self."

Mead provides a telling metaphor on this point: "[The mind and self are], so to speak, an eddy in the social current and so still a part of the current" (Mead 1962: 182). He clarifies the relationship of the body, and of society, to the mind and self:

The body is not a self, as such; it becomes a self only when it has developed a mind within the context of social experience…Mind arises through communication by a conversation of gestures in the social process or context of experience (Mead 1962: 50, emphasis added).

"Gestures"—acts, including vocal acts or language—draw a connection among the actor, particular acts, and the "objects" of the world (things and people). As examples: A hug joins two people; pointing one's finger indicates a particular object; speaking the word *cat* symbolically links speaker, audience, and cat. A full conversation of gestures makes and implies a range of connections. Such a conversation knits together a world composed of various things and people.

Conversation makes a place for each person among the people and things of the world by revealing that person's "connections:" daughter, good student, smart, middle-class, pretty, moral, short, Toyota Camry driver, and so on. In time, and after taking part in many conversations, the person gradually gains a sense of some constancy about his or her place in the physical and social environment. From the conversational process—from society—we acquire an active, self-conscious sense of our personhood that we call a "mind."

BOX 2.1

Nothing's left, nothing. When people come, we let them make an offering. Why not? But [God] no longer answers their prayers. The old ways are gone; the bonds are loosened. We go through the motions, but what of it?...*The radio has killed everything.*

(Duvignaud 1970:207, emphasis added, quoting a respondent in a small village in Tunisia.)

At a certain level, the mind functions—deliberating, facilitating, and inhibiting action—to *sustain a person's place in relation to others in the community,* and there is *an ongoing tie between person and community via the conversation of gestures.* Such mindful action modifies the exchange process in a way that specifically reflects the developing self and thus, by degree, modifies the general pattern of social group behavior. The mind constructs and alters the behaviors of the self directly. The mind alters the structure of the self, according to Mead, only indirectly as the behaviors of the self alter the organized relations with others.

Mead argues that, in interaction, the conversation of significant gestures creates a flow of meaning from the outer world of society to the inner world of the person and back again. But each time a meaningful act passes the boundary of the person on its way to the outer world, it has been "adjusted" to take the self–other situation context into account. He named this context the *generalized other.* Mead is clear that society is the source of the individual personhood we call the mind and self, that change in the structure of the self originates in alterations of society, and that those alterations in the pattern of symbolic interaction may be instigated by the self's behaviors.

The Implications of Mead's Theory for Understanding the Role of the Mass Media

Mead's theory is all about the influence of society on the self via the medium of face-to-face communication by symbols. In face-to-face communication there is continual and mutual feedback. Without consideration of the effects of mass media, a community of discourse creates values and sentiments. And these values and sentiments become a part of the individual mind and self. At the same time the individual is able to participate in the creation and determination of such community standards. Mead's theory describes a level of community intimacy that reaches into the very self. Mead's social psychology of mind, self, and society portrays almost no alienation, that is, no sense of detachment, distance, or disruption between the individual and community.

Enter the mass media. In Chapter 1 we discussed that one effect of the mass media has been to remove communication from face-to-face interaction. The flow of information is primarily in one direction because of broadcast technology: The Meadian feedback loop between source and self is broken. The world of language is no longer tied to a distinct community as the cultural world loses its boundaries. Images and symbols carried by the media from outside a community inevitably collide with the traditional symbolic processes of that community. Sentiment and value, which once came from a specific group and received their validation there, now come from everywhere, all the time, and in a multitude of contradictory forms. The intimacy of the former *generalized other* becomes more open to invasion by battalions of foreign symbols.

When the community is no longer the exclusive source of sentiment and value, Mead might say that the subtle yet powerful distinctions of belonging and membership dissolve. Fashions, trends, ideas, and values, created by the media to be attractive, rush toward the individual from multiple media sources. As community standards are mingled with other standards, the meanings of *appropriate* and *deviant* lose clarity and force.

The ties of community moral authority, implied in Mead's portrayal of the self-formation process, would relax as local and mass-mediated sources of authority compete. This competition for moral authority is analogous to the "chronic anomie" depicted by Durkheim. There would be a strong tendency to blend, and perhaps substitute, mass-mediated life with the Mead's community-mediated life of the mind, self, and society.

Mead might say that when the mass media *(1) violate the condition of feedback,* and *(2) hyper-expand the boundaries of the generalized other,* the (3) intimate communications *community is shattered,* leaving impersonal mass society. For Mead, all other more specific media effects can be derived from these three general effects. Let us look at further extrapolations from Mead's theory.

Within the cacophony of media-broadcast symbols, selves will still form, but a paradox surfaces. Meaning and experience are increasingly individualized (or privatized), even as the sources of meaning derive from a wider, more cosmopolitan, mass-mediated world. Why? The penetration of the mass media erases the natural commonality of experience within a community. Without a single, unified source of culture, individual selves attach to arbitrary symbols. These "foreign" symbols cannot then be turned into a language community for unifying validation. This process tends to increasingly isolate the self (from community), but the self then emerges as a primary standard against which experience is judged.

Media Related Outcomes Predictable from Mead's Theory

Some of today's most debated potential media effects are directly predictable from Mead's theory. First, some individuals become truly unattached to others because their *generalized other* is a haphazard, self-constructed mixture of symbols. These people are the unattached loners seen as odd and idiosyncratic. Second, a defined number of people find commonality around a stable set of fundamental symbols, attach to these, and withdraw from mass-mediated society seeking true, concrete community (e.g., a religious cult). As a matter of historical note: In the West, religious fundamentalism emerged at the same time as mass society. Fundamentalist groups are organized around a defined set of apparently permanent symbols, but exist in the midst of changing and challenging symbols. As a consequence they must expend considerable social energy in filtering out and condemning challenging symbols. Third, nongeographic, mass-mediated peer groups form, and create temporary "communities." Here individuals expend considerable energy deciding which symbols to include in their personal symbol set, including which "types" of people to include, all for the purpose of self-presentation. Much of this activity has been labeled "consumerism," "materialism," or the "art of conspicuous consumption." The basic social and individual effort is not different from the fundamentalism of a religious cult. Here, however, the individual is elevated above all else, and both the resulting groups and symbol sets are transient.

By degree, all three of these outcomes actually happen, although the latter is the most common. Temporary, nongeographic, mass-mediated groups can develop in several ways. We will examine three types: **topic circles, social interest collectivities, and lifestyle clusters.** We will move in order from the most to the least temporary.

Topic Circles
The media are capable of generating topics for conversation (e.g., sports, soap operas, news stories) that allow mutual external connections among people. These external connections substitute for the long-term internal biographical, kinship, and historical connections of the Meadian community. Community becomes portable and transient, a "virtual community" occurring whenever a media topic is evoked. That is, conversation becomes centered around regular media events, not around actual life events in primary groups.

As a consequence, life first becomes open to media metaphors. Then, in the extreme, life becomes a metaphor of the media: We increasingly live life among others as if we are characters in role-playing games, with special costumes for each facet of life. Actual games (e.g., Dungeons and Dragons) take on a new seriousness because they prepare us to slip into and out of guises in "real" life. Or, we present ourselves as fellow "fans." We individually broadcast, using logos on hats, T-shirt emblems, and other paraphernalia as minimedia. Such emblems provide identity in a world of strangers and provide a message of availability for a "pick-up game" in virtual community. Life and the world of the media blend into one big reality indistinguishable from a docudrama.

Social Interest Collectivities
Other types of virtual community are even more abstract because they need not exist in a face-to-face environment. Sometimes, during our individual search for meaning in the maze of available symbols, we attach to symbols and sentiments that rouse personal concern about things over which we have little influence or knowledge. Thus we "naturally" find ourselves empathetic with people in distant wars, starvation in central

Africa, worldwide lowering of sperm counts, holes in the ozone, and diminishing populations of amphibians. And so, for a time, until it grows tiresome, we want to save the whales (or the darter snails or the spotted owls).

Lifestyle Clusters

The media can also generate suggestions for *styles of life.* The mass-advertised, mass-produced array of consumer goods and services tends to form the basis of selection for the creation of lifestyles based on consumer preference. Where one shops, where and how one spends leisure time, where one lives and what services one requires, even one's religious "persuasion," when combined, tend to form sufficiently homogeneous and aggregated "clusters" of consumers to warrant highly targeted and profitable nine-digit zip code marketing.

These clusters can be understood as *neighborless neighborhoods* because residential segregation is based on lifestyle, not on social ties. For example, as new housing developments appear, they are segregated by price. They are further designed with distinct forms of appeal (apartment, single, townhouse, condominium, etc.) for separate "types" of people (young, old, single, family, etc.). Once built, they are rapidly populated by a large number of strangers—many of whom intend these dwellings to be temporary.

As individual tastes and incomes change, or as one ages, a lifestyle cluster can be discarded as easily as one trades in an old car for a new model. For some, the strongest ties are to current lifestyle, not to place or to people. The "clustering of America" (see Weiss 1988) would not be possible without mass-mediated information, and it is made more likely and more attractive by the effects of the mass media on mind, self, and society.

Mead wrote about communication as the origin of self from within comprehensibly small groupings of people. In such groupings, as described by Mead, there is *a union of cultural communication and life.* That is, communication occurs in small, closed feedback loops and is about *directly experienced* events, sentiment, and morality with immediate consequences and interaction with others met face-to-face. As we examined topic circles, social interest collectivities, and lifestyle clusters above, we were looking through Mead at contemporary forms of interaction.

In these three cases, we assumed Mead's principles of self-formation were accurate, but that *there was no longer a union of cultural communication and life.* Put differently, these three contemporary models of interaction depend heavily on the flow of (mass-mediated) *meta-information.* Mead's perspective allows us to understand the three models of interaction once direct communication feedback loops can be bypassed. His work, however, is a microlevel theory and cannot explain the range of social forces acting to place stress on stress community ties. Some of those larger forces, quite apart from the mass media, tend to shatter community and some tend to immunize community from media effects.

Mead's view of society did not include the complexity of existing, institutionalized class or status cleavages in community. His writings did not contain the concept of social power. Such actual structures would limit the power of the media to stress community, and they would filter media symbols through abstract but real social structures such as race, class, and gender relations. Thus, the outcomes described above have structural causes in addition to direct media effects. But the point here is not to isolate media causality from other related social forces. The point is theoretical: to describe the underlying pathways of a media effect, and to point to the social and social psychological tendencies of the media as they operate in society.

In this effort, Mead's work is remarkably helpful for someone who never wrote a word about the mass media. His ideas need to be woven in with those of the classical theorists to give both more strength. Although we cannot hope to accomplish a full theoretical synthesis here, the following summary will suffice for the purposes of this text.

Summary of Classical Theorists

We have discussed Marx, Durkheim, Weber, and Mead in order to understand the possible effects of mass media on society. These theorists were presented chronologically. As it turns out there is another, coincidental, type of progression represented. Each theorist places a different amount of emphasis on social structure versus culture. All use the concept of social structure as their base. Marx is very structural, Mead is the least. Durkheim and Weber, in that order, fall between Marx and Mead.

The structural emphasis of Karl Marx should be taken as a reminder that the media do not control the human world. Marx tells us that the media will have power when they broadcast cultural symbols that can take root in organized human relations. This power derives from the capacity of the media to provide meta-information beyond local and personal experience. Meta-information allows us to see beyond our immediate, personal lives. It allows us to identify with abstract structures larger than community. For Marx these abstract structures were those of the whole working *class* in the context of *modern, capitalist society.*

Durkheim would agree, but he adds three explicit qualifications. First, for Durkheim, relevant cultural symbols ("representations of the collective") act back on organized relations and help to strengthen and define social organization, without respect to social class. Second, Durkheim points out that the constant structural change that defines modern society implies a breakdown of structure. *This structural breakdown is not media-initiated,* but, theoretically, it can be sustained or accelerated by mass-mediated meta-information. This is so because, as a result of such chronic anomie, it is likely that broadcast cultural symbols act more directly on individuals and are less mediated by membership in stable social institutions. Third, Durkheim, like Mead, would say that the general "noise" of the mass media in the modern social environment provides a new symbolic basis of the individual mind and self. This basis is not small-scale community, but instead the sources are meta-information and large-scale society. Meta-information is nonetheless filtered and selected by autonomous individuals in particular social locations.

Overall, for Durkheim, social attachments modify mass-mediated cultural symbols and help individuals interpret them. The relevance and meaning of cultural symbols—and their effects—are regulated by experience in actual associations. Although media power grows under conditions of chronic anomie, the media message is refracted by the interpretations of millions of autonomous individuals. The effect of this potential for increased media power becomes, therefore, less directional and predictable.

Weber adds an interesting twist to our story about the interplay of structure and culture. He also helps us to understand more about why media power cannot lead to predictable effects. That is, one cannot predict from the particular message content of the media what long-term effects will result.

Weber reminds us that ideas can lose their connection to particular groups and can be incorporated into other belief systems. This is precisely the fear of those interested in preserving some set of traditions. In fact, the cultural realm of modern society is characterized by an enormous process of cultural recombination. This recombination goes on among ideas from both within and outside a society. The mass media aid in this process of recombination by continuing the rapid flow of ideas, without respect to group boundaries.

Weber admits that general cultural themes emerge and persist within the overall process of recombination. Ideas are combined that somehow appear to fit, without respect to original meaning or cultural origin. However, these thematic cultural directions are continuously creating antagonisms and resistance. Social movements rise up and alter, even if they cannot reverse, the direction and interpretation of the "offending" themes. Modern culture is "life" continuously evolving. It is not a stable life form. The constant recombining, juxtaposition, and opposition of ideas make long-term media effects fundamentally unpredictable. That is, any media themes—like the persistant message of exercise, health, and good nutrition, or that of excessive violence or the depiction of relaxed sexual morality—may produce altered behavior on the part of some people already predisposed to act. Some will model their values and behaviors on media themes, others will ignore the particulars of the media message, and still others will oppose these media messages. All of this reaction is going on at the individual level. What Weber points out is that every persistent cultural theme in modern society will provoke resistance by a *socially organized* opposition. The persevering communication of these opposing ideas will alter the cultural environment, leading opposition members, and a host of others, to energetically judge media content. As this new opposition awareness ripples through established social institutions—families, churches, Congress, clubs, political parties—and peer groups it will gain power, gain effect. Extreme elements of this opposition may well provoke their own organized opposition. And so on. In the meantime the media may alter their themes because of social pressures, provide program rating systems, or parents and V-chips (see Chapter 6) may change the accessible viewing content of the media.

The cultural content of the media can be judged, and it is. The content may and probably does have complex influences. But Weber reminds us that the media are not the basic causal elements of cultural threat to tradition. They are merely the social and material technologies for amplifying existing historical and cultural processes. These processes, though antitraditional, are just as fundamental to modern society as are its comforts and affluence. Weber tells us about these process on the largest scale, Mead describes the social processes that affect the flow of culture from society to within the individual and back again.

For Mead, both community and the individual mind–self are formed from such communicative interaction. Without consideration of the mass media, Mead considers the processes of community and mind–self-formation to be parts in an *intimate* (mutually influential) feedback loop.

As it was described in our interpretation of Weber, media alter already existing processes of communication. This would be true for Mead as well. Additionally, in Mead's terms, what the media do to communication is to remove the quality of real intimacy and break the feedback loop. Thus, the very basis of traditional community is diluted by rivalry with external symbols. Without strong community there is no single, unified source of culture for individuals to draw on during self-formation. There is no clearly defined "social eddy" in the flow of ideas to recycle symbols and sentiments. There is no limited social grouping to filter and interpret the influx of exotic symbols. These "foreign" symbols cannot then be turned into a geographically located, stable language community for unifying validation. Individual selves-in-formation must therefore attach to arbitrary, media-carried symbols. The self is increasingly isolated as a source and standard of meaning.

As a result, the media become a partner in the historical social processes of *individualization, privatization,* and *weakening of community* that characterizes a modern society. This sounds like a negative consequence and may seem like a loss to some individuals. Once again sociological theory can provide a bigger picture.

The Mass Media in a Societal Context

A modern society can continue to exist only as long as it remains able to adapt to the historical changes that it has set in motion. Communities and other intimate structures are conservative: They resist the changes that are inherent to modern society. The historical result is that community is not the structural basis of modern society. Communities are either artificial and temporary islands in mass society or they are remnants from the traditional past. The media did not bring about this dissolution of community. It was begun with the historical transition to industrial society. However, modern society may not be possible without two general tendencies within mass communication. Let us look at these two types of media effect on society.

Loss of Community and Increased Individual Responsibility

The mass media tend to stress the boundaries of community. The media thereby loosen conservative, change-resistant collective ties. By the same process, the media prepare the mind–self of the person for the flow of large-scale change. Neither one of these media potentials is comfortable, and both may be judged as bad at the small-scale level—our everyday lives. The media force us to observe the questioning of tradition. And they render individuals responsible for the selective consumption of cultural symbols. That is, *we are responsible for ourselves to an historically unprecedented degree.* We, not "community," must choose among the multitude of symbols and culture packages for those that we will incorporate into our selves and those that we will deny.

There is another side to this same coin. This forced responsibility frees individuals to be *adaptable.* Of course, freedom cuts in many unpredictable directions. If freedom permits an easier path of change for the sake of survival and growth, it also opens the world up to alternative behaviors and attitudes. Some of these may be criminal and dangerous forms of adaptation. Crime rates are always higher when community controls are weakened. Other adaptive alternatives may be judged as immoral by tradition. For example, we now have gay and lesbian enclaves in urban, suburban, and (for lesbians) rural areas. Consumerism is an adaptation that we judge as both good and bad. When we call it *materialism,* we see it as bad. When we call consumerism *shopping,* we see it as fun, good, and sometimes even therapeutic. Other modern alternatives we lump under categories perceived as good include leisure pursuits, mobility, and personal and political freedom.

Meta-Information for an Abstract Society

The media provide the meta-information necessary to organize and reorganize a modern, abstract society. Modern society is an abstract thing because of its size, tendency to incessant change, and vast complexity. The nation–state is a socially real abstraction that survives by talking about itself to itself. This is accomplished by massive public efforts to collect data (e.g., the U.S. census, opinion polling) and through the constant flow of mass media communications. This media-carried, societal self-talk includes more than the "serious" sources such as the news, educational programming, and documentaries. From talk shows and sitcoms to comedies and cop shows we obtain metaphors, accurate or not, about the range and morality of behaviors in modern society.

Marx suggests that things will never be the same. Weber informs us that in the long term change is constant and of unpredictable direction and pace. Continued societal adaptation is an inherent fact of modern life, aided by mass-mediated cultural communications. For better or for worse, and in spite of our hopes and traditions, change continues. Durkheim and Mead tell us that while it may not be possible to reclaim community as a central feature of mass society, our autonomous role in shaping our personal lives can be organized. Following Marx: If we organize around meta-information, temporary control of direction can be claimed. So far, we do this only sporadically, and almost never proactively. For example, we have Congressional hearings *after* something has become a problem. We, as a nation–state, rarely pass preventive or planning laws. It is as if some fundamental element of our culture encourages us to insist on a chaotic and unpredictable future. That is certainly what the classic theorists would suggest. Modern society is not a place to relax. The media are always watching. We must too.

3

Mass Media Effects I: Individual Effects

Up until I turned seven, I thought I possessed magical powers. I knew that She-ra had all the strength in the world, and even magic too. Jem was a rock star who led a double life thanks to her supernatural earrings. I figured eventually I would grow up and find a worthy occupation for my own special powers. It was a sad day when I began to realize that no streams of electricity shot out when I pointed my finger and squinted my eyes. Even when magic was out of the question though, I felt I would somehow grow to be as unique as each of my heroes.
—KRISTEN, COLLEGE SOPHOMORE

In 1993, Beavis and Butthead turned an aerosol can into a torch. Shortly thereafter, three Ohio teenagers imitated the act and set their room on fire. In the same year, two teenagers were killed copying a scene from a movie in which drunken college football players played a game of "chicken"—lying in the middle of a highway at night. The film producers removed that scene from the video version of the movie. In the fall of 1997, a teenage boy killed himself shortly after listening to a Marilyn Manson CD. His father believes the content of the group's lyrics was partly responsible. In December 1997, a 14-year-old boy, son of a church deacon and brother of the school valedictorian, opened fire on a student prayer group killing three students and wounding five. In the weeks that follow the media are full of stories that the killings may have been inspired by a similar scene from the film *The Basketball Diaries.* In response, the producers of the film remove the offending scene from the video version.

Beavis and Butthead have been blamed for anti-social behavior and sometimes violent behavior.

Could such violence have been caused by the mass media? If so, is it the reaction of a few disturbed individuals, or are the media turning us into an angry and violent society? If the media do have negative effects on society, how do we reconcile censorship of media content with our First Amendment ideals?

People spend much of their leisure time interacting with the mass media. Of the approximately 40 hours per week of free time available to the average person, 15 hours, or 38 percent, are spent watching television (Robinson and Godbey 1997:126). This is more time than is spent reading, socializing, and engaging in outdoor activities combined! Because people spend so much time involved with television and other media, and because of the potential power of symbols to evoke emotional involvement, it is assumed that the mass media *must* have effects on both individuals and the larger society—and those effects are often thought to be negative. Some, like epidemiologist Brandon Centerwall, believe that the mass media are a major destructive force in our society. According to Centerwall (1993:58), if television had never been invented, in the United States there would be 10,000 fewer homicides, 70,000 fewer rapes, and 700,000 fewer injurious assaults *each year.* No wonder the debate over mass media effects has been, and continues to be, a constant force in the environment of mass media producers.

While it could be argued that the debate has produced little meaningful reform, recent events, such as the mandating of V-chip technology and the voluntary television rating system, are indications the mass media producers must take public and political pressure seriously—if only to produce the illusion of real change.

In this chapter we will attempt to examine some of these questions. We will first look at the critique of popular cultural in general, and then examine what we know about the content of the mass media, particularly television. Finally, we will examine the evidence for and against media effects on individuals. This chapter will not be another polemic against the mass media. Rather, it will show that what is often assumed about mass media effects on the individual, both positive and negative, may be less clear than is often assumed.

The Critique of Mass Culture

Historical Roots

The negative evaluation of popular culture has its roots in the French Revolution when the social position of the aristocracy was challenged by the larger population. As the populace gained in equality, the upper classes relied on cultural choices as a way of distinguishing themselves from the masses. The use of cultural choices as a form of social status was heightened by the Industrial Revolution, which began in England in the eighteenth century and eventually spread to the European continent and then to the New World. The urban centers of industry drew a massive migration of European peasantry, fleeing an agriculture that could no longer provide a living, and seeking jobs in the new factory system. In America, the great urban migrations included waves of immigrants from overseas. Previously separate nationalities and religious types were now forced to compete for jobs. The conditions that greeted the new class of workers were awful. The factories were very dangerous and offered only long hours and low pay. For example, steel workers in the Pittsburgh area in the 1890s worked 12-hour shifts in temperatures that soared above 130 degrees, with no breaks for food or rest. In the various mills of Pittsburgh during this era, each year on-the-job accidents killed several hundred men and injured several thousand others.

Living quarters were overcrowded, dark, and filthy; they lacked water and sanitary facilities, and were filled with vermin. The early workers of industry had no comfort or security in their poverty. The pay for factory work was typically one dollar a day or less. Pay was so low that young children were required to work in the factories for the sake of survival. There were no school systems. Rates of death, accident, and disease were high, birth rates were low. The biological cost of city life was so great that their populations would have decreased had it not been for the continued migration of people who had no place else to go. Despite hazards, the numbers of city dwellers surged.

The tradition of *noblesse oblige* (the moral obligation of the nobility to aid their "inferiors") did not carry any meaning for the new class of capitalists. The American elite class was especially lacking in social responsibility because, with no history of U.S. aristocracy, there was no tradition of *noblesse oblige*. The feudal system was dying in Europe, but it left behind the ancient idea that property conferred special privilege and social authority. This legacy was thoroughly expressed everywhere in the new industrial order, both in law and by the great capitalist "robber barons" who considered themselves completely above the law.

The newly rich capitalists got the property, but did not take the age-old responsibility that went with it. The turmoil of the Industrial Revolution overlapped with the formation of nation–states in a era of transition to democratic government. All this structural change resulted in more than 130 years of revolutions, rebellions, riots, mob violence, and bloody labor strikes. On the U.S. side of the Atlantic, this era of fury lasted through the great strikes in the teens of this century. Among the various nations of European heritage, World War I and the Bolshevik Revolution in Russia seemed to end this epoch of chaotic alienation in the lower classes.

In the meantime, these years had been very good to the new elite classes. Their wealth was growing, they had spawned a small, dependent middle class very much swayed by capitalist values, and they were forging ties to the new democratic governments that consolidated the social power of the elites. The newly enriched groups could not or would not see beyond their own good fortune to understand the conditions of the working poor. The countless urban riots and labor struggles were to them moral outrages. The elites looked down and saw not the righteous struggles of people, groups, or classes. Instead, what they saw from their perspective were irrational masses engaged in formless turmoil, stirred by senseless and destructive impulses.

Ideologies were in place to foster such a view of the masses. This was an age that valued rationality both as the most evolved expression of human intelligence and as the driving principle behind the successes of science and industry. Further, Social Darwinism emerged to justify the differences among classes and to excuse lower-class conditions on the basis of natural law: the survival of the fittest. Not only did Social Darwinism absolve the elite of any moral responsibility, the presumed irrationality of the masses was a sign of moral unfitness. From this perspective, the masses deserved what they got.

Even as the wealthy viewed the restive stirring of the masses as senseless, they still sought a cause for the discontent. Enter the media.

The elite concluded that, not only were media (including newspapers, handbills, posters, pamphlets and, later, radio), lowering public taste, a few demagogues could amplify their views by cleverly inserting a political agenda into the emotion-laden descriptions of the plight of the masses. The elite came to believe strongly in the undermining effect of the media on high culture and social order. The other side of that same coin was the belief by radicals that the media could be used to rouse the people to revolt. Both sides saw the media as a powerful means for political influence over the great masses of people. Thus, out of the mutually antagonistic history of class relations came a widely accepted doctrine that justified a disparaging view of the masses and blamed upheaval on the power of the media. The conviction existed that control of the media was the control of a powerful manipulative, even coercive, force.

Two World Wars

This belief in strong media effects influenced media use during World Wars I and II. The media were directed by governments on both sides for the purpose of uniting their populations against opposing external forces. A famous World War I poster in the United States defined the enemy in stark form: A German soldier was painted holding his bayoneted rifle menacingly before him. On the bayonet, stuck through and dripping blood, was an infant. The bottom of the poster held the words "The Hun." The U.S. poster war continued through World War II ("Uncle Sam Wants *You*," "Loose Lips Sink Ships"). The Nazis employed every medium systematically, including radio campaigns, in a highly coordinated propaganda blitz (Herzstein 1978). Joseph Goebbels acted as the master propagandist for the Nazi Party. Goebbels saw "…propaganda as a pragmatic art, the means to an end, the seizure of total power (Herzstein 1978:69).

When the media were turned against the enemy in a methodical strategy of subversion, it began to be called "psychological warfare" or, later, "psi ops" (psychological operations). For example, during World War II the Japanese radio beamed the voice of "Tokyo Rose" and the Germans broadcast "Axis Sally" to seduce and weaken the resolve of American troops.

Whatever effect the media actually had in the propaganda campaigns of the two World Wars, they were viewed as the key to raising the largest armies in the history of the world and uniting all the resources of society toward the war effort. In the United States, the media were widely blamed for German citizens' seeming compliance with or participation in Nazi atrocities. Surely, rational, civilized people could not condone such acts without first being brainwashed.

In the years after World War II, during the Cold War, the Voice of America radio stations broadcast music and news across the "iron curtain." Some Voice of America transmitters were 20 times more powerful than the maximum allowed for any domestic stations, broadcasting with up to 1 million watts to an audience of an estimated 75 million. Unlike the Voice of America, with its reputation for unbiased reporting, Radio Free Europe, with ties to the CIA, largely transmitted Western propaganda into Communist countries. In return, Radio Moscow sent the Soviet message out in 64 languages. And during the Vietnam conflict, the enemy transmitted the voice of Hanoi Hannah to dispirit American troops. In return we dropped leaflets on enemy locations. One type had threatening pictures of B-52 bombers. These implied that next time something dropped from the sky it would be a bomb, not a leaflet. Still other U.S. leaflets described procedures for surrender and the benefits waiting for anyone who willingly did so. Once again, our government was acting as if the media could produce strong effects.

The War of the Worlds

The 1938 Halloween night radio broadcast of *The War of the Worlds* seemed to justify the belief in powerful media effects. Sponsored by CBS radio, this dramatic program created a panic that began among millions of listeners who believed the earth was being invaded by Martians. Research indicated that, conservatively, the program that night had an audience of about 4 million (Lowery and DeFleur 1995). Of those listeners, 28 percent thought they were listening to an actual news report and, of those, 70 percent (1.2 million people) were frightened or disturbed by the broadcast. The panic seemed to be a clear indication of the power of the media. Yet, not everyone who heard the broadcast believed the dramatic fiction was real—providing an early indication that media messages do not affect all people in the same way.

The Basic Critique

By the 1950s, the critique of the mass culture that had begun with the French Revolution produced the general argument that:

1. Industrialization leads to urbanization because factories and people converge in areas with adequate power, roads, and housing.
2. As people move to these large urban areas they lose their strong ties to community and family of origin.
3. People cut loose from community and family have fewer restrictions on their behavior and more readily seek the quick gratifications of permissive sex, crime, and vice.
4. Because of the higher standard of living brought about by industrialization, these unattached individuals also have more money in their pockets.
5. Businesses (including the mass media) spring up in an attempt to profit by nurturing and satisfying these unrestrained urges of the industrial masses.
6. The grand result: Society drifts away from high standards of morality and art and is thus opened to and permeated by the influence of images of sex and violence. Such images appeal to an alienated, debased audience, which, having lost contact with virtue, is easily manipulated by political opportunists, advertisers, and mass media programmers.

This argument, called "the critique of mass culture" (see, for example, Shils 1959), was popular during the 1950s, but elements survive today. Note, for example, the late Allan Bloom's 1987 best-seller, *The Closing of the American Mind.* Bloom's book is largely an attack on the concept of cultural relativism, which he associates with a lack of standards for moral conduct, and a call for a return to more absolute standards of truth and beauty. Whether or not you agree with Bloom's position, much of what he had to say harkens back to the 1950s critique of culture. For example, in discussing music, Bloom agrees with Plato that the power of music to arouse emotion must be tempered by reason. This must be done in order to appeal to what Bloom calls "higher purposes"—beauty, religion, or politics. The task for the arts is

Some social critics such as the late Allan Bloom have been disturbed by rock n' roll's ability to arouse frenzied passion in listeners.

to both provide pleasure and appeal to these higher purposes. Lamenting the loss of appeal of classical music to young people, Bloom contends that rock 'n' roll provides no such wedding of emotion and intellect. He refers to the popularity of rock as an addiction to a rhythm and lyric that stirs sexual passions while appealing to rebellion against parental authority. In discussing MTV, Bloom directly evokes the concerns of earlier critiques of mass culture as he writes, "Hitler's image recurs frequently enough in exciting contexts to give one pause" (1987: 74).

What is interesting about Bloom's position is not just its reprise of the earlier attack on popular or mass culture, but also the widespread endorsements it received—praise from critics writing for such publications as the *New York Review of Books, Wall Street Journal, New York Times,* and *Washington Post.* These endorsements, coupled with the popularity of his book, imply a continuing uneasiness with the content of popular culture in the United States.

There are other signs that, as a society, we are not completely comfortable with our mass-mediated culture. Note the persistent concern over sex and violence on television. This concern has resulted in a much criticized voluntary rating system for broadcasters and the government mandated V-chip for televisions. In addition, the past two presidential elections have seen first, Dan Quayle, and then, Bob Dole, criticize mass media entertainment. In 1985, Tipper Gore and the Parent's Music Resource Center (PMRC) worked to have rating labels placed on popular music recordings. Heavy Metal and Rap music have been particularly criticized for content allegedly damaging to fans and to society (see Ryan, Calhoun, and Wentworth 1997).

Because of its pervasiveness and popularity, most critical attention has focused on television. This attention began in the 1950s and has persisted now for almost 50 years. During those decades, television has been steadily accused of creating a variety of personal and social ills. There is much concern. But is this concern warranted? And can research help to answer that question?

The Search for Mass Media Effects

Early Attempts at Finding Media Effects

By World War II it had become common sense to assume that the media held the potential for powerful effects in mass society. Operating as a sort of magic bullet or hypodermic needle, the media were thought to have the ability to directly affect individuals in powerful ways. But common sense can be scientifically tested. Paul Lazarsfeld had escaped Nazi Germany on a Ford Foundation Fellowship. He was trained in psychological measurement and believed that mass society notions needed scientific evidence before accepting them as true. During the height of belief in powerful media effects, he began a careful research program of voter studies in Ohio and New York that, by the 1950s, led him to conclude that the assumptions of powerful effects were not accurate. When asked what had influenced their voting behavior, voters hardly mentioned newspapers, magazines, or radio. They reported that friends or acquaintances had been most influential. Another psychologist named Carl Hovland worked for the U.S. Army's Information and Education Division in its research branch. The mission of the research group headed by Hovland was to evaluate experimentally the effect of indoctrinational programs produced by the government. The Hovland group studied diverse media intensely, and came to conclusions similar to Lazarsfeld (Hovland et al. 1949).

Current Mass Media Effects Research

Concern over mass media effects did not end with the work of Lazarsfeld and Hovland. Mass media researchers developed new models to account for the seeming lack of direct effects, and research into effects continued unabated. Meanwhile, concern over media content and its effects has cycled on and off of the public agenda at fairly regular intervals. Reed Hunt, former chairman of the Federal Communications Commission, has been quoted in an article in *Atlantic Monthly* magazine as saying, "There is no longer any serious debate about whether violence in the media is a legitimate problem" (Stossel 1997). This is hardly the case. The author of the article goes on to state that "a huge body of evidence—including 3,000 studies before 1971 alone—suggests a strong connection between television watching and aggression" (87). As we shall see, there is, in fact, considerable debate about the extent, nature, and size of mass media effects.

Expected Effects

The mass media, especially television, have been suspected of having a wide array of effects on individuals and the larger culture. The litany of complaints against television is long. Commercial U.S. television is thought by many to increase the level of violence in our culture by increasing aggression in children and adults and by desensitizing us to violence. Our most used medium has also been accused of decreasing fantasy play among children, stealing time away from homework and other productive pursuits, creating a nation of conspicuous consumers, trivializing political campaigns and social issues, turning politicians into actors (and actors into politicians), misinforming or underinforming the public about important social issues, encouraging promiscuity, lowering attention spans, and stereotyping women and other minorities. Meanwhile, popular music and music videos, especially rap and heavy metal, have been accused of fostering Satanism, suicide, promiscuity, and violence against women. Even country music shared the spotlight when researchers seemed to find a connection between the popularity of country music in a given locale and the suicide rate (Stack and Gundlach 1992).

These concerns are the continuation of worries over mass media content that focused on newspapers in the 19th century, the movies as early as the 1920s, and comic books in the 1940s. Even the reading of fiction was once thought to be bad for children, although today you rarely hear that children are reading too much. What may be considered harmful at one point can be perceived as harmless or even beneficial at another point in time.

Heavy metal groups such as "Marilyn Manson" have been accused of damaging America's youth.

Nevertheless, many of the above concerns seem legitimate. In the next section we will examine some studies exploring the content of our most controversial medium, television. Then we will turn our attention to the effects of that content.

Television Content

Over the years there has been a fairly constant critique of the content of television. Sometimes it rises to near social movement status, while at other times it recedes more into the background—but it is always there. Sometimes it's about violence, sometimes about commerce, sometimes about sex, and sometimes about intellectual emptiness. Meanwhile, academics and representatives of various minority groups have raised their own concerns about the way various groups are represented on television. Television is our most popular leisure activity, and also the most criticized.

Stereotyping

One critique of television is that it presents a distorted demographic view of the real world. That is, members of a particular race, gender, social class, age, or occupation may not be represented in numbers corresponding to their presence in the real world. This is a problem because, it is argued, television provides the central social discourse of our society. It is the primary storyteller, the mythmaker, the supposed mirror of society. Thus, according to this rationale, to be invisible on television is to be invisible culturally and socially.

It is important to keep in mind that television programming is constantly evolving as the constraints of law, technology, industry structure, organizational structure, occupations, and market have their combined effects. Thus, content-analysis studies are extremely time-bound, although it is difficult to discuss findings in such a way as to get that across. It is, therefore, critical to remember that the studies discussed in this section refer to particular periods of time, and their particular conclusions may be more or less true for today. Nevertheless, these studies show that television, in one way or another, has consistently presented a distorted view of the world. For example, television has regularly overrepresented high-status occupations while paying little attention to how such an occupation might be attained (Ryan et al. 1988).

The most concern has been expressed about gender and ethnic stereotyping on television. For example, research has shown that during certain periods there have been three times as many white male characters as white females on television (Gerbner et al. 1980; Basow 1992). The ratio is about four to one in children's programming (Barcus 1983). According to some research, when television characters are women, they typically are young and beautiful sex objects, passive, dependent, dumb, and incompetent. In contrast, men are typically portrayed as powerful, aggressive, adventurous, and so on (Downs 1982; Wood 1994). However, as an indication of the constantly evolving nature of content, think about such characters as *Roseanne, Murphy Brown,* and Julia Sugerbaker of *Designing Women* in television comedy. In television drama, there have been such strong characterizations as Scully on *The X-Files,* Jeanie Boulet and Carol Hathaway on *ER,* Captain Kathryne Janeway on *Star Trek: Voyager,* and *Dr. Quinn, Medicine Woman.* And, in real life, there is Oprah. Men in general are not presented well on sitcoms. Many tend to be rather dim-witted, weak, or silly. For example, there is Drew Carey, the program *Men Behaving Badly,* Tim Allen on *Home Improvement* and, earlier, characters such as Cliff and Norm on *Cheers.* Do they fit the positive masculine stereotypes suggested in some research?

Other research indicates an underrepresentation of African Americans on entertainment television (Stroman 1989) as well as Hispanics and Asians. It is also argued that, when ethnic minorities do appear on television, it is in stereotypical roles or as villains (Lichter et al. 1987). It is true that positive African American male characters are rare in prime time, but there are Bill Cosby, Gregory Hines, Arthur "Lou" Fancy on *NYPD Blue,* Eugene Young on *The Practice,* and Captain Benjamin Cisco on *Star Trek: Deep Space Nine.* Interestingly, there are many more positive portrayals of African American males on daytime television.

Also underrepresented and stereotyped are the elderly. Despite the fact that older women greatly outnumber older men in society, on television it is just the opposite (Wood 1993). In addition, the elderly are typically portrayed as feeble, financially insecure, inactive, and sickly (Gerbner et al. 1980)—stereotypes that seem to ensure their marginalization in society.

Violence

Numerous studies show that our commercial television and movie images do, as critics suggest, contain high levels of violence. Studies have estimated some 6 violent acts per hour on prime-time television, and an attention-grabbing 18 per hour in Saturday morning children's programming (Signorielli et al. 1982). While figures such as these have become staples of various interest groups devoted to reducing violence or improving children's television, they have been criticized for failing to place violent acts in context. For example, in some cases violence caused by natural disasters has been weighted equally with murder and slapstick cartoon routines.

Studies by the Violence Assessment Monitoring Project (Cole 1996) have attempted to remedy this methodological problem. This ongoing project is designed to allow for independent monitoring by the UCLA Center for Communication Policy of the content of broadcast and cable television. The researchers have taken a comprehensive approach, examining every series, television movie, theatrical film, and children's program on network television, including 24 series from the UPN and WB networks (they did not look at news programs). In addition, every on-air promotion and advertisement aired during the programming was monitored. They monitored independent television in the Los Angeles area, a random two-week selection of public television, and eight cable channels (three pay and five basic) were monitored for randomly selected two-week periods. In all, some 3000 hours of television content were monitored in a single year. Finally, the researchers also monitored selections of top-ten videos available in stores, as well as a selection of video games.

Video games are another controversial form of entertainment for children.

Rather than take the traditional approach of simply counting incidents of violence—much objected to by television programmers—the researchers attempted to look at violence in context. They allowed that some violence might, in fact, be appropriate or used for comedic effect in such a way that it would not be taken seriously. It is clear that the very existence of a project of this scope, funded by the four broadcast networks, points to the importance of beliefs about powerful media effects in shaping the activities of mass media producers.

In September 1995 the UCLA Center released the first of three annual reports on the state of television violence. The report suggested that violence in programming created for broadcast television was not as prevalent as many believe. There was a greater problem with theatrical films (films originally released to theaters) shown on broadcast television but, even here, editing for television had greatly reduced the level of violence. Also seen as problematic were promotions for future programs. These often compressed several violent scenes which, although appropriate in the context of the actual program, seemed more violent when extracted from that program. Most disturbing to the researchers was the violence in films shown in theaters, in home videos, and on pay cable.

The UCLA researchers raised concerns that there is still too much violence on broadcast television, even though it is not generally graphic. They felt that, too often, violence was used on television as a solution to dramatic problems, especially in children's programming, and that violence occurred too early in the evening when children might still be watching. More specifically, they reported that, of the 161 television movies monitored, 23 (14 percent) raised their concern about the use of violence. Of the 118 theatrical films shown on television monitored, 50 (42 percent) raised concerns about the use of violence. These figures are in contrast to the approximately 121 prime-time television series monitored, of which 10 (8 percent) had frequent problems with violence and 8 (7 percent) had occasional problems.

The 1996 report showed considerable improvement over those numbers. The number of prime-time series raising concern dropped from 10 to 5 and, of those, two ran for only a few episodes during the season. In the first year report, 14 percent of television movies raised concerns about violence. In the second year this figure dropped to 10 percent.

One the most positive changes was that the number of theatrical films shown on television that contained what the researchers categorized as intense violence dropped from 42 percent to 29 percent. Despite this improvement, it continued to be the case that most serious television violence is in theatrical movies shown on television.

The problem of violent promotions, described in the 1995 report, was no longer seen as a problem in the 1996 report.

The researchers also saw improvement in the area of children's television, perhaps due, in part, to the implementation of the three-hour educational rule. The Children's Television Act of 1990 required three hours of educational programming for children per week as a condition for holding a broadcast license. However, broadcasters had used the term "educational" quite liberally, including such programs as *The Jetsons,* and *The Flintstones* as educational. In 1996, the FCC moved to prevent such abuses by more clearly defining educational programming, perhaps contributing to the difference found by the UCLA researchers.

The authors of the report expressed their greatest concern over what they term "sinister combat violence." This is violence that is central to the story, in which heroic characters glorify and use violence enthusiastically. While still of concern to the researchers, the number of children's programs featuring this type of violence dropped from seven to four.

The 1996 report described what the researchers considered a disturbing trend in the 1995–1996 season. This was the emergence of a genre of successful television specials containing real and re-created footage of animals attacking and sometimes killing people. While few in number, the researchers caution that the popularity of these types of programs may lead to their proliferation in the future. The Fox Network pioneered this genre of "reality TV" with its program *Cops.* The network has taken the reality genre to new levels with its *Greatest Car Chases* series. The third segment in the series climaxed with graphic footage of a truck driven by a teenager and his girlfriend being hit broadside by a tractor-trailer rig, killing them instantly.

The UCLA report offers a number of possible reasons for what the researchers believe is the improving picture on television violence. These include, (1) the raising of the issue prominently in the political arena—including two White House summits (2) public opinion data showing public concern, and (3) the establishment of the monitoring process itself. The simple fact that an extensive and very public monitoring process is in place may have altered the behavior of the producers. These three factors together make it clear that concern over media content and its effects is an important factor in the environment of mass media organizations.

In January 1998, the Center released its third and final report. Data from the 1996–1997 television season showed that the number of network series raising frequent concerns over violence had dropped to two (compared to nine in 1995 and five in 1996). the number of series raising occasional concerns had dropped as well—from eight in 1996 to six in 1997. However, as predicted in the previous report, violent "reality specials" proliferated in the 1996–1997 season.

But before we rejoice too much over the improved picture regarding television violence, it should be pointed out that not all researchers agree with these interpretations. Just months after release of the third report, another group of researchers using a different methodology released findings suggesting an *increase* in prime-time violence over the same period studied by the UCLA researchers (Mifflin 1998).

The Evidence against Effects

Despite the commonsense notion of mass media effects, and despite the comments of numerous media critics, the search for powerful media effects has been less than successful. Two comprehensive reviews of the effects literature illustrate this point.

In an extensive review of the literature on media effects, McQuire (1986) found some surprising results. In examining areas where there were *intended* media impacts, McQuire found that few studies showed effects that approached statistical significance. This means that few findings could reasonably be assumed to have *not* been due to chance. And those that did reach significance actually explained very little of the variance in the variables being studied. In other words, the studies were unable to demonstrate much in the way of media effects, and those effects that were demonstrated were small. This was true for each of the following areas in which there was a conscious effort to create media effects.

1. Commercial advertising effects on consumer behavior. Despite the billions of dollars spent on media advertising, few effects could be demonstrated.

2. Mass media political advertisements. McQuire again found that studies showed few effects. Some results even suggested that what relationship there was between political advertisement expenditures and campaign success was actually the opposite of what is commonly thought. Because political incumbents tend to be elected, they also tend to draw the most support. It may well be that their large advertising budgets are more the result than the cause of their success! The studies reviewed indicated small effects that were limited to those who were late in making up their minds about a candidate, to lesser known candidates, to minor office races, and the ads were just as likely to influence voters to vote against a candidate as for the candidate. McQuire concludes: "In sum, it has not been established that political ads have sizeable effects on the amount or the direction of voting" (183).

3. Other types of political coverage. Concern is often expressed about the *way* U.S. media cover elections. The elections are often treated as a horse race or some other sporting competition in which the emphasis is more on who is winning than on the substance of the issues. Of more specific concern has been the networks' practice of projecting winners in national elections from East Coast results before West Coast polls have closed. It has been argued that voters on the West Coast may alter their voting behavior based on East Coast results or exit polling results. McQuire reports that there is little support in the research that the public actually is affected in this way.

4. Public Service Announcements. Whether the goal is to discourage smoking or to encourage the use of seatbelts, the studies reviewed by McQuire once again indicate little or no direct relationship between exposure to public service announcements and changes in behavior.

Of course not all media effects are intended. Indeed much of the concern over media content has to do with *unintended* effects, especially violence. Nearly everyone except the programmers themselves agrees that there is significant violent content in the mass media. Yet, when McQuire examined some of the best studies done on the effects of violence in the media, the results were the same—few studies showed effects that reached statistical significance and, in those that did, the magnitude of the effects amounted to no more than a few percentage points. And the greatest effects were found in controlled laboratory experiments, which usually do not simulate real-world conditions well.

A 1996 comprehensive review of the literature by sociologist Richard Felson (1996) reached similar conclusions regarding the relationship between media content, exposure, and violence. Felson notes numerous contradictory results in the research. He writes, "The reason media effects (on violence and aggression) are not consistently observed is probably because they are weak and only affect a small percentage of viewers" (Felson 1996:118).

Other areas where television is thought to have important effects did not fare quite as poorly in McQuire's review of the literature. For example, as noted above, numerous studies have shown that television's depiction of the real world has been seriously distorted. Historically, television has underrepresented and negatively stereotyped women, African Americans, the elderly, and other minorities. Research on the effects of these portrayals seems to show that heavy television viewers do, in fact, exhibit perceptions that are in line with these distortions.

The Cultivation Effect

The best-known explanation for this phenomenon is the "cultivation effect" (Gerbner 1986). In a series of studies, Gerbner and his associates at the Annenberg School discovered that television overrepresents the level of violence in society and distorts the reality of who is most likely to be a victim. In particular, women, the young, the old, and some minorities are most likely to be victimized on television. According to Gerbner, rather than causing most people to be violent, this distortion cultivates in heavy viewers, particularly members of victimized groups, feelings of mistrust, alienation, gloom, and a sense that the world is a "mean" place.

The Annenberg studies show that heavy viewers possess perceptions of the world that more closely correspond to the televised world than do those who watch less television. Thus, heavy viewers are more likely to possess stereotypes of minority groups corresponding to those on television, and are more likely to perceive a "scary world" in which they perceive that they are in greater danger from crime than they really are. Gerbner and his associates argue that these perceptions are "cultivated" in heavy viewers through their television watching. While the effects are not large, they are consistently statistically significant. This seems to be a clear example of negative effects of television content.

However, there is controversy regarding these findings. Causal direction is problematical. It could be that media writers hold the same stereotypes as the general public, or that their marketing knowledge about what sells leads these writers to mirror attitudes with commercial value. This would suggest that heavy viewers already possess attitudes and beliefs similar to those portrayed on television, rather than acquiring them from television. Or, regarding the tendency for heavy viewers to see a "scary world," it could be that heavy viewers come from neighborhoods and demographic groups more likely to experience crime and violence. It could also be that heavy viewers watch more TV *because* it conforms to their world view. There are other problems with these findings that suggest the need for further research (see Hughes 1980; Hirsch 1980, 1981).

McQuire contends that even pornographic imagery does not have clear effects, despite the fact that it seems intuitive that it would. And, if pornographic material does not have obvious effects, this calls into question the concern over the comparatively mild erotic imagery of broadcast television. McQuire's findings are supported by those of a Presidential Commission (U.S. Government 1970), which found at most very small effects of pornography on behavior, and Felson's (1996) review of the literature.

Television and Children

In addition to the great concern over the effects on children of violent and sexual content in the mass media, the media have been accused of negatively impacting the cognitive and academic functioning of children. Again, the results are contradictory. Many studies seem to show negative effects. However, a 1988 report, *The Impact on Children's Education: Television's Influence on Cognitive Development* (Bennett et al. 1988), reviewed 165 studies and found little support for the idea that television is bad for children cognitively and academically. The studies showed no evidence that children are overstimulated by television, or that children who do *not* watch television spend most of that time in more worthwhile pursuits, or that children do a poorer job on their homework if they do it in front of the television. It is true that children who watch more television tend to read less, although it is unclear whether that effect is due to television itself or to parental modeling. The researchers found weak evidence that television shortens children's attention spans and contradictory evidence of the effect of television on imaginative play. Regarding the latter, some studies show that children who watch more television are less creative in their play, while other studies indicate that children use televised images to stimulate imaginative play.

The Evidence for *Effects*

As noted at the beginning of this chapter, there is widespread belief in the power of the mass media to influence a wide range of attitudes, beliefs, and behaviors. We have also seen that some extensive reviews of the literature do not support that belief. In addition, there are other reviews of the literature that support the idea of limited or no effects (see Freedman 1984, 1986, 1988). However, still other reviews of many of the same studies draw just the opposite conclusion (see Comstock and Paik 1991; Friedrich-Cofer and Huston 1986). One of those is a review by Paik and Comstock (1994) in which the researchers use a methodological technique known as "meta-analysis" that allows for the statistical analysis of the findings of groups of studies.

Paik and Comstock conducted their analysis on 217 studies dealing with the subject of mass media exposure and content and its effect on aggressive behavior. Their analysis results in some very different conclusions than those of McQuire (1986) and Felson (1996). Paik and Comstock find a statistically significant relationship between exposure to violent programs and various forms of aggressive behavior. This means that whatever differences in aggressive behavior exist between those who are exposed to more television or other violent programming and those who are not is *not* random or simply due to chance. According to this study, there *is* a relationship between exposure to television violence and antisocial behavior.

While statistical significance tells us whether or not there is a real effect, it is not a measure of the size or importance of that effect. One way to determine the size of an effect is in terms of the amount of variance explained. That is, how much of the variation in observed or reported aggressive behavior can be explained by a variable such as media exposure? Paik and Comstock conducted a statistical analysis of the data and concluded that, overall, about 10 percent of the variance in aggressive behavior in a sample could be explained by media exposure. Given the limitations in trying to study something as complex as media effects, this is a rather sizable effect. However, their results differed widely depending on the type of study examined. They report that 16 percent of the variance in aggressive behavior in laboratory experiments was due to being exposed to a violent stimulus, compared to 4 percent in time–series studies (in which effects are traced over a period of time) and 3 percent of the variance explained by media exposure in survey studies. One possible explanation for these discrepancies is that laboratory experiments have been heavily criticized for creating artificial conditions under which aggressive acts are more likely to occur. We will discuss that issue in greater detail below.

Another interesting aspect of this study was that the researchers looked at effect sizes for different *types* of effects. The researchers looked at several kinds of aggressive behavior:

1. Simulated aggressiveness: defined as playing with an aggressive toy, use of aggression machines to deliver a simulated shock, or stating an intention to perform an aggressive act.
2. Minor aggressiveness: defined as physical violence against an object, such as a toy, verbal aggressiveness, or noncriminal violence against a person.
3. Illegal activities: burglary, grand theft, or criminal violence against a person.

The results of this analysis are quite interesting. Again, effect sizes vary by method used. And again, experimental studies showed, by far, the greatest effects. For laboratory studies examining simulated aggressive behavior, the overall effect is 11 percent of the variance explained by exposure to violent media content. For all studies examining minor aggressive behavior, the overall effect is 10 percent of the variance explained, and for all studies examining criminal behavior, the effect was 3 percent.

For policy purposes, the findings regarding criminal violence against others are most important. After all, this has been the most damning critique of television: that it causes the level of violence to increase. Paik and Comstock found that surveys indicate the effect of media exposure on criminal violence (homicide, suicide, stabbing, etc.) was less than one-half of one percent of the explained variance. This leaves over 99 percent of the variance in criminal violence unexplained by media exposure.

What you make out of this depends on your point of view—a variation on an old cliché, "Is the glass 99 percent empty or 1 percent full?" Paik and Comstock conclude that the overall effect of media exposure on aggressive behavior is of moderate size, and the effect on illegal activities is small. Some, such as McQuire (1986) and Felson (1996), might argue that the overall effect of 10 percent of the variance explained (assuming that number is accurate) is small, and the effect on illegal activities is minuscule. It depends on your point of view. Perhaps any effect on criminal behavior is too much.

In either case, causality is still a problem. For example, individuals who engage in criminal activities typically do not hold regular jobs and therefore have more time to watch television. Individuals with violent dispositions may be drawn to violent programming. Only the experimental studies give some indication of causality, but those types of studies have their own problems. More generally, a major problem with meta-analysis is that it cannot undo the numerous methodological problems in the studies it is grouping together.

What are we to make out of this confusing array: moderate, weak, or nonfindings of mass media effects? McQuire (1986) and Felson (1996) offer a number of possible explanations for salvaging the idea that the mass media indeed have effects.

Methodological Explanations

Because of the complex methodological problems involved, it is difficult to draw firm conclusions from mass media effects research. For example, it is often the case that independent variables in mass media studies are poorly measured. A measure of television exposure may be as crude as asking a respondent how many hours per week he or she watches. It seems almost certain that it may be more important *what* someone watches, what they are doing while they are watching, in what context they watch, and so on. Such information is difficult to obtain. People don't always remember what they watch and have difficulty estimating how much they watch. Studies of children's viewing habits are particularly suspect in this regard. Some rely on parents' reports of their children's viewing and, as Felson (1996) points out, there is a low correlation between parents' reports and children's reports. Even if the researchers have an accurate measure of how much television is watched, do they have enough variation in television viewing in their sample to develop meaningful categories of level of viewing? That is, it may not make much difference if someone watches 10 hours or 20 hours per week but it may make a difference if they cross a higher threshold—say, 40 hours. If those watching 20, 30, or 40 hours per week are lumped together, the effect of the highest exposure will be masked.

Dependent variables are also often inadequate. Measures of aggressiveness may lack validity. For example, in an artificial laboratory, such measures as attacking a "Bobo" doll or simulated shocking of confederate subjects may be encouraged, either overtly or more subtly, by the researcher. A subject may perceive that the researcher either is expecting aggressiveness, an expectation that the subject feels obligated to fulfill, or at least the subject may feel that the researcher is giving permission to be aggressive. In experimental research this is known as the **sponsoring effect.** In laboratory settings there is no likelihood that aggression will be punished and the aggression is not real in its consequences. It is likely that most individuals who react aggressively in an experiment would not do so in a normal social environment, even after receiving the same stimulus. Measuring "aggressiveness" outside of the laboratory is even more problematic. Often researchers rely on potentially biased reports from teachers or peers or self-reports. In any case, it is not clear whether effects are being masked or exaggerated by such measurement problems.

Another problem is that, even when a correlation is found between media exposure and some effect, the causal direction is often difficult to determine. For example, as we saw with cultivation analysis, does watching television cause heavy viewers to feel like they are more likely to be victims of violent crime, or is it that people who already feel vulnerable, the elderly, for example, are more likely to stay home and watch television, or is it both? Are violent people more drawn to violent programming and therefore watch more than less violent people?

Outside of the experimental laboratory there is also the potential for spurious relationships between television watching and behavior. There may be a spurious correlation between a child's viewing and later aggressiveness because children who are closely monitored by parents may be less likely to watch television and less likely to commit aggressive acts. Felson points out that researchers typically do not control for need for excitement, level of fear, commitment to school, intelligence, and other variables that may influence the effect of media exposure. For example, Wiegman et al. (1992) have found a negative relationship between intelligence and both media exposure and aggressive behavior.

Beyond these types of methodological problems, there is much to be learned about the whole process of how people interact with the media. This process may have much to do with whether or not we are able to perceive effects. It has been fairly well demonstrated that viewers tend to seek out information that supports their view of the world (see Klapper 1960). More controversial is the possibility that people actually attempt to avoid exposure to media content that they find distasteful, or that is not in accordance with their beliefs and values. It seems likely that this would depend on a number of factors, including the discrepancy between the person's values and the material, the level of curiosity, and so on.

The growth of cable television with channels specifically targeted to certain lifestyles may make selection even more possible. Similarly, it could be argued that, because mass media messages pervade our society at such a high level, direct exposure is not necessary. In a sense, each one of us is exposed through our friends and associates, even if we do not view the material directly. If their attitudes and beliefs are influenced, and they are significant others to us, then this will have an impact on us as well.

Summary

We have seen that there is a widespread and longstanding belief in the power of the mass media to influence behavior. Yet, the research on the subject of media effects has yielded confusing and contradictory evidence. This does not necessarily mean that the media *have* no effect. It may mean that the effects are too complex to discern using the tools we have been using thus far. There are, in fact, reasons to expect that the mass media *must* have an effect, even if that effect is difficult to discover empirically. After all, we have all had the experience of leaving the grocery store with an item that we neither wanted nor needed until we saw an advertisement extolling its virtues. Or perhaps you have found yourself wearing a particular hairstyle or item of clothing that you saw on *Friends*. We know that a single 90-second story on the nightly news about some new "cure-all" herbal supplement can clear store shelves of that product in just a few hours. And, when Oprah Winfrey picks a book for her on-air book club, sales soar, and when she does a program on mad cow disease, cattle prices fall. The quote that opened this chapter is one of many collected by one of the authors that suggest that people believe that the media have had effects in their lives and can provide specific instances of influence. This seems to be a case of a discrepancy between what we feel that we know and what some interpretations of the research show.

What we can say is that, if there are effects of the mass media, they are difficult to measure and are complex and probably subtle in nature. This should not be surprising. Looking back to our discussion of sociological theory and the mass media, it is easy to see both that we should expect an effect but not expect that effect to be a simple one. The nature and quality of the message, the context (from societal to individual) within which the message is received (if it is received at all), and characteristics of the person exposed to the message all moderate the influence of the message.

If we accept the questionable assumption that the mass media have clearly negative effects on individuals, a key question is whether these effects are large enough to justify the efforts our society puts into attempts at regulating the media. Is it possible that the media are being made the scapegoat for more complex problems that might be more difficult to solve than regulating television programming? Whether the effects are real or not, the belief in effects is real in its consequences. Ratings systems, V-chips, and CD warning labels all illustrate the fact that this belief is a major constraint in the environment of mass media producers. Media producers cannot escape the fact that there is widespread concern about what they do. And this concern makes it necessary to select and edit content with critics of the media in mind.

4

Mass Media Effects II: Societal Effects

*Welcome to the Digital Revolution, a curious revolution
if ever there was one. Its target is not the levers of political
or economic power but rather the dials on your television
and buttons on your PC. Its weapons aren't guns or street
protests but cutthroat commerce and high-risk finance.
It promises not deliverance from oppression, but rather
entry into a high-tech utopia so advanced it will make
the gee-whiz gadgetry of the Jetsons seem more like
the simple stone tools of the Flintstones. And ironically,
while aiming to empower the individual with hybrid
"tele-computers" that deliver a host of new information
and entertainment services, the Digital Revolution will actually do more to alter the shape of government, the economy,
and the American way of life than even the most radical
social activists have imagined in their wildest dreams*
—BURSTEIN AND KLINE 1995:32–33

The year was 1987, the place, the small town of Midland, Texas, an unlikely location
for the world's attention to be focused. *Newsweek* reporters Evan Thomas and Peter
Anin (1997: 34) describe the scene:

> *Jessica McClure was almost 1½ when she fell down an eight-inch-wide well
> in her aunt's backyard. Her mother had gone inside—just for a moment—
> to answer the phone. For 58 hours, nearly 100 rescue workers labored to
> get her out, drilling a shaft 29 feet down and five across. Diamond-tipped
> drill bits snapped on the bedrock; the progress was slowed when the drill-
> ers, exhausted, broke down and sobbed because they could hear the girl,*

still alive, singing nursery rhymes and crying for her mother. While she was being pulled free, inch by inch, by a paramedic using K–Y lubricating jelly, 3.1 million people were watching live on CNN—at the time, the largest audience ever to watch the cable news service.

Jessica McClure ("Baby Jessica" to the mass media) survived, but the lives of townspeople were changed forever. Jessica's parents divorced. The man who pulled her to safety appeared on *Oprah,* judged the "G. I. Joe American Heroes" contest and, according to Thomas and Anin, became intoxicated with fame. He committed suicide in 1995. Meanwhile, the townspeople divided into factions over whose stories would be told in the Hollywood movie.

Of course not all of the problems faced by people in Midland are due to media attention. But there is plenty of anecdotal evidence, from the bombing in Oklahoma City to the death of Princess Diana, to suggest that when media attention is turned on people and places, things change. Not because of any particular message—as was the concern in the previous chapter, but because the media change the context within which people interact with each other (an audience of local townspeople expands into millions), create status differences, and dispense or withhold recognition and money. These are not just effects on individuals, they are social effects, altering the framework of social interaction.

We saw in the previous chapter that, while it makes sense that mass media messages would have impacts on individual behavior, such effects are difficult to show empirically. This is due to both the complexity of the ways in which the media might affect the individual, and the limitations of methodologies for uncovering

The death of Princess Diana highlighted issues pertaining to media invasions of privacy.

effects. What we do know is that the history of human beings has been a history of developing new technologies to solve the problems of living. And we also know, as Max Weber pointed out long ago, that each new technology brings with it unintended consequences, a new set of problems to solve. Even if the exact dynamics of how media interact with daily life are not yet fully understood, it is clear that these new technologies and new ways of communicating have given us solutions to some of our old problems, as well as a whole new set of challenges and opportunities.

In some ways, societal effects are easier to see than are internalized individual effects. For example, just cruising through a mall with video stores, music stores, computer software and hardware stores, and electronics dealers, it is easy to see how the mass media have changed the way people entertain themselves and receive information. It is easy to see that, where once riding alone in an automobile would normally put you out of touch with others at home or work, now the car can become an extension of home or office through the technology of the cellular phone. It is easy to see that where once people limited their discussion of emotional trauma in their privates lives to family members, small therapy groups, or close acquaintances, now virtual support groups on the Internet provide new environments for such interaction. In this chapter we will look at some of the ways in which the media have changed our social world.

New Ways of Communicating

Impersonal

As we saw in earlier chapters, technology has provided human beings with vast new ways of communicating across time and space. In traditional societies communication was almost entirely face-to-face. Face-to-face communication provides multiple layers of messages from words and gestures, to body language, to facial expressions. More often than not this communication is carried out in the context of a real relationship and a context that is well known to the participants. Thus, there are a variety of ways of extracting meaning from that communication. Another important element of this comparatively very personal type of communication is that it is potentially interactive. Each person, to some degree, can press the other for clarification, further information, and so on.

New technologies have altered one or more of these elements of face-to-face communication. The written word removes most of everything but the obvious content. While the context may be well understood in the particular time and place of the document's creation, it becomes less obvious as it moves outside its own culture and time period. For example, Wendy Griswold (1987) has shown how the novels of West Indian writer George Lamming have been interpreted differently by literary critics from the West Indies, Great Britain, and the United States. It is often the case that context, contributing to meaning, must be added back in by experts specializing in a particular cultural genre. To the modern reader *Gulliver's Travel's* may seem to

The mass media change the context of communication.

be a simple fable, but to readers in the 18th century most of the scenes and characters had political and social implications.

One way of describing these effects is to say that much of modern communication is impersonal, while much communication in traditional society is personal. But it is not quite that simple. Technologies such as television and the Internet are capable of mimicking elements of face-to-face communication. Television, for example, shows visual images of human faces that can, especially in advertising and newscasts, seem to speak directly to viewers. Messages are often designed to appeal to familiar situations and strong emotions. Thus, modern societies are awash in communication that appears to be personal but lacks some crucial elements of the personal. From a societal standpoint, one of the most crucial of these missing elements is the ability to judge the accuracy of the message. Because of the anonymity of developed society, we cannot be sure of the authenticity even of face-to-face messages. The mass media can exaggerate this problem. We are constantly exposed to messages from speakers we do not know for purposes we are not quite sure of.

Political and Economic Control

Another characteristic of mass-mediated communication is that, in many places in the world, it is communication for profit. In other places it is politically controlled. In either case, the idea is not simply to convey information but rather to serve powerful interests in some way.

There are some obvious societal effects of this. In a politically dominated media system, it is likely that what is transmitted is designed to serve the interests of those in power. As we will see in the chapter on industry structure, even in the United States, where most of the media are privately held, some would argue that the overall effect of the media is to maintain the legitimacy of those in power (see, for example, Giddens 1987).

Likewise, in profit-oriented media, the message is skewed toward legitimating consumption and attempts at manipulating demand for particular products. As we will see in Chapter 9, in the process, sometimes even sizable audiences can be ignored if they do not have consumer power.

Speed and Volume

Not only are the media bombarding us with messages rooted in economic and political agendas, they do so at incredible speed, over vast distances, in enormous volume. If nothing else, this means that people have large amounts of information coming into their lives that they must deal with in some way, even if dealing with it means ignoring it. Increasingly, in modern society it seems that the problem is information overload rather than a lack of information. Sorting out information, assimilating it, handling discordant information, these are the central problems. It also means that we are more connected to the world outside our immediate environment than ever before. Many people are more connected to the distant world than to the world right around them. How is this possible?

One factor is the decline of "community" in large-scale societies. One of the characteristics of modern leisure is a high degree of privatization (Rojek 1985). This means that people in developed societies spend a large amount of their leisure time in their homes interacting with the mass media, video and computer games, the Internet, and so on. They do this instead of congregating in public places. Part of this is due to the allure of these leisure activities, but it is also due to conditions in the larger society. People often move several times in their lifetimes and are unlikely to reside near their family of origin or the friends they grew up with or met in school. In new locations they are likely to rely primarily on their spouse and children for companionship. At the same time, public places, especially in urban areas, are often perceived as dangerous. Ironically, there is an interaction between this perception and reality. When people stay in their homes rather than frequent public places, those public places are often taken over by deviant activities. Fear of the deviant activities then makes people even more reluctant to go out. As we saw in the last chapter, some (see, for example Gerbner 1986) would argue that the mass media contribute to this cycle by cultivating fear in heavy viewers.

Further compounding this problem is that, in many cases, truly local media may not exist. With the decline of face-to-face communication in local areas, those without a local newspaper, radio station, or television station may be cut off from local news, all the while tuning into satellite broadcasts from around the globe (meta-information). A possible effect is a lack of awareness and interest in local issues (local off-year election turnouts typically vary from 10 to 20 percent of eligible voters), precisely as political trends push more and more decision making to that level.

Time Use

If the mass media have no other effect, they certainly have altered patterns of time use. We know that people spend more of their leisure time interacting with the mass media than doing anything else. In fact, the most important thing about television is that while people are watching it they may not be doing something else. The U.S. General Social Survey data from 1993 indicate that people spend an average of nearly three hours a day watching television. Because this is primarily passive time, one wonders how many books have not been written, songs composed, paintings painted, or inventions discovered because it was easier to turn on the television and watch reruns of *The Andy Griffith Show.* More realistically, how many books have not been read, household conversations missed, family outings not planned for the same reason? It is certainly true that television is a very easy and involving form of leisure activity.

Television had a major impact on time spent with other mass media. In the years prior to the popularization of television, it was the radio that was at the heart of home entertainment. Television quickly ate up large segments of time that had been devoted to radio listening and radio would not begin to recover until the 1960s. Likewise, with the advent of television, movie attendance declined and newspaper and magazine consumption went down. In 1955 the U.S. Department of Health, Education and Welfare reported results from a survey on how other media were affected by television. This study showed that, after the purchase of a television set, magazine use declined 41 percent, newspaper use declined 18 percent, and radio use declined 57 percent (Brody 1990:269).

Of course television is not immune to encroachments from other media. It appears that video games and, more recently, Internet cruising, have begun to take bites out of the amount of time spent watching television.

However, if we simply look at the time spent on television and other mass media we would be missing a significant portion of their impact. The mass media, especially television, become part of our way of ordering the world. What industrial work has done for the rational ordering of the workday around fairly rigid time schedules, first radio, and then television, have done for the ordering of leisure time. It is not unusual for individuals to schedule their leisure time, sometimes their entire day, around the scheduling of their favorite programs. We know that young children stay up later than they have in the past and some observers attribute this to the influence of the television schedule: Popular programs often do not start until 8 PM. It is interesting that, although the VCR held the promise of liberating us from the tyranny of the program schedulers, people rarely use the technology in that way. Few people actually use VCRs for "time shifting," recording a program for later viewing. Most use the machine for playing back prerecorded videos.

This may have something to do with what people perceive as the complexity of the technology. However, it may also have something to do with the role that television plays in creating ritual events in our lives. Popular programs become the focal point of these rituals in which family and friends either gather together or at least know that the others are watching the same program at a particular time, the "topic circles" predicted from our discussion of Mead in Chapter 2. Even watching in physical isolation may have the effect of connecting one to a community of other viewers in ways that watching a time-shifted tape may not.

Globalization and Shared Identity

As we shall see in Chapter 7, the mass media today are truly global. Not only does ownership sometimes transcend national boundaries, programming flows at an ever-increasing rate across penetrable borders. Beamed down from satellites, carried by cable or telephone wire, shipped in crates and carried by trucks, pirated in back rooms and warehouses, cultural products are shared quickly and easily around the world.

Take, for example, some Roper data reported by Walker (1996). In 1995, data were collected that examined various activities done in the previous day by people in six separate regions of the world: North America, Latin America, Western Europe, Central Europe, the former Soviet Union, and Asia. Excluding work and sleep, in every region, the only activity more likely to have been performed than TV watching was toothbrushing. Television watching ranked higher than reading, listening to the radio, showering, or bathing.

The mere fact of placing television at the top of leisure activities globally may have some effect, but more important are the commonalities in content around the world. As developing nations have adopted television technology, it has proven quite difficult to provide viable local programming. Television production, especially of credible dramatic programs, requires large investments in technology and production, and the creation of technological and artistic expertise. Inexpensively available, slickly produced programming from the developed countries (especially the United States) is an easy substitute for creating a local TV infrastructure.

The mass media are increasingly able to penetrate every region of the world.

Local programming is further hindered by the voracious appetite of television. It requires enormous, expensive resources and technical expertise to fill all available airtime on all channels with ever-changing content. Traditional sources of drama, dance, music, and other cultural expressions are quickly used up by the medium. To cite an example from the United States, break dancing, after a long history of development in African American culture, became a highly visible component of the larger popular culture in the 1980s. For a period of time this cultural expression seemed to be everywhere: in music videos, motion pictures, documentaries, and even in McDonalds commercials. As a result, the public became bored with it and it dropped from popularity. What had been a long-evolving folk expression of creativity became merely cliché and "out of style."

It is not just television that crosses borders. Music has become an international business as well, with world sales reaching nearly $40 billion. The importing of music produced by multinational corporations has had profound impacts on local music, in some cases wiping out the local music industry entirely.

The outcome of all of this is a real threat that the culture receiving these products will be seriously altered or become secondary to that of the producing nation. This is not just a problem for developing nations, as witnessed by Canada's attempts to limit the influence of the United States on its cultural industries. An editorial (August 10, 1997: F2, excerpted below) in the *Toronto Star,* entitled "Ottawa Must Be Firm on Protecting Culture," is illustrative of this concern over cultural contamination. The editorial attacks Canada's leadership for failing to protect Canada's cultural industry, in particular the magazine industry, from U.S. competition. The editorial suggests that the Canadian government insist on the following points in negotiating with the Organization for Economic Co-operation and Development on trade agreements:

- Culture should be taken off the table, not just exempted from the agreement. It is not negotiable.
- Canada should make common cause with countries such as France that are determined to resist the homogenizing influence of Hollywood.
- If the United States refuses to accept the right of other states to protect their own forms of cultural expression, Canada negotiators should leave the talks.

What is sometimes called **cultural imperialism,** the domination of one culture by another, is not just an issue for developing nations. As the above editorial suggests, even developed nations fear that their culture will be swept aside or assimilated into the tide of material emanating from the United States. Such concerns may be warranted. For example, Fine et al. (1995) demonstrate that popular books published in Canada differ little from popular books published in the United States. The researchers attribute this fact to a strong U.S. presence in Canadian publishing, as well as to the mass market strategies of publishers.

As the Canadian example suggests, the preservation of local cultures is difficult and rarely fully successful. The question often becomes, "whose culture is to be preserved?"

Often a variety of subcultures or folk cultures exist within the boundaries of a nation–state. Yet, the mass media are by definition designed to cut across such boundaries. Countries usually end up elevating a few of their folk cultures, at the expense of others, as they attempt to develop a mass medium. Cultural diversity is often best accommodated in state-run systems that do not need to develop a generalized market. However, technologies such as fiber-optic cable and satellite direct broadcast open the possibility of more easily accommodating diversity, even in commercial systems. For example, large cities in the United States now typically carry Hispanic and Asian programming on their cable systems.

Local programming has been growing as media systems around the world mature. However, U.S.-produced programs still enjoy enormous success worldwide. When one of the authors of this book recently had the opportunity to teach a seminar in Holland with students from eleven different countries, one of the most popular shows among members of the group was *The X-Files*. Other programs, such as *ER* and, in an earlier period, *Dallas*, have enjoyed tremendous worldwide success. The general rule among producers is that action movies and dramas seem to translate particularly well cross-culturally, and comedies translate the least. This is because humor tends to be much more culturally specific than violence, which is fairly easily understood by everyone. Among teenagers worldwide, the most popular programming after movies is MTV. However, MTV has adapted to cultural differences by adopting regional variations. Thus, in Europe there is MTV Europe and in Japan MTV Japan and in India MTV India. These variations retain much of the familiar look and feel of U.S. MTV, with only a portion of the same artists.

Watching Dallas

Similarities in programming, however, do not necessarily lead to the globalization of culture. A study by Liebes and Katz (1993) on audience interpretation of the television show *Dallas* suggests that local culture has an effect on the way such programming is received or understood. The researchers looked at the impact of the program on four ethnic groups in Israel—Arabs, newly arrived Russian Jews, Moroccan Jews, and kibbutz members. A comparison study was conducted in Japan where the program had failed to attract an audience. The researchers found that the program, despite its complexity for people living in other countries, was quite popular—viewing was an important part of social life for many people and it became a major source of conversation in social gatherings—but it was interpreted differently according to one's culture. While most study members treated the program as real—that is, accepting that people really live as portrayed on *Dallas*—at a general level, the more modern and educated the group, the more they reacted to the program at an intellectual, analytical level. More traditional groups had greater emotional involvement with the program. Arabs tended to interpret the program as a morality play, highlighting differences between American culture and their own. The Russians were most critical of the program, emphasizing its manipulative aspects and its inferiority to the writings of Pushkin and Tolstoy. The Americans and kibbutzniks engaged the program at a more playful level. The Japanese did not care for the program because of its fast pace and the fact that each episode did not end with harmony among family members.

Likewise, the international students in Holland "read" *The X-Files* in different ways. For example, students from developing countries were more likely to believe that characters Fox Mulder and Dana Scully were real people in situations that were based on reality. This anecdotal example, as well as the *Dallas* examples, points out the adaptability of culture—the tendency of people to remain in their own cultural frame. The subtle influences are undoubtedly assimilated into viewers' perpsectives, but mass-marketing of cultural products is unlikely to result in a single world culture.

Global Marketing

Kline (1995) has outlined some potential effects of global marketing on world culture. **Global marketing** is the purposeful transcending of national boundaries in the marketing strategies of large multinational corporations. As part of this process, **consumerism** has become a driving force in the social life of many cultures. That is, it is primarily through the purchase of goods and services that people create status, identities, and entertainment, and provide meaning in their lives. And, anything that can be turned into a commodity and sold will be sold. Anything: food, clothing, history, childhood, religion.

Kline argues that, worldwide, the media are more commercialized than ever before. Therefore marketing and product promotion are more important than ever in the mass media production process, and the overall impact of massive marketing on other cultures needs more study. Of special concern to Kline is the fact that children and their play are being targeted by marketers and, increasingly, through alliances between various types of producers. Spurred on by the lucrative practice of tying children's television programming to toy license agreements, an increasingly larger portion of worldwide marketing has focused on children. As the editor of an industry publication devoted to children's advertising put it, "There is not a company on the globe that does not have some vested interest in marketing to kids" (quoted in Horovitz 1997:2A).

In recent years there has been a shift in the strategy of global marketers. One of the most successful global campaigns in history was the Coca-Cola "teach the world to sing" campaign. The campaign consisted of advertisements that were virtually the same in every country. Today it is more likely that campaigns and products will be altered to fit local cultures. Kline refers to this trend as the movement from global to **glo-local** marketing—the global parallel to the practice of "narrowcasting."

However, there is a question as to whether such differences of local marketing are really meaningful or whether they are mostly trivial as compared to the underlying consumerism messages. If meaningful, then this is illustrative of the power of local cultures. If mostly trivial, then the mass-marketing of products around the world may indeed lead to a globalization of culture. What certainly is true is that, especially for young people around the world, consumerism is increasingly a positive value, as they

Cultural symbols are exported from the United States and consumed by young people in widely varying contexts around the world.

seek status and create identities through the consumption of a remarkably similar set of mass-produced products—including Coca-Cola and Levis jeans.

Parents and Children

The mass media have had an effect on social relationships as well. For example, the media penetrate into the relationship between parents and children. We have already seen that bedtimes may be altered by the effect of mass media schedules. Even if parents resist such pressure, it becomes "just one more thing" they have to deal with in raising their children. Likewise, advertising aimed at children may create desires that parents must respond to in some way. Children view some 20,000 ads per year, many of them aimed directly at them. Advertisers spend considerable time, effort, and money trying to find out more about the private lives of children. Some parents find themselves running from store to store and waiting in long lines to find the latest fad toy, whether it be "Tickle Me Elmo," "Beanie Babies," or "Mighty Morphin Power Rangers." Some parents may resist, but they are under powerful pressure when other parents do not resist in a culture that equates buying with caring.

Many children seem to be highly status conscious and very aware of the relationship between brand names and status. One of the authors knows of an incident in which a first grader came home crying after being teased by classmates because her doll was not a *real* Cabbage Patch Doll (it wasn't). In another incident, a junior high school child was teased for wearing a discount store brand of tennis shoes. Anyone who has experienced a toddler in a supermarket tantrum over some cereal made like little chocolate donuts knows the impressionability of children and the tension this can create in the parent–child relationship.

Likewise, the relationship between parents and children is used to sell products to parents. Commercials tell parents (and, less directly, children) that if they don't buy a certain kind of tire or use a particular brand of gasoline they are endangering the life of their child. Another advertisement depicts a young man going off to college only to flunk out of school. Why? The ad tells us it was because he did have his own personal computer. Such advertisements attempt to influence the buying patterns of parents by linking love and guilt with the purchase of a product.

In the previous chapter we saw the difficulty in linking mass media messages to changes in specific behaviors. However, when the mass media deliver content to children that parents disapprove of, this must certainly affect the authority of parents and the relationship between parents and children. The mass media are agents of socialization that may compete with parents when parents' values differ from those of the media. Children may be exposed to the high levels of violence or sexual behavior on television or in music, either at home or elsewhere, well before parents intended or expected such exposure to take place. The way activities are portrayed may not be what parents want. For example, television sitcoms frequently use scenes with sexual display, casual sexual encounters, and a sort of immature locker room approach to sexual matters. Many parents want other attitudes and values portrayed to their adolescents, who are exploring the world of sexual relationships.

All of this suggests that the mass media regularly expose children to points of view other than those their parents grew up with. For example, Lichter, Lichter, and Rothman (1991) argue that the mass media have a distinct "liberal" bias on social issues such as gender, race relations, and homosexuality. They believe that this bias clashes with "traditional mainstream" values held by most Americans. If this is the case, most Americans are not opposed to being entertained by actors behaving in ways they do not approve of for themselves. Similarly, Prindle and Endersby (1993) have shown that a sample of Hollywood opinion leaders were more liberal than the American general public on political ideology and social issues (e.g., abortion and homosexuality). A new genre known as "advocacy sitcoms" has emerged as in the attempts to normalize homosexual behavior on programs such as the much-publicized *Ellen*. It would appear that this program was out of step with the majority of the public. For example, according to General Social Survey data from 1993, 67 percent of the respondents in this national survey believe that sexual relations between adults of the same sex are always wrong or almost always wrong (Chapman 1994). Not surprisingly, once the main focus of the program became Ellen's homosexuality, ratings dropped, and the show was subsequently canceled.

Lichter, Lichter, and Rothman (1991) believe that the liberal bias on social issues is directly linked to the urban elite background of media workers. If the bias that these researchers describe exists, then many parents may in fact find themselves in conflict with the mass media as agents of socialization of children.

The Internet

The proliferation of home connections to the Internet creates many new opportunities for children to be exposed to material their parents do not approve of. For example, between 2 and 3 percent of Internet sites deliver pornographic material. This small fraction still means that there are thousands of such sites—the fast growing type of site on the Internet. From a parent's point of view, the number of sites is not as important as the ease with which they can be reached. Particularly problematic is that children may accidentally stumble across these sites while using search engines to look for other types of material. For example, entering the search term *toys* in the search engine Infoseek results in a listing of nearly 40,000 links. Of these links, approximately 7,455 are sites that display sexual material or sell sex-related products. These include a site that advertises "The Good Looks Sex Machine Dual-Action Double Climaxer" and "Porn Link," a site that advertises links to the "best adult sites that you can get free on the net." While it is true that getting into one of these sites requires clicking on the link and then on another link after various disclaimers, curious children have temptations that were previously less available. There are software products that, when installed on a home computer, can block access to these sites, but the effectiveness of these programs is not guaranteed.

It is not that all parents are incapable of dealing with these pressures; many *are* capable. But the point is that consumerism, as well as the pervasive sexuality and violence of the mass media complicate the relationship between parents and children— even those who are able to say no.

Not all media effects on relationships are negative. In some families the television can be a focal point, what has been called the "electronic hearth" (Tuchman et al. 1978). This metaphor suggests that just as families once gathered around the hearth for fellowship and conversation, the modern family comes together around the television set to share a common experience. It has been suggested that this type of experience may even be more conducive to interaction than sitting together and reading individual books. This is because family members viewing the same program are likely to interact in the sharing of their experiences.

However, this scenario may be an artifact of a particular moment in mass media history when there was a very limited range of broadcast programming—just the three major networks and PBS—and when most families owned only one television set. Today, in an era of almost unlimited programming choice that is much more narrowly targeted, it is not unusual to own two and more television sets. The average number of TV sets per household in 1994 was 2.2. In many families, children and parents have their own sets in their own rooms and watch separately.

Similarly, music is, more often than not, generation-specific and consumed in the isolated environment of the Walkman or Discman. It is always amazing to see a couple out for a walk or jog with one or both wearing headphones—beside one another and yet not together. The Internet too is primarily an individualized experience. All of this suggests that the privatization effect of the mass media, which has moved leisure experience out of the public arena into the home, continues within the family unit itself to divide members from each other.

Agenda Setting

It has been suggested that events covered in the mass media are perceived by the public as being the most important. Thus, even though the media may not be able to directly change opinions, they do set the public agenda. Studies support the idea of a modest relationship between media attention and public interest (Shaw and McCombs 1974). For example, research on voting behavior indicates that political issues emphasized in the media are those deemed most important by voters.

But the question is this: Do media cause public interest in an issue, or does public interest cause media coverage? This is a problem of "causal direction." Establishing causal direction is difficult because media producers try to attune themselves to the interests of the public. However, some statistical techniques, such as lagged correlations, do show that the media can increase public interest in an issue. The question of causal direction assumes the mass media are not part of their audience's climate of opinion. Local newspapers, radio, and TV stations clearly attempt to reflect their intended audiences, exactly because they are local. National media compete for audiences and try to gauge the interests of the nation, but they cannot possibly reflect the hundreds of ideologically diverse U.S. locales.

Coverage increases awareness and concern which, in turn, may lead to even more coverage. At some point, however, the issue is resolved or, more likely, media producers suspect that the public has tired of the issue and coverage recedes. Thus, while the media may help to create and perpetuate controversies such as "acid rain," "global warming," or the "hole in the ozone layer," at some point the public becomes saturated and loses interest. What sometimes happens is that extensive media coverage of an issue may lead to public burnout well before the problem is resolved, as in the case of people who are "sick of hearing about the environment."

Of course it is not just perceptions of public interest that drive media coverage. Media producers are often responding to each other as much as to the audience. After all, they are concerned about prestige and business competition. Thus, the "if the *New York Times* covers it it must be important" syndrome tends to drive coverage as well.

An important point here is that the actual importance of the problem in the real world is not a direct factor in the amount of coverage (Funkhouser 1973). Rather it is the *perception* of what might be the audience's interest that drives the process. For example, according to the Center for Media and Public Affairs (1997), recent research suggests that while the homicide rate was decreasing by 20 percent in the United States in the mid-1990s, television coverage of murder, driven by the O. J. Simpson Case, increased 721 percent! In fact, one out of every twenty network news stories during the period 1993–1996 was about murder, and crime stories were the top category.

As we saw in the previous chapter, linking media content to specific behavioral and attitudinal changes is difficult. There is no doubt, however, that at a higher level the kinds of things people pay attention to and consider important are influenced in part by information gleaned from various media sources. The amount of influence depends on at least four factors: (1) the nature of the message (how well is it constructed.); (2) the medium (music, TV, newspapers, etc.); (3) the issue itself (how relevant is it?); and (4) the characteristics of audience members (have they already made up their minds? Do they have alternative sources of information?).

Social Movements

The agenda-setting function of the media is an important component of social constructionist and resource mobilization theories of social problems. The basic idea of these theories is that social problems are not simply "out there" as the most important issues in society. There are, in fact, any number of issues available to compete for public attention. For an issue to become defined as an important social problem a number of things must occur. Principal among them is that an individual or group must adopt the issue as their own and actively work to promote the issue to the public and to policymakers. Groups that are likely to be most successful are those that mobilize such resources as volunteers, money, communication networks, and, most importantly for our purposes, media attention. Thus, social problems researchers explicitly acknowledge the importance of the media in understanding the menu of social problems before the public at any given period of time.

Framing the News

In keeping with this perspective, researchers such as Molotch (1970) and Gitlin (1980) have conducted studies on how social activists have attempted to be both the authors and subjects of media attention on such issues as an oil spill in Santa Barbara, the safety of nuclear power, and the Vietnam conflict. Activists may take various routes, including public demonstrations, to induce media coverage. However, just as important is the effort to control the nature of that coverage. There are, after all, many different ways to slant a story. Some elements are left in, others left out. Some are emphasized and some de-emphasized. On television, the images selected, the narrative, the tone of voice of the reporter or news presenter, body language, and even the order in which stories are placed in the newscast all contribute to our understanding of the story. For example, Ryan and Sim (1990) have shown that network coverage of art and artists tends to place art stories near the end of the broadcast, creating stories that ridicule fine art and artists and link artistic production to bureaucratic waste. This process of slanting stories in one direction or another is called **framing.**

A demonstration can, and often is, framed in such a way as to discredit the participants. Some events, such as the Million Man March on Washington, may be generally framed positively but others, such as the 1997 Promise Keepers March, are not. Todd Gitlin (1980), in his work on the organization called Students for a Democratic Society (SDS), shows how media coverage can have a profound effect on an organization attempting to engage in social change. In the mid-1960s, early coverage of the SDS and its antiwar activities attempted to trivialize the movement while emphasizing internal dissention and the marginal character of the participants. Later, other elements were added to this negative frame, including a focus on Communists in the movement, violence, and the highly inflammatory symbol of the carrying of the Viet Cong flag. The overall impression was of an extremist movement harmful to the public good.

Gitlin argues that this coverage only focused on certain elements of SDS, but in doing so created a type of self-fulfilling prophesy. New members were attracted to, and expected to find, the organization that they had seen portrayed on television and in the papers. These members looked, behaved, and thought in ways that corresponded more closely to the media image. They were, as Gitlin (1980:30) describes them, "less intellectual, more activist, more deeply estranged from the dominant institutions" than were the original members. Their estrangement from dominant institutions was often reflected in unconventional clothing and hairstyles and the conscious use of profanity. They were also more narrowly focused on the antiwar issue than the broad social program of the original members. As they moved into leadership positions they directed the organization in such a way as to fit this new model. Thus, Gitlin argues, media coverage successfully and unintentionally modified an organization to match the media frame.

Political Campaigns

Whatever the magnitude of the effect on voters' behavior, media coverage now plays a major role in political campaigns. Campaigns focus much of their activity on maximizing positive TV coverage for their candidate and negative coverage for the opposition. Because of this, candidates are chosen at least in part for their media-friendly characteristics. Reporters and media analysts believe that former President Ronald Reagan was the master of manipulating the media. He was dubbed "The Great Communicator" for his media charisma. Some suggest that this power contributed to more negative coverage for former President George Bush and for President Clinton because reporters vowed never again to be so manipulated. President Reagan was a tough media relations act to follow.

The emphasis on popularity polls and the "horse race" approach to political coverage has also been suspected of impacting the political system. The media in the United States have been accused of focusing more on who is ahead and who is behind than the substance of political issues. In part, this is due to the complexity of such issues as healthcare and the economy. It is difficult to reduce this complexity to the types of short stories that will hold the audience's attention. It is particularly difficult given the production conventions of commercial television that limit most news stories to a few minutes at most. This problem has been worsened by personnel reductions in news divisions, which have reduced the opportunities for reporters to develop expertise in a particular area. Conversely, the ups and downs of political careers, scandals, and relative positions in the polls are fairly easily represented. Thus, media formats and perceptions of the audience prevent the media from wading into and teaching complex issues to the public. At the same time, it is easy for politicians to take advantage of the complexity of issues and the limited media formats and expertise to slant issues in particular ways.

The belief in the power of media images has led to huge expenditures on media advertising by candidates and parties. However, as noted in the previous chapter, it is not all clear that such spending is dollar-for-dollar effective. For example, the strongest candidates in terms of public and party support are also the ones who are likely to have the most money to spend. Further complicating the issue are numerous examples of candidates spending more than their opponent on media advertising and still losing—including the fact that then-candidate Bill Clinton was outspent by both President George Bush and third-party candidate Ross Perot. The sheer volume of exposure, beyond a point that ensures recognition, is not as important as the framing of that exposure. Nevertheless, the power of mass media campaigns is illustrated by the fact that both Ross Perot and Steve Forbes (a candidate in 1996) were able to buy and induce enough coverage to establish themselves as credible candidates outside of the two-party political structure. An important lesson must be noted. Media coverage proved to be a partial substitute for traditional political party organizing.

A secondary effect of the current state of involvement in mass-media political campaign is to divert considerable funds to them. Even though individual effects on voters are hard to show, these are large amounts of money that could be spent in other ways, including expanding opportunities to truly educate voters and increase participation in the political process.

Another potential effect of the mass media in the political arena is the effect on communication between political actors. The Iran Hostage Crisis (November 1979–January 1981) is a good example. During that crisis the media were more than passive spectators. The potential for media coverage helped to precipitate the crisis—providing motivation for the hostage-taking. Once the coverage began, it helped to escalate the hostage-taking into an international incident. Media coverage may have also increased pressure to undertake an ill-fated airborne rescue attempt. What is particularly interesting is that the militants, the governments, both of the United States and Iran, used the news media as a vehicle of communication with each other. In several ways, the media became active participants in the incident.

The Legal System

The mass media have developed a close relationship with the legal system. The legal system has become the source of raw material for both news and entertainment media products. Much of what is defined as news focuses on issues of crime and law. Reporters scan the legal system for cases that might in some way appeal to the public interest. These tend to be sensational murder trials. *Sensational* can mean a number of things. Crimes are sensational when they involve a celebrity, or are particularly gruesome. Newsworthy crimes often involve killings that defy conventional stereotypes, such as a mother killing her children or murders committed by children or by middle-class citizens.

Prosecutions and trials of public officials or business leaders or lawsuits involving widely consumed products are also common raw material for the media. Some programming, such as *Cops* on the Fox Network, bridges the gap between legal news and entertainment. Fictional entertainment programming (e.g., *Nash Bridges, Law and Order*) portrays the legal system as an arena in which individual, organizational, and societal conflict are played out, mediated, and resolved.

This is not a one-way interaction. The media are increasingly intertwined with the day-to-day operations of the legal system. There are numerous examples of this interaction. Media framing of a particular story may influence public opinion in such a way that jury selection becomes difficult. Beginning with the Rodney King case in 1992, there has been increased concern that juries will consider public opinion in reaching a verdict. Fairly or unfairly, jurists in both the Rodney King and O. J. Simpson criminal cases have been accused of carrying out racial and personal agendas through their verdicts. At the same time, attorneys attempt to use the media to sway public opinion in favor of their clients, while building national celebrity status for themselves.

Two specific criticisms have emerged regarding mass media coverage of courtroom trials. One criticism is that most coverage is by its very nature partial—especially in the broadcast media. Thus, the public has a sense that they know what took place in a trial when, in fact, the jury was exposed to considerably more material than was reported. This disjunction may make the jury's decision incomprehensible to those not exposed to the entire trial. Some have argued that this phenomenon could be alleviated by the use of cameras and live coverage in the courtroom. But "gavel to gavel" coverage may not be the solution that it appears to be. Studies of the O. J. Simpson criminal trial suggest that few viewers had the time or inclination to watch all of the coverage. Exposure was still partial yet created in the audience the illusion of having seen the full trial and a false sense of expertise on the issues and evidence.

A second criticism is that, increasingly, the mass media have intruded into the legal process in an attempt to "get the story." News programs and magazines, financed by large organizations and locked in fierce competition for audience, are willing to spend large sums of money for exclusive material on sensational stories. One outcome of this has been the paying of witnesses for their story. Known as "check-book journalism," this phenomenon has led to situations in which critical witnesses sell their stories to the media, sometimes even before talking with the police. Police are then left in the embarrassing position of following the media to the story.

Even entertainment programming can have an effect on the legal system (Hans and Dee 1991). Programs like *LA Law* and crime dramas such as *NYPD Blue* may create unrealistic portrayals of the legal system and occupations within that system. In entertainment programming crimes are usually solved, and guilt or innocence is clearly established. Attorneys are mostly highly paid professionals in designer clothes who spend most of their time engaged in exciting courtroom interchanges. No wonder that the popularity of such programs correlates with ups and downs in law school applications. Never mind that most attorneys do not live the lifestyle portrayed on these programs, that most cases are not solved, that there is considerable ambiguity in the process of establishing guilt and innocence, and that most attorneys spend only about 5 percent of their time in the courtroom.

Privacy

The mass media intrude into private lives. In a sense, this is a partial return to an earlier way of being. Throughout most of history there was little notion of a "private life." Lives were intertwined with extended family and community to a degree unheard of today. Like the community of old, the words, voices, and images of the mass media penetrate into every corner of our lives today. The difference is that this penetration is *not* that of a real community with shared experiences and a core of shared values and beliefs. Once more, it is a one-way interaction between parties who have never met and never will. It is communication to be sure, but it is not a relationship. As Silverstone (1995) has described it:

> *The box in the corner is part of the furniture—a hearth—an indispensable focus for what remains of family life, a site (among others) for the construction of individual identities. Its images and narratives endlessly play and replay the dreams and nightmares of contemporary domestic life, as advertisements and sitcoms, chat shows and soap operas offer a chorus of*

seductions and seditions, the murmuring of public voices in otherwise private domains.

Nowhere is media penetration into the private more obvious than when the media change private grief into public spectacle: disaster victims, survivors, and their relatives are brought before the camera to bring their tragedy to the world.

Occasionally the media greatly magnify private intrusions by other public institutions. The FBI wrongly accused Richard Jewel of being the Olympic Bomber who struck the 1996 Olympics. The media promptly exposed every detail of Jewel's life, with framing that made him appear guilty. The FBI later admitted there was no good evidence against Jewel and made an unprecedented apology. Thanks to media coverage Jewel must struggle to restore his life and reputation.

Sometimes, being exposed to media attention can be particularly devastating when an act carries greater than normal social stigma—as in the case of child molestation. For example, once one is portrayed in the media as an "alleged child molester," a verdict of not guilty is not enough to remove the stigma. Further, to seek any sort of celebrity, even in the name of public service, is to give up any hope of a private life. Presidents and members of Congress are hounded by the press over issues that many would argue are irrelevant to their public life. And of course there is the interesting phenomenon of talk show guests who make their private lives public in the quest for celebrity. Some people see media celebrity of any sort as an accomplishment.

Summary

In this chapter we have looked at how the media influence society. The mass media have changed the way every person lives. Hours of every day are spent engaging the mass media through newspapers, radio, TV, magazines, recorded music, and books. Mass media have enlarged the volume of information, the range of topics and information sources, and generally regulate our access to the world beyond our face-to-face encounters. The mass media give us topics to talk about with our parents, friends, and children.

In a number of ways the mass media have changed the dynamics of personal relationships. They give us the historically exceptional flood of private information about strangers. We let TV and video games "babysit" our children while we go about other business. But we also must guard our children from these babysitters. We caution children against media overuse, try to keep them from inappropriate content, and negotiate over their demands for products pushed directly to them by advertisers. Thanks to the presence of the media in the most intimate moments, lovers can have an "our song." Family members can spend time together or escape from each other by using the media. And, by the way, who commands the remote control?

The mass media tend to elevate consumerism, harness public interest, and shape the form of political life. They can help raise political candidates out of obscurity, that is, candidates not supported by one of the two major parties. Their broadcasts cut across cultural and national boundaries, raising fears of culture loss and homogenization. They frame issues and facts, slanting the information that we have to work with as we construct our personal understanding of the world around us. Media overexposure can trivialize vital issues before the underlying dilemma can be fully explored or solved, but they can also make us aware of important social problems that might otherwise have gone unnoticed. The moral messages contained in media programming cannot possibly be coherent with the increasingly diverse religious and ideological backgrounds of a mass audience. These messages are then subject to attacks from those whose beliefs they threaten. Yet these mass-mediated moral messages are far from universally subversive to the traditional moral order. The same media that carry sitcom messages of casual sex have carried themes that extended the inclusiveness of democracy and civil rights. The same news programs that seem to fixate on crime and violence also may raise our awareness of environmental crises and other important social issues. The mass media are no single thing, neither all good nor all bad. The mass media are complex in their messages and complex in their effects.

Part II

The Production of Culture

5

Mass Media Technology

Welcome to the Datasphere, Mr. Gutenberg.

*I was on the stage of New York City's Town Hall
with an audience of 1,500 people. I was behind a
lectern, and in front of the lectern was this computer.
And I gave a very short, minute-and-a-half description
of what was wrong with the technosphere, how it was
destroying the biosphere. And then I walked over and
got this very powerful sledgehammer and smashed
the screen with one blow and smashed the keyboard
with another blow. It felt wonderful.*
— *"NEO-LUDITE" KIRKPATRICK SALE,* WIRED MAGAZINE
INTERVIEW, JUNE, 1995 (KELLY 1995:166)

Right now the GM Hughs Electronics geosynchronous DirecTV satellite is pouring
energy out of the heavens. The broadcast "footprint" is coast to coast in the United
States. This "bird" alone bathes you in one billion bits per second. There are other
satellites, of course, and ground-based stations for radio and TV. At no time in
human existence has the environment been more dense with information-carrying
electromagnetic radiation. And by the way, it's six A.M. and my newspaper was just
delivered. Welcome to the datasphere, Mr. Gutenberg!

Communications satellite in orbit.

Technology and Media Technology

Technology

Technology is a word so common that its meaning is taken for granted: a useful machine. It is true that in common sense we tend to anchor our meaning of *technology* with examples or images of machines. Sometimes when a word is just a part of everyday life, the range of its actual uses goes unnoticed. Let us take a few paragraphs to explore the meaning of the word *technology*. We must do this because this chapter is not just about the machinery of the mass media.

Very generally, science expands our knowing and technology expands our doing. A nail is an important piece of technology for anyone needing to join pieces of wood quickly and easily. McDonalds is a useful technology for anyone needing to eat quickly and easily. If one studies the use of nails in constructing safe buildings, the reading soon transforms mere nails into a class of fasteners and into the focus of engineering-based guidelines for fastening *systems*. Likewise, fast-food restaurants are vast, efficient *systems* of food distribution and meal production. The nail is primarily a *material technology*, fast-food restaurants are complexes of social and material technology. The strategy of an army and the bureaucratic hierarchy that manages Exxon are primarily *social technologies*. Each of these examples represents *an invention that expands our power to do some task*. A sociologist by the name of Jacques Ellul broadly defines *technology* as *all the methods we have thought out that help us to do any task more efficiently (1970)*.

Media Technology

As societies grow in population, in geographic size, or both, they literally become massive. If a massive society is to continue functioning and survive, it—like its much smaller historical counterparts—must engage in internal communications. The massive society must still be able to know, unify, and correct itself even when it is too large for a fraction of its people to actually meet face-to-face. The technology of the mass media help us to perform this necessary communications task more efficiently. And, whereas the history of mass communications is most often told in terms of the inventions of its central, material technologies (the printing press, the television, the magazine, etc.), each mass medium is actually a vast system of social and material technologies. *Each mass medium represents a large-scale transformation of social and economic relations.*

To use a mass medium to communicate about ourselves, we create or "spin-off" new jobs (graphic artists, "paperboys," sound technicians, reporters, etc.), new skills (multitrack recording, acting, directing, announcing), new statuses (celebrity, VJ, talkshow host, news anchor, mass audience, etc.), we make new uses of other seemingly unrelated technologies (the bicycle distributes newspapers, the interstate highway distributes books, the school system prepares journalists, satellites relay television programing, etc.), and invent a cascade of accompanying, compatible technologies (book superstores, the Walkman, the bass cannon, etc.), each with *its* own spin-offs. In addition to employment directly in media industries, many jobs are indirectly or partly affected by the mass media industries. For example, food service jobs that produce movie theater popcorn sold to theaters, newsstand owners, cleaning services that have contracts with radio stations, TV and VCR repair work, car stereo installers, paper company employees who make newsprint, and so on.

Let us conclude this illustration of the not-so-obvious large-scale media transformation of society with a glance at media-related employment. There are just over 8 million U.S. jobs in media industries (the great majority of these are in the print media). This figure represents 6.7 percent of the employed labor force. A very conservative multiplier (4.00) can be used to estimate jobs affected by, but not directly in, the mass media industries. Then, we have an indication that about 27 percent of all U.S. employment is related in some way to talking about ourselves, to ourselves. (See Table 5.1 for more economic information.)

To communicate on a mass scale, we transform our social world massively to deliver the content of any particular message. *A mass medium is a massive and complex technological transformation of society.* It is this sociological perspective on mass media technology that prompts observers to say that "technology has its own powerful dynamic" (Jacques Ellul), that a modern society composed of systematized institutions and values is like an "Iron Cage" (Max Weber), or that the "medium is the message" and the "massage" (Marshall McLuhan). Welcome to the datasphere, Mr. Gutenberg!

Before Mass Media

In the beginning of history was the word. History, by definition, begins with the written word. The Sumerians (an ancient civilization located in what is now Iraq) were the first to invent writing 5500 years before the present (BP). In their writing each symbol stood for a word, more or less, so to write or read, one had to memorize hundreds, even thousands, of symbols. Because writing and reading were so difficult to teach, literacy was confined to a small part of the population. That was all that their civilization required to record civic and business affairs.

Two thousand years passed before the Canaanites—called Phoenicians by the Greeks—invented a phonetic alphabet (3500 BP). The Canaanites were the supreme seafaring nation before Greek civilization began to flourish. They traded and had other political dealings with both the Babylonians and the Egyptians. Like the Sumerians before them, the Babylonians and Egyptians had complicated written languages. It may be that the path of least difficulty between two complex writing systems is the design of a third system in which symbols stand for sounds, not ideas. That way any spoken language can be represented by the same writing system. This was the perfect compromise for a nation of great traders, but especially so for a world in which civilizations were increasingly connected by trade and treaty. The

TABLE 5.1   Media Societal Transformation

6.7%	Proportion of all U.S. employment in media industries
27%	Direct and indirect media employment as a percent of all U.S. jobs
$169 billion	Direct mass media revenues
3.4%	Mass media portion of GDP (output of entire U.S. economy)
$670	Per capita annual media expenditures
9%	Percent of all household discretionary income spent on mass media
70%	Percent of consumer entertainment dollar going to mass media

(Adapted from U.S. Department of Commerce, Bureau of the Census, 1995.)

phonetic alphabet was a quantum leap for communications, and it was an early demonstration of the law of progress by compatibility (discussed below, Principle Seven).

Another breakthrough in the sheer tedium of written communication came three thousand years later (546 BP). The German inventor Johannes Gutenberg brought the phonetic alphabet together with cast-metal, movable type, a new ink he invented that adhered to metal characters, and a screw-and-lever printing press (adapted from an Italian wine press). By 1450 Gutenberg had perfected his printing method so that it was commercially efficient. In many ways the printing press technology marked the beginning of the European Renaissance, or cultural rebirth.

The Gutenberg press could print entire pages. Setting the type was slow, but it was sure and simple. Gutenberg's method was used almost unchanged until near the end of the 1800s. A world increasingly dependent on the flow of knowledge was demanding faster production and the mass reproduction of the written word. Many attempts were made to mechanize the printing process and, finally, in the 1880s Ottmar Mergenthaler, after emigrating to the United States from Serbia, successfully mechanized typesetting. His **Linotype** was installed in the *New York Tribune* in 1886. The technological basis of the first truly mass medium was up and running 436 years after the invention of the printing press, and only 110 years BP.

Both Gutenberg's and Mergenthaler's methods made use of molten metal for casting into type. Metal is not the best means for the optimal combination of printing speed and flexibility. During the 110 years between the first commercial use of the Linotype and now, printing technology has changed considerably. Offset printers and optical printers have almost universally replaced the Linotype. Indeed, since their introduction in 1946 (only 50 years BP), we are into the fourth generation of optical printers. Now, borrowing from computer technology, digitized typefaces and precision laser energy provide rapid, high-resolution commercial printing.

Seven General Principles of Media Technology Development

The brief history of one mass medium tells quite a story beneath the words. **First,** society drives the technological change of a media invention. The ideas and tools of the lone inventor are prepared by history. Every invention is dependent on an historical accumulation of other inventions and the social changes they have brought about. Invention is the vertical (historical) integration of previous inventions and their social consequences.

Second, society provides the need or market for a media invention. After Gutenberg, the next several centuries produced major events that forced open the natural self-enclosure of societies. These same social changes increased immeasurably the need for information carried best by the printed word. Look at what happened during the next two centuries: the Renaissance (it increased levels of education throughout Europe and produced an estimated 30,000 new book titles), the religious foment of the Reformation in the next century, all the seafaring exploration and colonization of the "new world," and the political turmoil of the various democratic revolutions of the eighteenth century (one of which founded the United States), not to mention the Industrial Revolution. All of these history-making events begged for the increased flow of information that only the printing press could provide.

Third, the information medium is more than a response to society (first principle above). The new communications medium becomes part of the necessary processes of societal maintenance and change. Western societies became Western civilization partly because the printing press allowed relatively rapid information reproduction. Westernism was spread and stored in the "memory" of books and periodicals. The printing press helped *bring about* the Protestant Reformation. Martin Luther's "95 Theses" represented a local protest by a parish priest deeply concerned with abuses by the Church hierarchy. Local, that is, until a few of his friends made copies on a printing press and distributed them all over Europe. Because of the printing press, a local protest became a social movement.

Fourth, the time frames between major media inventions grow shorter as we approach the present. Two thousand years passed between the invention of writing and use of the phonetic alphabet, three thousand more years went by before Gutenberg's press. These are unimaginably long periods of time. Remember, our nation is just over 220 years old. After these ancient times, things speeded up. There was a mere (!) 400 years from Gutenberg to the Linotype, a twinkling of 60 years elapsed to the first generation of optical printers in 1946, and since then four more optical technology generations have brought optical printing into the computer age.

Fifth, each major step in media progress requires the interweaving of an ever wider array of technologies and social institutions. The first principle above emphasized a kind of vertical integration of technology from the depth of history to an invention. This fifth principle implies a *horizontal* integration of technologies and institutions. Let us compare Gutenberg with modern printing, say in journalism. Gutenberg combined knowledge of alphabets, printing, wine presses, and metallurgy with his own creative twists, borrowed money from individuals, and hoped the local economy would support the commercialization of his press. In contrast, printing in today's journalism is dependent on the chemical, machining, paper, computer, and aerospace (for the satellite transmission of stories to the newspaper from globally separated sites) industries. Also intimately involved in getting that paper to your doorstep are local electrical power companies, school systems (for training newspaper personnel), trucking companies (for distribution), telecommunications (for the transmission of a digitized, formatted paper to remote printing sites), advertising corporations, legal firms, insurance companies, and banking businesses. The horizontal integration goes on. Science provides research for continued advancement, the political and legal institutions offer a changing environment for publication, and a complex economy provides a large marketplace for sales and for competition with other media forms. And so on!

Sixth, every communications technology requires a means of carrying its message and a destination prepared to receive it. An example of a carrier might be paper and ink. A rapid printing press without an abundance of paper and ink could not be a mass medium. Similarly, for destination, there must be a literate audience with enough money to purchase copies on a regular basis. Another example: Radio stations must have regulated airwaves in order to keep their signals from becoming entangled, and consumers must invest in radios and have the time to listen. This sixth principle would seem to be a truism, except in its relation to the fifth one. We will consider this relationship next.

Seventh, we can consider two corollaries to principles five and six. The more complex the media technology, the more widely invested society becomes in its form (because of horizontal integration), therefore: (1) the harder fundamental change becomes (a clean shift in basic technology); and, (2) the more any potential technological changes must show compatibility with the existing form. Together, we will call them **The Law of Progress by Compatibility.** (In economics this is called "increasing returns"; urban sociology has demonstrated that this principle underlies urban development.)

Let us consider the case of **TVs, HDTVs,** and **VCRs.** Almost every U.S. home (98.2%) has at least one television (there is a total of over 200 million televisions in the United States), and that TV is turned on for an average of seven hours a day. Yet as a piece of modern technology it is old. Despite its age we are not about to throw out our TVs for some newer, technologically different version of video. TV qualifies as an established media technology by any cultural or economic standard. Therefore all the technological changes related to TV must cater to its technology: analog signal reception, 525 interlaced scan lines on the screen (United States), and a 3-by-4 aspect ratio (a nearly square picture, United States). This standard dates back about 50 years BP for black-and-white transmissions; the same standards were adopted about 40 years BP for color transmissions.

High Definition Television (HDTV) represents a different television technology. In the United States, HDTV signal transmission would be digital to obtain signal compression into one VHF bandwidth and to suffer less apparent signal distortion. HDTV would process over 1000 interlaced scan lines bringing higher resolution to the pictures, and the screen aspect ratio might be 9-by-16, as in Europe and Japan. Every television owner and each video rental store has a stake in current television technology. To simply switch to HDTV would require at least two major modifications, the first one being very expensive. Every existing television set would have to be scrapped and much more expensive HDTVs would have to be bought (estimated cost of the first-generation HDTV is $3000–$10,000), or broadcasters, cable companies, and satellite systems would have to send out two types of signals. Neither is financially feasible for most consumers of TV fare. Second, all available video material in the 3-by-4 format and would have to be displayed with black vertical strips (called "curtains") to mask each side of the 9-by-16 screen. Consumers would have to put up with all of this just to obtain a more defined television image. To give HDTV a market chance (the industry has a lot of research and development money tied up in this system), and to prevent consumer revolt (it took ten years for people to start buying color TVs after color programming began), the Federal

Communications Commission (FCC) has ruled that HDTV systems must be capable of being received in 525 scan lines on conventional sets. That is, the FCC is requiring *compatibility.* (Digital broadcasts may have begun by the time you read this book. A digital-to-analog set-top converter is available to allow you to see the picture on your old set, without the increased resolution.)

So, we see the corollaries of the seventh mass media technology principle being played out in TV technology: the inertial resistance to fundamental change and the compatibility requirement. It may be that HDTV is not even a necessary technology. Cable companies are switching to digital technology. This would be a business expense (e.g., new decoders at the consumer's TV) offset by better, all-weather signal reception at the company antenna, and most importantly, the capacity for carrying more channels and a variety of consumer services. This may slightly reduce picture quality at the consumer's TV. Further, Digital Direct Satellite systems, begun in 1994, beam digital signals direct to consumers. This means that willing consumers would have to purchase or lease a small (about 18 inches) satellite dish and a decoder, the latter device as an add-on to their existing TVs (like the cable box or VCR). The advantages of DSS for the consumer are substantial, particularly in areas not served by cable. (Currently about 30 percent of U.S. households cannot be wired cost-effectively with cable. Many of these same areas are remote and receive weak signals from the network affiliates and other local stations.) Well over 100 channels can be accessed, reception would not be affected by rain or lightning, unless a heavy thunderstorm comes directly between the receiver dish and the satellite. According to the DSS technical manual for consumers, the system will provide a reliable signal 99.7 percent of the time. This translates into about 26 hours of signal loss spread out over the entire year—the equivalent of cable. Compared to the older and very large analog satellite dishes, the DSS dish is much less visually intrusive, the picture quality would be excellent (VHS quality or better), and the system would be expandable to include the additional services, including a high-speed data port for computer access to the "information superhighway." Technologically, both digital cable and DSS can provide near studio-quality viewing resolution on existing TVs. These alternatives to an HDTV switch offer versatility with high-quality images (pictures almost indistinguishable from the HDTV standard). These digital technologies follow the **Law of Progress by Compatibility.** They are *options* for the consumer, and do not force the obsolescence of an existing consumer investment. Certainly, the little 18-inch dishes are already starting to show up everywhere outside the reach of cable. HDTVs are coming as a consumer option, not as a sea change in home entertainment technology. Which would you bet on? The HDTV revolution or the digital evolution (a slower switch by consumers)?

The Video Home System (VHS) format of the **Video Cassette Recorder (VCR)** is the most spectacular economic success story in the history of consumer electronics. In only about 20 years U.S. consumers alone have bought over 100 million VCRs. This apparatus first and foremost is compatible with the TV. It also increases the flexibility of the basic TV technology. Tens of millions of households around the world now have VCRs. The VCR is so popular it needs no introduction. And it can be said that, "As we all know," VCRs allow time-shift viewing of TV programming (although viewers do not much use this choice), many VCRs have a scan feature that can "zap" commercials out of recorded programming, and we all love the home viewing of movies shown in theaters, cheaper and on demand. Who has not seen this message at the beginning of a rented movie:

> *This film has been modified from its original version. It has been formatted to fit your TV.*

That is not all. Millions of these homes with VCRs also have camcorders. This, "as we all know," permits people to record and then view on their TVs their child's first steps or the family vacation, all without the trouble of film processing and the hassle of setting up a projector.

Hollywood now pays attention to the needs of the same TV viewers who were once seen as profit-robbing foes. Movie rentals have now become a major market for film studios, expanding the audience size, profits, and the time during which a movie earns revenues (shelf life). Movie rental for the VCR has itself become a very big business. With over 25,000 movie rental stores in the United States (more than the number of theater screens), the average citizen lives no more than about 10 miles from the nearest video outlet. And given population concentrations, most of us have the choice of going to several such stores without traveling 10 miles from home.

Technological improvements in VCRs, even going digital, are made with compatibility in mind. New digital VCRs (and camcorders) integrate easily into the prevailing system because of their compatibility with existing TV technology. The VCR is more than a success story based on the existing integration of TV into the fabric of society. The VCR and the camcorder widen the range of horizontal integration and further entrench TV technology.

The Internet

The Internet is an amazing crazy quilt of interconnected users and nodes. It is user-driven, can be added to (a personal Web Page) by any interested individual, and it is decentralized by design; therefore, in the accepted sense, the Internet cannot be defined as a mass medium. Yet isn't a web page "hit" by hundreds of thousands of users a mass medium? The Internet is not even a medium of the "masses"; its uses are too individualized and personal. Maybe it is something new, both mass and personal. Whatever its category, *the Net,* as it is affectionately called, is too much of a communication phenomenon not to be discussed. And it is constantly evolving, so it is good to know its history.

The decentralization of the Internet means there is no single hub or "authority" through which all messages travel. So, the Net is not even designed like the user-driven but very centralized phone system, although the long-distance phone system is being redesigned to be more netlike in its ability to route around damage. Fundamental design differences still divide the two information-movement systems. If you are accessing the Internet from a modem, the phone system treats your use as a "call" and your phone line is "tied up." If someone tried to call you they would get a busy signal. When your Net access gets to a node on the Net, your use does not "tie up" any lines. Information on the Net travels in digitized, addressed packets allowing many people to drop packets into the same line. Once again, the phone system is moving in the technological direction of the Net. The "Call Waiting" service option on your phone gives you direct experience with a digitized information packet. While you are talking on the line, the phone company's computer can phase a digitized packet into the analog signal of your call. And without disturbing that signal or interrupting the call, the computer lets your phone know that there is another call waiting. The phone beeps to let you know.

People pay to get an address and to get connected to the Net. The best part of the Net is its central mystery: No one is sure who pays for what; the Net itself *seems* to be free for most uses.

Three avenues of development have merged to create the Internet as it exists today. They are the personal computer, the basic concept and initial network, and the World Wide Web (WWW). We will look at each of these in turn.

Personal Computers

Physicist John V. Atanasoff, inventor of the digital techniques that underlie our computers, died in 1995. During the 55 years between his invention and his death, the world of information changed. And so has the world of computers. The original computers were used in WWII to compute tables for artillery trajectories. (An artillery shell travels such a distance and stays up so long that the earth actually rotates under it. Unlike a rifle, artillery is not just "point and shoot." Think about this and you will see how complicated accuracy can become.) The original computers were huge (perhaps 30 tons) and prone to regular failure as their vacuum tubes went bad. Scientists knew that computers could be reduced in size. A 1949 *Popular Mechanics* article predicted that, "Computers in the future may weigh no more than 1.5 tons." Then came transistors and printed circuits, and college students of the 1960s could hold in one hand a calculator with more computing power than possible for the 30-ton WWII behemoth, ENIAC. Then came microchips. Entire computer processor circuitry, transistors and all, became part of a silicon flake no larger than a thumbnail.

There were only 150,000 computers in the world in 1972, and these were for very specialized scientific or military use. Computers for the nonexpert became available from Apple and Commodore in 1977. These had hardwired BASIC language. This was a big "so-what" for most American consumers. Many people were very impressed that computers were for regular people, but they just did not see them for regular consumers. We had little to say in BASIC. Simple word processors and

Today's laptop computers are more powerful than the room-sized ENIAC of 1946, considered by many to be the first true computer.

spreadsheets began to be a part of built-in software, but it was all very crude. Most often your TV acted as the monitor, and any disk drives were separate boxes. It all had to be hooked up for every use because there was no place for all this junk in the living room.

About 1980, Steven Jobs introduced a computer with a *Graphical User Interface* (GUI). With its mouse, on-screen buttons, and icons, some of the burden of "machine interface" was shifted from the user. GUI and other changes helped to increase the compatibility of computers with users. That computer was the Macintosh. It was the future, if copycatting is some measure of the influence of its GUI approach. Four years later IBM introduced its version of the home computer, the PC. That was the name that stuck, even if Apple Computers had the friendliest system. Now there are in excess of 30 million computers in the United States alone. U.S. computer makers are shipping nearly 13 million new computers per year out to the world. By far, most of these are PCs, but that number includes super computers, mainframes, midrange, and workstations. Now more Americans make computers than build automobiles. Since 1990, U.S. firms have been investing more in computers and related communications hardware than they have spent on all other capital equipment combined. Software is America's fastest growing industry.

If you, the reader, are 20 years old, you are considered young. The computer as-we-know-it is just about your age. This stuff is new!

A New Window on the World: The View through a Monitor

The Internet

As we watch a movie or read a novel, we become emotionally connected to the story and its characters. Real fear, joy, anger, sadness, or even sexual interest are experienced. In short, we begin to live in the world of the medium. In literary circles, this experience is called the "suspension of disbelief." This world is nowhere. On the Internet we go nowhere. Yet we move into *cyberspace* (a term coined by science fiction writer William Gibson in 1984). We suspend disbelief and travel (or *surf*) to distant sites. We *chat* with others, who, outside of this *virtual reality,* may not be as they seem. We can become a virtual person, equal in stature to all other virtual persons. A child can become an adult, or vice versa. Man can be woman, a woman can be a man:

> *The record is quite clear: I'm male. A heterosexual male at that. But the record is limited, for life as I've known it lo these many years now ends at my modem. Once I call up my online service and beam myself into cyberspace, everything changes—in addition to the recognizably male identity I use to communicate with people I know, I have another persona. I'm a woman. Well, a virtual woman (Jesse Kornbluth, 1996).*

On the net, we can go to the White House or to the Santa Fe Institute, or read the latest *New York Times.* We pull information off the net, and put information on; it is not pushed at us. This is the difference between being a user and being an audience. The Internet may be the ultimate in modern personal and individual communication; it is just not communication with anyone we know in real time and space. On the Internet we can be part of a *virtual community* with a *virtual address.* (Just *where* is my mailbox if I can look in it and check my mail anywhere in the world?) How we are able to go nowhere so fast, and still get somewhere, that is the story of the Internet.

The father of the Internet is Larry Roberts. Unlike Edison and Marconi, Atanasoff (computers, mentioned above) and Roberts are never mentioned as historical figures of significance. Let us examine the story.

The Cold War was a period of chronic threat between Communist and non-Communist blocs of nations. The major players were the United States and the Soviet Union because each had an enormous arsenal of nuclear-tipped missiles. The cold war began after WWII and lasted until the sudden collapse of the Soviet Union in 1991. During the Cold War the United States wanted to create a communications network that would not crash in the event of a nuclear strike. An arm of the U.S.

Defense Department, called Advanced Research Project Agency (ARPA), was in charge of development.

A think tank called the Rand Corporation was called in on the project. This is where Larry Roberts enters the picture. Roberts's strategy for the crash-resistant network dates to about 1964. The network was to have no hub (central authority). Messages were to be packetized so that each packet, forming a part of the message, could travel from point A to point B, following a different route, if necessary. Damage on the network would be interpreted as the signal to find another route to point B. The packets would be assembled ("multiplexed") at the destination point B, as text or in some other form. The net itself is formed by the linkage of dedicated host computers. Each computer contains the authority to determine the route to the next node or to the destination. The first net was military, ARPAnet, but its principles were attractive to many at universities and in businesses. Local area nets multiplied during the 1980s. Many local nets linked to other nets because of communications speed, savings, and convenience.

In the late 1980s the National Science Foundation built five supercomputer centers to give academic researchers access to the best computing power in the world. The five regional centers were linked into a net using ARPAnet principles, now called Internet protocols (IP). Local university nets were chained together to link with the closest regional supercomputing center. The IP nets were quickly used for purposes unrelated to supercomputing. Inter- and intra-university E-mail was born. The savings brought by abstaining from the telephone and conventional mail (*snail mail*) induced many businesses to invest in equipment and network connections in the early 1990s. Now the Internet is worldwide, a vast network of networks. The Internet is not North American anymore. (A consortium of U.S. universities is now in the first stages of creating Internet2. The original Internet is too overworked for efficient research use.)

More than 95 thousand networks were part of the Internet by the first quarter of 1996. There were more than 4 million host processors. Thirty-five percent of the host nodes are outside the United States. By some measures, the parts of the Net outside North America represent its most rapidly spreading fabric. No one knows how many users there are. A 1995 estimate places the number at 26 million users.

A word should be mentioned about security or privacy on the Internet. Any information transmitted, including credit card numbers, can potentially be intercepted and stolen. Mailboxes can be snooped by hackers or by the FBI, and individual computers or local nets can be entered by unauthorized people who have the knowledge to do so. The only secure information transmissions are those that are encrypted. Until very recently, encryption was not a financial or technological option for most PC users. Now encryption software is cheap, but all communicating parties must have the same software. Further, it is illegal to send encrypted information outside the United States, with the banking business being an exception to the law. Organizations protect their systems by building (software) *firewalls* that stop unauthorized entry.

World Wide Web (WWW)

The World Wide Web is what makes the Internet, the Net, and more than a tough hike on a back trail in unexplored wilderness. This is one lane on the *information superhighway*. The Web was developed only in 1990 at the European Organization for Nuclear Research (CERN). It was originally a means for scientists to share documents. The WWW is the newest format on the Web. By 1995 the WWW was the fastest growing feature of the Internet.

The WWW allows computer users to rapidly and surely *navigate* the Internet, using software *browsers*. A browser is a program that allows a user to travel among websites, explore websites, and download data. *Hypertext* features are integral to the WWW. Hypertext allows a user to jump between related ideas within the same document and creates *links* between documents, even documents located at different sites. The jumps are easy: Point to a highlighted word (or other marker in a nontext document) and click with the mouse. You may retrieve a document from 12 thousand miles away. It is just as easy to *back out* and land at your starting point. *Web sites* are places to visit on the WWW. Some sites have *home pages* that belong to particular organizations or to individuals. Negroponte (1995) estimates that Web sites are doubling every 50 days and that a new home page comes on-line every four seconds (232). Web sites and home pages offer every imaginable kind of information. How about a trip to the Bell Laboratory Museum (WWW.bell-labs.com)? Perhaps you would prefer gossip, real-time discussion groups, hobby clubs, virtual dating, cyber-dancing, organizational descriptions of E. I. du Pont and other corporations, news, weather, sports, database access (law and medical libraries, Supreme Court Decisions, etc.), access to elected officials and their documents, shopping and advertising, pornography (made illegal as of February 1996, by the Communications Decency Act, then the Act was found unconstitutional by the Supreme Court in June of 1997), civic networks, fortune-telling, on-line subscriptions to magazines and scientific journals, on-line encyclopedias, software, and art. The list goes on and it multiplies faster than anyone can track it.

Roadblocks in the Cruising Lane of the Information Superhighway?

In May of 1995 the National Science Foundation (NSF) started the process of ending its oversight and support of the nation's main Internet "backbone" technology. At the same time, largely because of the popularity of the World Wide Web, the number of users and the complexity of the net are both increasing. Numerous public and private companies are assuming the former role of the NSF. These companies include Sprint, MCI, Netcom, UUNET, and, recently, AT&T. Each of these corporations now claims ownership of separate portions of the Net. The situation is analogous to multiple companies owning parts of a giant interconnected rail line. Despite

---

BOX 5.1

There it is again. Some clueless *fool* talking about the "information superhighway." They don't know *jack* about the Net. It's nothing like a superhighway. That's a bad metaphor. But suppose the metaphor ran in the other direction. Suppose the highways were like the Net. All right! A highway *hundreds* of lanes wide. Most with potholes. Privately operated bridges and overpasses. *No highway patrol.* Two hundred thirty-seven onramps at every intersection. *No signs.* Wanna get to Enseñada? Holler out the window to ask directions. Ad hoc traffic laws. Some lanes would vote to *demolish* single-occupant vehicles.

No offramps.

Now *that's* the way to run an interstate highway system.

(Jim Vandewalker. *Wired.* March, 1996.)

private ownership, some parts of the rail line are open for the use of all companies. Each company keeps usage patterns on its sections secret (even the common carrier portions), and no company wants to upgrade its section because other companies will benefit by its costs. All that is known is that the number of train trips is growing rapidly. It sounds like a recipe for gridlock and accidents.

MCI has already experienced a "data brownout" that left many users on the West Coast without Internet connections for one and a half hours. Anyone using the Net is already familiar with connection delays and data loss in peak traffic hours. Sometimes the Net just seems sluggish and peculiar things happen, like disconnects, identical WWW searches coming up with different results, and addresses not always working. The weakest points on the Net are its NAPs (network access points). Currently, there are 15 NAPs in the United States. A NAP is where the Internet service providers and major telecommunications companies connect to exchange the digital data packets that make up Net traffic. Executives and engineers in the Internet industries know the Net is now strained by its traffic load. Most think that enlightened self-interest will force companies into the necessary technology upgrades. (MCI, for example, has already started.) But it is possible for any access provider company to simply withdraw from the market, if the risks seem to outweigh the probability of profit. The first lane of the information superhighway is a work-in-progress.

The Internet and the Media

All things are possible in cyberspace, so why not a soap opera. It's got sex, skin, angst, ghosts, and a "Cyberian" husky who gets all the best lines. More than that, this soap has characters who get advice from their fans—on E-mail! The show is called *The Spot* (http://www.thespot.com). *The Spot* mixes photos, text, video, and sound in a multimedia, hypertext presentation of cybersoapy hardbodies. There are also hypertext buttons that advertise products (e.g., Honda, Activision). As of this writing, you can go to *The Squat* for a parody of *The Spot*. Type in http://theory.physics.missouri.edu/~georges/josh/squat to follow the lives of five genetically commingled, educationally challenged bumpkins who all share a trailer with a horse. You can also rush through cyberspace to get daily summaries of the "real" TV soap operas, or take your chances with soap trivia contests. Users can post comments on a variety of shows, from *The Simpsons* to the *Rush Limbaugh* show, or engage in discussion groups about shows. Many TV news shows have home pages where daily news can be retrieved and comments can be posted.

The Internet mingles the mass media and individual people in substantive ways not possible only a few years ago. There is more. There are no media time slots. There is no separation between performance and audience, because on the Net the distinction does not exist. It feels different. *The Internet/mass media connection is less passive, less mediated, and asynchronous when compared to the mass media alone.* This means the information comes on-demand and at the will and convenience of the user. Similar to the horizontal integration of the mass media, the Internet is a symbol of parallel technological growth, consumer investment, and (cyber)culture. Internet use may be preparing society and the individual, culturally and technologically, for a new format in entertainment and information.

Computer technology in all its forms, and the growing familiarity of computer skills within the population, create their own societal **horizontal integration.** As the mass media become more digital (less analog) in their transmission, the **compatibility** of the two forms increases. As the software of Net browsers becomes more sophisticated, the two otherwise parallel lines of technological development might begin a more rapid spiral toward each other. There are many possibilities for technological evolution, but two come to mind.

The first line of growth does not exclude the other. The first is that the user goes to the media site and digitally retrieves a performance (movie, sitcom, soap, the 1990 Super Bowl, etc.). This need take only seconds in digital form. The same retrieval could be done automatically by a software agent. A second potential merging of the two technologies might come in the form of what Stewart Brand called **broad*catch*ing** (1987). This scenario has the mass media broadcasting in digital form and pushing an information-rich bit-stream into the air or down a fiber-optic pathway. Your home computer "catches" all the bits, selecting the few you might want and discarding all the rest.

The retrieved shows or text could be viewed at any time and in any order. The economics of these possibilities would probably be based on bits retrieved, not minutes on-line. Some media performances might be pay-per-view, like movie rentals today. Others might be free for the viewer, with advertisers basing their support on very accurate measures of bit retrieval. In other cases, such as on-line magazines and newspapers, the cost could be shared between readers and advertisers, as it is currently with printed paper copies. In the digital world, however, it is possible to exclude advertisements from retrieved information, a kind of "A-chip" action on the bit-stream by a software agent. This makes cost-effective advertising a problematic feature of media economics.

Industry is already preparing the necessary microprocessors and other hardware components. Time Warner Enterprises president Bob Pittman has said that, "The computer industry is trying to make their computers full motion video and the TV people are trying to make their TVs smart. We're both coming to the same location." A recent NEC (Nippon Electric Company) ad in a national magazine poses this possibility: *In ten years, people will ask "What are televisions?"* The ad pictures a future multimedia system that would bring the world to your living room, run your household electrical systems, act as a videophone (now widely available on new PCs), and enable you to "catch your favorite episode of *Star Trek*" (now also possible on your PC). Given costs and the current horizontal integration of TV, a 10-year timetable may a bit hopeful and too revolutionary. And too, all of this sheer access has to be accomplished easily, with "friendly" software more obviously and intuitively directed than today's VCRs. Otherwise, each consumer must ask not "what is television," but how much expensive unused capacity she or he is willing to buy. No doubt there will always be a need to simply sit back, relax, and just be entertained passively. The media formats may evolve, but couch potatoes are a stable evolutionary form. They are us, and we are the consumers.

Whatever the actual pace of change in media participation, the direction seems clear. Access will get more personal and individual. We will have the choice to shift back and forth between "user" and "audience." Technology is giving each of us the option of being an individual. Economics heads those same technological capacities toward creating each of us into a demographic unit of one. The fused outcome of these split tendencies will no doubt be variable, depending on how much attention we as individuals want to devote to shaping our own media experiences.

The Symbiotic Medium of Advertising

Symbiotic is a term from biology. It refers to a mutually beneficial relationship obtained by the close association of two dissimilar organisms. Here, we are using the term as an analogy to refer to the relationship between advertising and various other media forms. The relationship is simple. The mass medium delivers an audience to the seller of a product, the seller gives financial support to the medium for the opportunity to address the audience. Advertising is an important part of the mass media in the United States. We will devote all of Chapter 9 to exploring the relationship between the media and advertising. However, advertising is also sometimes thought of as a medium in its own right. This is so because in the midst of another medium, an advertisement creates an episode of different perspective and experience. That is, the audience reacts to the ad in a different way from the information in the surrounding medium. Advertisers bank on the likelihood that this shift in experience will nudge audience members toward a moment of heightened attention.

In that moment, advertisers attempt to persuade audience members to buy a particular product, vote for a certain candidate, or agree to an idea.

The key to advertisement is to arouse interest, usually in the form of some emotion. Because the intent most often is to encourage a consumer purchase, the ad must invoke emotions of need: envy, lust, greed, and empathetic pride. It is the emotion that forms a consumer's *identification* with the ad and constitutes the episodic quality of an advertisement's moment of audience attention. The emotion is what "grabs" you. Often, but not always, there is little information and even less new information in an ad.

A short note on information is important. The federal government and most states prohibit deceptive or unfair ads for consumer goods. Common sense would make the criterion of "deceptive" the relative truthfulness of the information content in the ad. For the law, the yardstick is whether the consumer is harmed. There are no similar restrictions on political advertisements: No law forbids even the most blatant falsehoods or distortions. Public pressure is the primary enforcement arm of U.S. advertisement regulation. Public opinion may be direct, forcing existing ads out of the media. Or, public opinion may be anticipated in judgments by the National Advertising Review Board or by media executives who deem an ad unfit. It is fair to say that in most ads, effect, more than truth, is the goal. As a result, the technology of advertisement is primarily directed toward the creation of emotional effect. Hence, a wide range of graphical technologies and related skills support the production of advertisements.

In the cases of MTV and some children's programming, advertisement and entertainment blend into one media experience. MTV has changed forever the way popular musical creations are promoted. Many children's shows are very tied to toy and game sales. Children's movies such as *Pocahontas* arrived in the theater, and stores were already filled with movie memorabilia. Video games like *Mortal Kombat* are turned into movies, with each advertising the other. The computer-animated *Toy Story* has become a line of toys. In these examples advertisement is perceived as entertainment. On the other hand, the Home Shopping Network, along with its rivals like QVC Fashion, and infomercials are pure advertising put in a creative format. Here, also, advertisement is perceived as entertainment. Thus, advertisements require a widening range of technologies.

Advertisers also have an indirect interest in the technology of the mass medium carrier (e.g., TV, radio, magazine, etc.) for the ad. The concern is for *reach* (number of people who perceive the ad at least once), *target reach* (number of people within specific demographic categories who perceive the ad at least once), and the *frequency* (the average number of times each person is reached). A third area of advertising technology is *direct mail* advertising, the fastest growing segment of the industry. Here computers and other automated equipment generate highly specific catchment areas for particular advertisements. This is done by matching lists of names with area codes, nine-digit zip codes or phone numbers, and sorting these by income, occupation, sex, age, and so on. Advertisers can then pinpoint potential consumers. Direct mail is relatively expensive to use for advertising. Its targeting capacity makes it attractive and, as measured by percentage increases in revenue share, it is the fastest growing ad medium. This, despite the tendency for most direct mail ads to be discarded before they are opened.

The carrier media vary widely in their advertising qualities. TV offers the most complete message with sound, moving pictures, and personality. It gives extensive reach for comparatively low cost. TV is not specific as to target, however, and it cannot offer a record of the ad (a copy of the product name, a discount coupon, a telephone number for orders, etc.). Radio is a better targeting electronic medium. Radio audiences are specific in terms of geographic location, age, or interest groups. (In 1996 the Federal Communications Commission was finalizing a plan for satellite-delivered, subscriber radio known as digital audio radio—DAR. It would serve the entire United States and listeners would have to buy a new car radio and a disc-shaped antenna.) Offering only sound, radio is the most limited medium, but it is inexpensive. Newspapers are good for specific geographic exposure and deep reach in their home areas. Magazines can support more attractive advertisements than newspapers, and have a more specific target reach. Both newspapers and magazines offer hard copy records of ads. This can increase reach and frequency. (Magazine executives sell their space to advertisers based on the premise that magazines will be passed around and will be reread.) Print media also allow easy return reference. (The consumer can come back to the ad at will to reread it, or to get coupons, or to obtain order blanks and 1-800 numbers.)

TABLE 5.2   Percents and Destinations, U. S. Advertising Revenues

LOCAL	% Local	% National	% Total
Local Newspapers	50.6		21.8
Local Broadcast	27.7		12.0
Local Yellow Pages	13.2		5.7
Other Local	8.3		3.6
NATIONAL			
Four TV Networks		12.6	7.3
National Spot TV		9.8	5.7
Cable & Syndication TV		4.7	2.7
National Radio		2.6	1.5
National Magazines		9.2	5.3
National Newspapers		4.5	2.6
Other National Media		56.5	32.8

(Adapted from *McCann Erickson Worldwide Insider's Report,* 1994.)

Publishing: From Corporations to the Desktop

Books

Books are the oldest form of a real language, high-capacity, portable, cultural information storage and retrieval device, other than human beings. The above sentence is kind of a joke. It seems like such an overblown description of something so commonplace as a book. Yet as old and as familiar as the book is, it still can be considered an important information technology. And, of course, there is a mystique about books. The two people writing this text have written a couple of other books, apiece. Whenever this fact comes up in conversation with nonacademics, we suddenly become Authors and somehow different, momentarily, in their eyes. "How could you possibly do that?" and "I don't think I could ever do that" are common, immediate responses. It seems many people would like to be authors, yet most feel lacking in the "right stuff" for authorship. People still line up in bookstores to have their personal copies of books signed by the author. We listen to authors as if they have special insight and know things we do not. *Authority* and *author* come from the same Latin root meaning "the right to give commands." An author is frequently called an authority.

Book appearance is also part of the mystique. The expensive hardback in a dark, rich color with no graphics on the cover (words alone), and with a sewn binding carries more prestige and authority than the paperback, with a glued binding, rough paper, and plenty of graphics on the cover. This is the difference between, say, *The Handbook of Elementary Particle Physics* (to invent a title) and a romance novel titled *Total Seduction* (a fictional name suggested by a graduate student Jennifer Scherick). What we perceive is this: The more impressive the binding, the greater the authority of the work.

Writing, by definition, marks the beginning of "history." Writing has been recognized by many "authorities" as the key to the historical civilizing process for societies. The book, in many ways, is the coherent form of that process. The technologies, physical materials, and social structures behind book publishing have changed considerably. The book still looks and functions the same. The book is a physical reflection of its society and changes in its underlying technology: from the book hand-copied by monks on parchment (or individually formed and pressed paper sheets) and bound in leather to a vinyl-bound *Bible,* electronically printed by laser on mass-produced paper with highly specialized characteristics that ward off wear and oxidation. The technology of books transforms as we change, but so too the contents.

As literacy spread, along with electric lighting, the paperback book began large-volume publication (particularly in the late 1930s and early 1940s). As leisure and affluence became a part of everyday life in the 20th century, the bulk of published books moved from the realm of religion, intellectuality, and high moral stance to the modern novel with themes offering escapism and entertainment. As communities dissolved and we became more alienated and self-concerned, novels began to explore the psychological and emotional realities of characters, and more books were written in various self-help categories (see Ryan, Wentworth, and Chapman 1994). The "sexual revolution" of the sixties brought us more books about our various forms of sexuality, problems with sex, and that "revolution" made more explicit sex common in respectable works of fiction. As society grew more abstract, diverse, and mobile, novelists began to rely on symbols as much as on realism, and novelists started to experiment with noncontinuous time sequences and with variable points of view.

Books now appear in nonpaper forms. Audio recordings have become quite popular. The computer revolution brought reference books, especially, out of the paper medium and into digitized formats. Most word-processing programs incorporate what formerly were paper books: a spell checker (one venerable function of dictionaries; some digitized versions contain word definitions), a thesaurus, and a grammar checker. You can purchase a combined dictionary, spell-checker, and thesaurus that looks like a handheld calculator. Your desk space need no longer be reduced by these three or four paper reference materials. The home bookshelf used to be graced by encyclopedias, atlases, world fact books, and compendia of familiar quotations. These are now available in multimedia versions as CD-ROMs for the home computer. If we understand that paper and printing expenses combine into about one-half of the cost of bringing a book to a reader, then we see the values of the CD-ROM format to publishers. Paper versus plastic is the difference between dollars and pennies.

The technology, form, content, and perspective delivered by the books of a given era tell us something about ourselves. Books open a window on what we know and feel, show us how we relate to each other, and display our hopes and fears. Books remind us of our capacities for good, for evil, for change; and they reflect what the vast forces of history take from us in our need to preserve some continuity. Books, as a species of communicative technology, create both a personal journal of and a technical manual for civilization.

All of this societal change has swelled the size of the market. Between 40 and 60 thousand *new* book titles are published annually in the United States. The annual sales value has increased from $343 million right after World War II to $21 billion in 1997. Publishing organizations both grew and shrank. Those that grew got very large, and many became part of international parent companies that controlled several media types (e.g., Time Warner, see Chapter 7). Those that shrank did so to exploit market niches left open by the mass volume, large, corporate publishers. By the mid-1990s there were at least 25,000 book publishers in the United States (some with a highly literary focus survive because of foundation grants). In Chapter 7 we will examine more closely some of the changes in the publishing industry and effects of those changes for culture production. The social technology of book distribution has also changed to meet market needs. Bookstore chains blossomed in the 1960s, wilted, and then bloomed in the 1980s. These now seem to be evolving into book "superstores" in the 1990s. A superstore typically stocks niche books as well as those of the larger publishing houses. Once inside a superstore you can browse for hours, ask a clerk to do a computer search for an author, title, or subject, and sip your favorite espresso while reading periodicals in the integrated "coffeehouse."

Newspapers

The modern newspaper is no single thing. It comes in two typical sizes, tabloid and broadsheet. The latter is the larger size and it is what we most often think of as a "real" newspaper. Newspapers are usually published in short, regular intervals. The most common intervals are daily or weekly. Worldwide, perhaps 60,000 newspapers exist (about 7,200 of them are published daily) with a combined circulation of an estimated 500 million. There are large areas of the globe where the newspaper is rare. Europe has about one-third of all newspapers with about one-half of the world's total circulation. North America also has about one-third of all the newspapers with a circulation equal to one quarter of the global circulation. The United States has about 1,500 daily newspapers (circulation: 60 million) and approximately 8,000 newspapers published at intervals other than daily. Newspapers range in perspective from the general dailies (e.g., *Miami Herald, USA Today*), to trade dailies (e.g., *Variety, Women's Wear Daily*), to the sensationalist (e.g., *The National Enquirer*). Other papers are narrowcast for very defined markets: the military, a college campus, a prison population, or a minority group.

Some U.S. papers are national in circulation, with either a more national or an international focus. Other papers are more local in circulation and focus. The two national newspapers in the United States with the largest circulations are the *Wall Street Journal* and *USA today,* each with a circulation of about 2 million readers. A few United States papers enjoy very strong reputations nationally and internationally for the quality of their reporting. These "prestige dailies" would include *The New York Times, Washington Post,* and *Los Angeles Times.* They stress foreign and national news, analysis and interpretation, politics, science, economics, and culture. Their stories also tend to be longer or have more detail than the stories in many local papers.

Newspapers have staff reporters who research and write stories. Many papers also rely on organizations called **press agencies** and **press syndicates.** These organizations form a network of bureaus and reporters around the country and the world. They gather news stories and some provide **features** (e.g., comics, "syndicated" columnists, pictures, and "fillers," short items or facts that can be used to fill a column when a story does not). AP (the Associated Press; operated as a cooperative by a large group of newspapers) and Reuters are the most familiar press agencies in the United States. United Press International (UPI) was a major rival of AP until it filed for bankruptcy in the early 1990s. The largest news syndicates (owned by newspapers) are those of the *New York Times* and *Los Angeles Times / Washington Post.* Major syndicates specializing in features include *King Features, United Features,* and *Knight-Ridder/Tribune News Service.* Perhaps the most familiar foreign news agency is the Russian ITAR-Tass press service. Agencies and syndicates distribute their materials to subscriber newspapers for a fee. All use electronic telecommunications technology for distribution.

U.S. newspapers are showing a strong tendency to consolidate. In 1978 over 60 percent of U.S. papers were owned by chains. By 1987, about two-thirds of U.S. papers were financially controlled by an ownership chain. In the mid-1990s chain ownership accounts for about 75 percent of U.S. newspapers. In Chapter 7 we will examine this process and its potential effects in greater detail.

Newspapers are printed on cheap, rough-surfaced paper called **newsprint.** Only a small proportion of a newspaper is filled with accounts of events—the actual news. Headlines, commentary, pictures, cartoons, and advertisements account for nearly 50 percent of the space in a newspaper. Advertising revenues account for about 75 percent of a newspaper's revenues (you pay the other 25 percent of the cost). In fact, over 24 percent of total advertising expenditures in the United States go to newspaper advertising. Newspapers get almost 85 percent of their advertising dollars from local businesses.

The newspaper is perhaps the most celebrated form of the press in U.S. history. It is an old medium, backed by sophisticated printing and telecommunications information technology. The dailies and others together reach well over 20 percent of the population. It is a cheap and diversified (despite consolidation by chains) information source that generally matches itself well to the interests of its readership. Newspapers today present their readers with a breadth of news, professional commentary, letters to the editor, entertainment, sports, weather, politics, and cultural information unknown in previous times. The venerable newspaper remains one of the most important media for discovering and redefining values and ourselves.

Periodicals (Magazines)

The principal form of the modern periodical is the magazine. (The scholarly journal is another type of periodical.) Magazines are bound, paper-covered, and issued regularly.

TABLE 5.3   A Glance at U. S. Newspaper Readership

Per Capita Newspaper Circulation, By U.S. Region

New England	.28	East Central	.236
Mid-Atlantic	.283	North Central	.249
Mid-South	.196	Mountain	.21
Atlantic South	.17	West	.216
South Central	.19	District of Columbia	1.53

(Adapted from *Editor and Publisher Year Book,* 1992.)

The most familiar magazines are published weekly. It was not until the turn of this century that the price and popular appeal of magazines were sufficiently low to qualify them as mass media.

Now it is estimated that nearly 95 percent of all adult Americans read magazines every month, and each of us is likely to have at least opened and glanced at several different magazines per month. Magazines receive about 5 percent of the total advertising monies spent in the United States, and that amount is $7 billion annually. Gross magazine revenues are about $14 billion annually. The top 20 magazines have a combined circulation of about 110 million copies. There are over 10 thousand magazines published in the United States, with an increasing trend toward narrowcasting for highly specialized markets. Supermarkets are a major outlet for magazine sales. Waiting rooms (e.g., at a dentist's office) are a major means of multiplying readership, so that the Magazine Publishers Association estimates that each issue of the average magazine is read by 3.8 people.

Magazines tend toward either *general interest* or *special interest.* Most general interest magazines have very familiar names to Americans. Examples include *Reader's Digest, TV Guide, National Geographic, Ladies' Home Journal, Woman's Day, Time, Playboy, Sports Illustrated, Ebony,* and *People.* Examples of special interest magazines include *Runner's World, Vibe, Byte, Nickelodeon, Sesame Street Magazine, X & Y Magazine, The Cross Stitcher, Wave Rider, Fangoria, Baywatch, Classic Crossword Puzzles, Gun News Digest,* and *Herbs for Health.*

The *Ladies' Home Journal* was founded in the 1880s. *Time* became a quick success after it was founded in 1923. *Mad* was started in 1952, followed one year later by *Playboy* (whose first centerfold was Marilyn Monroe). *Ms.* appeared in 1972 as a popular expression of the contemporary women's movement. In 1974 *People* magazine was published as a highly successful spinoff of the "People" section in *Time* magazine.

Desktop Publishing

Desktop publishing is a name for a process that is only recently possible. We can grant that the introduction of the relatively inexpensive laser printer in 1985 marks the beginning of desktop publishing. Probably the most common publication from the PC is the simple newsletter. However, almost any level of sophistication is now possible. A combination of software programs—some for graphics (including clipart software libraries with tens of thousands of fully scalable images and photos) and others for layout (including libraries of fonts), scanners, color printers with at least 600 dpi (dots per inch) resolution, "video capture boards" (that allow a computer user to "grab" full color images from any video source, including your TV and camcorder), and access to downloadable Internet graphics makes the publication of a very sophisticated magazine within the reach of many would-be publishing entrepreneurs.

The Electronic Cauldron: Telecommunications

Telecommunication means to communicate via a technology over some distance. It generally refers to telephone, radio, and television communication. Such communications occur by sending transmissions through the air or through some type of cable (cable examples: paired copper wires, coaxial, fiber-optic). "Airwave" messages go from a transmission antenna to a receiving antenna. In the cases of commercial or police radio the process is a very direct airwave broadcast. Cellular phone and cable TV messages follow a complex mix of transmission routes. Cordless, in-home phones transmit through the air for no more than several hundred feet, then by cable, but may take to the air again for highly directional microwave transmission (between phone company antennae) or to reach a cell phone. Long-distance calls are very likely to switch cable types from electrical to optical and back again, and can be transmitted to a satellite for an airwave connection to a cellular phone located anywhere on the planet.

The Airwaves

We hardly stop to consider it. The airspace seems so vast. Yet that space is a scarce resource when we begin to divide it up into bandwidth partitions for telecommunications. That space must be carefully allocated to prevent interference occurring among the many uses of the airwaves. **Bandwidth** refers to the frequency range required to carry different types of electronic or radio signals. In general, the more complex the information to be carried, the wider the necessary bandwidth. A **channel** is the household name for a particular set of information bandwidths. In practical terms, bandwidth or channel is the specific set of one or more frequencies required to complete the desired broadcast at the receiver. For example, a color-TV channel requires a frequency for the audio and a frequency for the video, and the two must be separated by yet another frequency range to keep the two from distorting each other (producing static in the audio and "snow" in the video). The bandwidth for color TV is over one thousand times wider than for telephone transmissions. HDTV requires a bandwidth 7500 times wider than a telephone conversation. Each channel must also be separated from other channels to prevent distortion. What is the importance of this? Let us use a very crude analogy to explain.

Suppose you were out in the desert lying on your back looking up at the sky. And suppose further that you could see each bandwidth in a horizon-to-horizon slice marked off in the sky by a different color—like a rainbow. You would see narrow slices of color for cell phones and pagers, slices for military transmissions, slices for taxis, CB radios in trucks and ham radios, slices for each AM and FM radio broadcast station, slices for TV stations, and separate slices each for terrestrial and satellite services, and so on. Unlike a rainbow, our slices must be separated from each other to keep the colors from mingling and creating interference. As the uses of airwave transmission multiply and the complexity of signals increases, the sky fills up with slices of color. We run out of room for more uses. As we shall see in Chapter 6, 50 years ago the Federal Communications Commission allocated bandwidth simply to prevent signal distortion. Now, in addition, the FCC must be the steward of an increasingly scarce and valuable resource.

Cable

Remember that, by the term *cable,* we mean solid medium signal transmission by electrical or optical impulse. Bandwidth is a concept that can also be applied to a carrier medium. That is we can gauge the potential bandwidth capacity of a cable type. For the transmission of typical analog signals, the pair of copper wires in a phone line has a very narrow bandwidth capacity: It is just fine for voice transmission, but not much else. Coaxial cable has a wider bandwidth potential for analog transmission and it carries VHS quality television signals. Fiber-optic cables, which are now just as cheap as copper wire to install (including all the electronic hardware for sending, amplification, and receiving), carry digital signals. Theoretically, the bandwidth of fiber optics approaches infinity. It is now possible to deliver 1,000 billion bits per second of information. This is an impossible amount to consider directly in any meaningful way. By analogy, Nicholas Negroponte (1995) describes this quantity as a potential for transmitting one million TV channels through a single fiber the size of a human hair, all at the same time. He says all issues of the *Wall Street Journal* ever published could be transmitted in less than a second. This, he says, is 200 thousand times faster than copper phone lines.

Digital and Compressed Signals

If analog signals were converted to digital and digital signals were "data-compressed," the effective bandwidth of every channel and medium would be increased. Existing bandwidth allocations would be able to handle more and more kinds of information. Signal loss and distortion would be diminished.

Telecommunications industries, whether it is your local phone company or cable provider, AT&T or an international multimedia corporation, whose name you may never have heard, are all poised to enter a mixed media market and offer as many types of services as can be made profitable. This could include interactive TV, pay-per-view movies, remote library research, traditional phone service, global video phones, E-mail, magazines, video games, in-home banking, on-line medical information services, on- screen programming and navigation guides, and so on. Note that all of this focuses on your TV—your "home entertainment appliance." Watching television may never be simple again. All of this depends on our spending more time and more money in the multimedia world. But the technological and market questions boil down to this: What transmission medium (and hence which corporations) will bring all this to us? Will it come digitized on the airwaves? Will it all pour out of the TV coaxial cable? Will the phone lines take us where no telephone company has gone before?

The Switch?

The datasphere is getting more crowded and filled with more complex information. The technologies and the possibilities are changing. Data compression, signal digitization, fiber-optic cables, and Digital Direct Satellite systems (mentioned earlier in this chapter) are beginning to mix and match. Given the scarcity of room on the airwaves and the increasing capacity of cable types, especially fiber-optic, a number of experts and lawmakers are considering a major shift in transmission: **The Negroponte Switch.** This is not a name coined by MIT professor and media guru Nicholas Negroponte. It is a name for a concept, coined by George Gilder (a technology writer and visionary), and it stuck. Professor Negroponte suggests that a trading of places between cable and airwaves is a reasonable future to expect. He believes that we should save the scarce airwaves for very remote or mobile receivers. What is in the air now will go to cable, and what is in cable may well go to the air. Whatever emerges from the technology will depend on what is distributed and who wants to buy it. It is a buyer's world. The consumer will sort it all out. In the final analysis all this wonderful technology is just a distribution system.

The Datasphere: Media Content, Content Media

What we buy out of that wonderful, technological distribution system is its content. We buy it with our time, with our interest, and with our money. That distribution system delivers its content into the datasphere. *Datasphere* is a term from the first chapter of *Media Virus!* by Douglas Rushkoff (1994). *Datasphere* seems to mean a world saturated by media content, a world in which it is entirely possible for most people to spend as much time with media programming as in conversation with other flesh-and-blood people. The datasphere is not a neutral world. Its messages are designed to influence. Our news, weather, sports, comedy, docudramas, cops and robbers (or drug dealers) shows, and music—in short, the bulk of our cultural references—come from the media.

We use the media to babysit our children while we do other tasks around the house. The media keep latchkey children company after school and before their parents get home from work. The media are represented first thing in the morning on our doorsteps and distract us as we drive to work. The media can make an empty house seem more inviting when we are home alone. The media bring us a glimpse of political candidates, provide us with soaps and sports so that we have common interests around which to form our conversations. The media take the fantasy and reality of the actual, diverse world and present them to us inside the datasphere.

There are still people alive who can remember the time before there was a data-sphere, a time when the media could be left behind. There are people who can remember stable communities, more or less insulated from the wider world. There are many others who, out of nostalgia, loathing, or fear, wish for a return to the time of community. Many people believe that the media are at the center of responsibility for the destruction of community. Many others feel that every day their beliefs and values are slapped in the face by media content. They feel that the media have a powerful allure that destroys traditions at the core of community.

When things in society do not seem to be as they should, we like to find something to blame. Lately, media messages have been assigned a lot of accountability. We say there is too much explicit sex, violence, bad language, incivility, and irresponsible behavior displayed in the messages of the media. Conversely, we say that there is not enough of human good. These are of course the very things we think are wrong with society. Are we simply trying to "kill the messenger" when we are told these unpleasant or abhorrent things about ourselves? Granted, media messages are not neutral and balanced, and do have an independent effect on society. Granted, if things are to get better (by some definition, but whose?), we have to start somewhere. And for many that "somewhere" is the mass media.

As a society we are not willing to accept that the same technological transformation of society (from an Agricultural to an Industrial to a Post-Industrial Service/Knowledge economy, all, roughly, during *this* century) that brings so much material well-being can also have a downside. There is no free lunch. The growth of the mass media is only a part of an even larger transformation of society. This larger shift is a monumental "creative destruction" of the past on the way toward some unknown future. This larger shift has created large new classes (the middle class and the underclass), and an increasing distance between the wealthiest and the poorest. It has been the platform for a greater political and legal inclusiveness (the successful civil rights movements of so many minorities) that in itself is threatening to many others. And this larger societal shift furnishes the world with an ever-new array of technology.

Summary

Trends in media technology, as discussed in this chapter, appear to be leading us toward greater *flexibility*. We are approaching the capability of moving at will between being part of a passive "audience" and having the alternatives of a "user." We are approaching a time when media technology will allow us the opportunity to construct our own datasphere. From V-chips to digitalization, from a greater reliance on computers to narrowcasting, from "broadcatching" to becoming a demographic unit of one, all these create the chance for higher levels of selectivity in what information we wish included in our world. What the current mass media do not ever ask of us is personal responsibility. What personal programming demands is *effort* (even granting that the newer technologies will be easy or "transparent"), *vigilance,* and *responsibility.* Technological flexibility in the media should empower us to choose the level of personal programming we desire.

But what of the ways the media function positively for society? We mentioned at the beginning of the chapter that a massive society still needs to have internal communications. Only by conversing with itself can a society know, unify, and correct itself, even when it is too large for a fraction of its people to actually meet face-to-face. *The technology of the mass media help us to perform this necessary internal communications task more efficiently.*

Many people feel that the media contain too much that is bad and not enough that is good. These are the exact things many also think are wrong with society. The media will not let us ignore the facts of life. If we do not like something about life and the media make it difficult to hide ourselves from it, maybe we will work that much harder to change what threatens our peace—and not merely blame the media. The media have a substantial positive impact on the economy and on job production. Media industries contribute $169 billion or 3.4 percent of the Gross Domestic Product. Over 8 million jobs are directly related to the media.

Lastly, consider an implicit theme of this entire chapter, *change.* Modern and even postmodern societies are all based on never-ending, chronic change. Change is at the heart of our survival, growth, and continued adaptation. How can anything grow and not change? How can one increase in wealth and not change? How can one adapt to an emerging world economy and power structure and not change? If the media actually have the power to weaken or destroy tradition as is alleged—however frightening and distasteful this might be—then the media help to loosen the very bonds that hinder change. Still, evolving culture will point the way: Society drives the technological change of media invention (Principle One, from the beginning of this chapter). Media technology merely opens us to the possibilities of our future. Welcome to the Datasphere, everyone!

6

Regulating the Media

The Internet is at a very different time and place in China. The Internet is tiny here—about 300,000 users. It's under the thumb of the government, which controls all access, screens content and makes users register with the police (Maney 1997:1B).

The Barnes & Noble bookstore chain has been indicted on obscenity charges for selling three books that feature photographs of nude children. The books by photographers Jock Sturges and David Hamilton have received some critical praise, but a Tennessee county grand jury claims they may violate state obscenity laws (Greenville News, November 24, 1997:2A)

All societies regulate communication in some way. Communication is too essential to the process of social cooperation to remain uncontrolled. Regulation can be either formal or informal. At the most subtle level, communication is regulated by the rules of language, the culturally determined categories for describing the world. For example, in Western culture, we do not have words for easily distinguishing between our father's parents and our mother's parents. In some other cultures, such a distinction can be made linguistically, reflecting the fact that, in the kinship systems of those cultures, distinguishing between maternal and paternal grandparents is important.

Communication may reflect status and power differences in society. Thus, we often speak in different ways to our friends, our family, and our boss. Sometimes males and females use language differently, as do the old and the young and members of certain subcultures. The point is, because human beings are inherently social beings, communication is never entirely unregulated. Like other types of human behavior, it is constrained by social rules.

As societies grow and become more complex, communication is regulated more formally through laws and other written regulations. For example, laws may exist to protect individuals or groups from defamation. These are laws designed to protect a person's good name and reputation from false assertions.

Other laws may prohibit treasonable utterances against the state, or attempt to preserve certain standards of morality. In the United States, and in most other countries with broadcasting technology, the creation of broadcasted goods is treated very differently from the creation of other goods, such as automobiles or microwave ovens. Governmental regulation, to varying extents, controls entry into the industry, use of communication technology, content, and ownership of cultural products. As we shall see, these types of restrictions can have particular importance for the day-to-day functioning and quality of the mass media.

Government Regulation

Freedom of the Press

Of all the mass media, the print media are the most free of government regulation. The First Amendment (1791) of the U.S. Constitution guarantees freedom of the press: "Congress shall make no law…abridging freedom of speech or of the press." Subsequent to the First Amendment, court decisions have made this restraint binding on state governments. Freedom of the press means the right to gather and publish information or to write opinion without government control or fear of punishment. A free press acts as a check on the power of government. The press also provides people with a means to be informed as citizens who are active in their own governance.

The right of press freedom, while not absolute, applies to every form of printed or broadcast material, not only to newspapers. In the United States, printed materials, and newspapers in particular, are seen traditionally as being the media with the most voluntary audiences, and tend to have the fewest restrictions. Broadcast media, while coming under the First Amendment, tend to be more regulated. Broadcast audience members are legally seen as having less absolute control over what is broadcast into their home.

The meaning of a free press is constantly being argued and modified in U.S. court decisions. It does not apply for obscenity and pornography or in cases of overriding national security when publication would create a "clear and present danger" to the vital interests of the United States. And, when prejudicial pretrial publicity may form as a result of news coverage, a judge has the authority to bar the press and the public from controversial criminal proceedings.

The press is most free in the United States and in Great Britain, including the Commonwealth nations (e.g., Canada, Australia). Freedom of the press is also very strong in Western Europe, parts of Latin America, and Japan. The rest of the world lags behind. Where democratic movements occur in the world, they beget national pressure for press freedom. Where press freedom is not strong, the press is controlled by censorship or used by government as an organ of propaganda. For example, on August 2, 1987, the *New York Times* published an interview with Woo Sang Ho, the president of the student body at Seoul's Yonesi University. Woo criticized the South Korean government and the United States involvement in his country (*Asia Watch* 1988). Later that month, Woo and several other students were arrested on charges of violating the South Korean "Act on Assembly and Demonstration." Woo was further charged with slandering the state by making his comments to the *Times* reporter and to other international journalists. In December of 1987, the Korean press reported that Woo had been sentenced to four years imprisonment. He was subsequently released, arrested again, and placed on probation in 1988.

It is impossible to imagine an incident like that happening in the United States today. But that does not mean that the press here is totally free. Despite the high legal status of the press in the United States, practically speaking, what the press publishes is influenced by the public, business (particularly advertisers), government, and the editorial policies of the publisher. Direct government pressure in the United States is rare, but it can happen. For example, in 1971, the *New York Times* began publishing a series of articles on *the Pentagon papers*—a massive top-secret history of the United States' role in Indochina. Commissioned by then Secretary of Defense Robert S. McNamara and leaked to the press by Federal employee Daniel Ellsberg, *the Pentagon papers* contained 3,000 pages of narrative and more than 4,000 pages of documents covering the history of U.S. involvement in Indochina. Informally, President Nixon refused all further interviews for himself and his staff with the *New York Times,* and commissioned a burglary of the office of Ellsberg's psychiatrist. Formally, the Justice Department obtained from a U.S. District Court in New York a temporary restraining order against further publication. The *New York Times* and the *Washington Post,* which had also begun publishing articles on the history, appealed, and on June 30, 1971, the U.S. Supreme Court ruled 6–3 that the right to free press overrode any subsidiary legal considerations, and permitted publication.

Regulating the Spectrum

Compared to the print media, broadcasting is less free of governmental control. By *broadcasting* is meant messages sent by radio or television waves through the atmosphere and primarily intended for reception by individual television or radio receivers. Messages intended for reception through cable or satellite dishes are treated differently than broadcast signals, and film is primarily self-regulating.

Broadcasting is more regulated than print or cable partially due to the fact that the broadcast spectrum is a limited, but extremely valuable, resource. This spectrum can only be divided into a limited number of broadcasting channels, and demand far exceeds supply. New technologies may alter this in the future, and regulation is already under powerful attack—but for now the spectrum remains a scarce resource.

The spectrum is a scarce resource because the nature of broadcasting technology is such that, without proper controls, one broadcasting signal can easily interfere with another. In the early 1920s, as commercial radio began to develop, there was near chaos in the industry. At times, amateur, nonprofit, and commercial radio signals merged together in an indecipherable jumble. The commercial radio industry sought the government's help in sorting out the mess. The industry was interested not only in sorting out spectrum use, but also in securing the place of private commercial radio by driving out many of the nonprofit stations. The result was the Radio Act of 1927, passed by Congress. The act created the Federal Radio Commission with licensing and regulatory powers and established the important principle of public over private ownership of the spectrum. This paved the way for the more comprehensive Communications Act of 1934.

The Birth of the FCC

The Communications Act of 1934 created the Federal Communications Commission (FCC) with authority over the broadcasting, telephone, and telegraph industries. The FCC now consists of five members, each appointed to a five-year term by the President. The terms are staggered in such a way as to minimize the influence of any one President on the composition of the Commission.

One of the FCC's first duties was to oversee the technical division of the broadcast spectrum. The broadcast spectrum is limited by our technological ability to encode, send, and decode information of particular wavelengths. The lower frequencies were assigned to AM radio, the next higher band to FM. Still higher frequencies were assigned to VHF television broadcasts and radiotelephone communication. The highest band (UHF) was set aside for future television development.

Because of the limited space and the tremendous demand for the use of that space, the FCC's primary power comes in the form of the granting or withholding of broadcast licenses. These licenses are given out for free, but carry the almost automatic guarantee of major profits from the sale of advertising. Not surprisingly, they are in great demand. Because spectrum space is so limited, broadcast channels are, in effect, government-created oligopolies.

With each new broadcast technology, pressure on spectrum space increases. To get a sense of how quickly new technologies can eat up the spectrum, each FM station takes 20 times the space of an AM station, and one television station takes up space equal to the entire AM band!

When new technologies come along, the FCC must allocate portions of the spectrum to accommodate them. For example, the Commission is hoping to stimulate the development of digital TV by giving broadcasters a second channel for that purpose. In return for the giveaway, the FCC received commitments from the National Association of Broadcasters to build at least three stations in markets serving one-seventh of the country by November 1998, one-third of the country by April 1999, and one-half by November 1999.

Some consumer groups, estimating the value of the additional spectrum space for broadcasters at $100 billion, have criticized this plan. These groups would prefer that the new spectrum space be auctioned to raise funds for children's television and other public interest projects. This has been done with other portions of the spectrum. For example, in 1998, the FCC raised hundreds of millions of dollars auctioning licenses in the 28 Gigahertz range to companies that want to offer consumers wireless voice, television, and Internet service over Local Multipoint Distribution Service (LMDS). Such auctions simply serve to highlight the giveaway of HDTV. And, because new digital technologies will allow HDTV to be packed into a small portion of the new spectrum space allocated to each broadcaster, there is also concern that the remaining space will be used by the broadcasters for subscription services such as pagers and cellular phones.

Licensing

The granting by the FCC of a license to use the broadcast spectrum does not confer ownership of that space or an absolute right to use it. The courts have made it clear that a broadcast license is not a personal property right but rather provides for the temporary use of public property. The rules originally stipulated the licenses were for three years with possible renewal. In 1981, the licensing period was extended to five years, and now it is eight years. While renewals are usually granted, they can be challenged by other license applicants or others who believe the station is not fulfilling its obligations to serve the public interest. This was the case when, in 1998, the media watchdog group Rocky Mountain Media Watch petitioned the FCC to revoke the broadcast licenses of four Denver television stations. The group contends that the stations' local news programs contained excessive violence while ignoring or underreporting important social issues, elections, the arts, and education.

With the Federal Communications Act of 1934, the FCC was mandated by Congress to develop criteria for choosing among broadcasting license hopefuls. These criteria were to be based on serving "the public interest, convenience and necessity," a phrase carried over from the Radio Act. The FCC made three central assumptions in defining the public interest:

1. The basic purpose of broadcasting should be the creation of an informed public. The right of the public to be informed takes precedence over the right of the government or any individual to broadcast their own particular views.
2. It is assumed that the best way to create an informed public is by presenting it with a diverse array of opinions and information about a particular subject. Thus, it is important not to overly concentrate access to broadcasting in the hands of the few.
3. Broadcasting needs to be sensitive to local needs.

The stated goal of the FCC is to create an informed public through the broadcast of information emanating from diverse sources and relevant to local needs. Ideally, it attempts to carry out this goal through its licensing procedures and other rules designed to promote competition, diversity of content, and localism.

The Fairness Doctrine

One attempt to encourage diversity was the Fairness Doctrine of 1949. This FCC ruling mandated that broadcast stations fairly present all sides of important public policy issues. In a sense, the FCC, supported by the Supreme Court, was taking the position that the right to free speech on the part of the broadcasters must be secondary to the right of the public to be informed. However, rather than providing the free exchange of information, some have argued that the Fairness Doctrine might actually have had the opposite effect (Krattenmaker and Powe 1994). Forced to provide all sides to controversial issues, often at their own expense, the broadcasters sometimes choose not to cover the issues at all. The result of such criticism was that, in 1987, the Commission repealed the Doctrine.

Equal Time

The Communications Act of 1934 stipulated that, if a broadcaster allows one political candidate airtime, he or she must allow other candidates time under similar conditions. If free time is granted to one, then free time must be granted to the others. Similarly, if one candidate pays for time, others must have the opportunity to also pay for airtime. However, a controversy arose as to whether coverage of the activities of incumbents necessitated the granting of equal time to nonincumbent candidates. In order to deal with this problem, the FCC, in 1959, exempted news programming from equal-time coverage. In 1983, candidate debates were classified by the Commission as news events and therefore also became exempt. This meant that stations were not required to give equal time to candidates not included in the debate. However, if a station editorializes on behalf of one candidate, other candidates must still be given equal time to respond.

Promoting Diversity

Both the Fairness Doctrine and the equal-time provision of the Communications Act of 1934 were intended to promote the diversity of sources of information. This is in accordance with the assumption that a diversity of sources is a public good. More generally, the FCC has been given the mandate to promote diversity through control of spectrum allocations and rules of station ownership. The assumption is that greater diversity of ownership will promote greater diversity of programming.

Racial Preferences

One example of this principle in action is the FCC's policy that gives preference to racial (but not gender) minority applications for ownership. This is done by providing incentives for selling stations to members of racial minority groups. Such preferential practices, however, have come under serious political attack.

Political candidates' debates are exempt from equal-time regulations.

Ownership Rules

The FCC has also regulated the number of broadcast stations that a single owner can have in a particular market. Since 1970, the Commission has allowed ownership of only two AM or two FM or two television stations within the same market. It also made it impossible to own a radio station and a VHF television station in the same market. However, the FCC now allows for ownership of up to 8 stations in markets with 45 or more stations, 7 stations in markets with 30 to 44 stations, 6 stations in markets with 15 to 29 stations, and 5 stations in markets with fewer than 15 stations.

The FCC also controls the number of television broadcast stations that can be owned nationwide. In 1996 the FCC eliminated a rule that a single owner may control no more than 12 stations. It also raised the national audience-reach limit from 25 percent to 35 percent. The Act retained existing rules that forbid one company from owning two TV stations in a local market, or a newspaper and TV station in the same market, or a newspaper and cable system in the same market. The Act also maintains the ownership ban of a cable company and a broadcast company in the same market.

The rules are more lenient for national radio. In the radio industry, the restrictions on the number of stations owned nationally have been eliminated. However, these rules are still evolving. The Justice Department has already forced modifications in mergers that would give a radio group more than 35 percent of ad revenue in a single market, and the Chairman of the FCC has expressed concern over the number and scope of mergers. Congress, on the other hand, has worked to relax rules even further.

This whole concept of ownership in media industries and its effects will be explored further when we examine the structure of media industries in the next chapter, but, for now, the important point is that ownership rules were originally intended to promote diversity of information sources. The assumption has been that diversity of information sources was intended to lead to a more informed public. While diversity of sources is still a stated goal of the FCC, the agency has now taken the position that, because of new technologies, concentration of ownership is not a serious threat to that diversity. The nearly unlimited capacity of fiber-optic cable, direct satellite reception, and various forms of digital communication have threatened to make scarcity of spectrum space obsolete as a justification for regulation. At the same time, the popularization of a conservative, free-market, antigovernment ideology in the political arena has made regulation unpopular.

Other Diversity Rules

Other rules that are intended to promote diversity include rules intended to maintain some independence between affiliates and their parent networks (affiliates do not *have* to air network programs), rules concerning program acquisition, and rules limiting the amount of network-produced programs that can be carried by affiliates. Regarding the latter, until recently, the FCC has protected independent program producers by severely restricting the network's ability to make and distribute their own programming. Networks can now both create and distribute their own programs, and, as a result, an increasing percentage of network programming is self-produced. Nearly all new programs announced for the 1998–1999 season on the three major networks are "in-house" productions.

Regulation and Media Mergers

The relaxing of ownership and program acquisition rules has led to a frenzy of merger activity in mass media industries. In 1995, Walt Disney Company announced a takeover of the ABC television network for an estimated $19 billion. The very next day The Westinghouse Corporation announced its takeover of CBS. Quickly, Turner Broadcasting and Time Warner followed suit. The Disney/ABC deal was then the second largest takeover bid in U.S. history. In buying ABC, Disney acquired not only a television network, but also eight television stations, twenty-one radio stations, cable channels such as ESPN, A&E, and Lifetime (adding to its own The Disney Channel), seven newspapers, and several magazines. Thus, this merger provided the kind of concentration of ownership that the FCC has long tried to prevent.

In addition to being a result of the liberalizing of ownership rules, analysts believe that one reason for Disney's move was the removal, noted above, of restric-

The Walt Disney Company takeover of the ABC television network sparked a wave of media mergers.

tions on networks airing their own programs. Independent program producers like Disney have feared that the networks might begin producing the bulk of their own programs in order to reap higher profits, freezing out independents in the process. By buying ABC, Disney is assured of a broadcasting outlet for its products. At the same time, ABC is assured of a ready supply of quality programming.

Regulation and the Rise of FM Radio

Often, the relationship between regulation and content is indirect and not easily detected. For example, Fornatale and Mills (1980) have highlighted the fascinating relationship between FCC regulation and the development and content of FM radio. Despite the superior sound quality of FM, its inventor, Edwin Armstrong, had to struggle to obtain frequency space from the FCC for his invention. Originally turned down, Armstrong, with the backing of CBS, eventually obtained frequency space and went on the air in 1939. However, in order to reserve space for wartime communications, the FCC froze all station allocations in 1942. At that point in time, AM radio was clearly dominant over the newer FM technology, with 909 AM stations on the air compared to FM's 30. Because of the freeze, FM was not able to develop during the war years. To make matters worse for FM, after the war was over, the FCC shifted FM to a different part of the broadcast spectrum. The 500,000 receivers already in the hands of consumers were suddenly obsolete. Fornatale and Mills show how, despite FM's superior sound quality, this change created a negative image of FM as an unstable technology. Understandably, given the shaky early history of FM, consumers were reluctant to invest in new equipment.

Later, with spectrum space for AM becoming more scarce, the FCC worked to expand the audience for the new technology. The FCC accomplished this in several ways. One was to allow for "simulcasting" on AM and FM radio. This meant that stations were allowed to broadcast the same material simultaneously on both bands. Simulcasting provided an incentive for broadcasters to experiment with FM. This was because companies that already owned an AM station could broadcast in FM without the cost of developing new programs. The primary costs involved were limited to those associated with obtaining the new equipment. Of course, this policy was not helpful to independent FM stations not attached to AM stations.

A second way to increase the audience for FM was to allocate FM stations enough frequency space to allow for stereo broadcasting. This, coupled with FM's already superior sound quality, made FM attractive to the serious music listener. A third strategy was to set aside a small portion of the broadcasting spectrum for educational radio stations. This publicly funded, noncompetitive environment gave FM a chance to win listeners over to its superior sound quality.

The example of FM is important because it shows how a regulatory body can take an active role in the success or failure of a new communication technology. As we shall see, in this case, the actions of the FCC did more than just promote the new technology, these policies created a context within which the actual programming *content* of FM radio was altered.

By the mid-1960s, FCC policies had given FM a foothold in the industry. The FCC now moved to end simulcasting in cities with populations over 100,000. Aided by the success of public radio with its heavy airplay of classical music, the growing appreciation of the superior sound quality of FM stereo, and the introduction of FM car radios in 1963, the regulatory body felt that FM could now stand on its own. This was important not only because of the FCC's mission of promoting broadcast diversity, but also because the AM spectrum was nearly full. With the demand for new licenses continuing unabated, FM offered an alternative for prospective owners.

The FCC's decision to end simulcasting had an important effect on the content of popular culture. As explained by Fornatale and Mills, in the period immediately after the end of simulcasting, the FM stations had yet to attract advertisers on their own. The advertisers were not convinced that there was sufficient audience to justify buying airtime on FM. This meant that, unlike AM radio, where advertising filled up much of the time every hour, the possibility existed in FM radio for long periods of uninterrupted airplay. As a result, songs too long for AM's strict format and entire albums were played by the FM disk jockeys who felt no pressure to please advertisers. At the same time, musicians reacting to the new format were freed to write longer songs and record concept albums. This was quite a departure from the standard practice of including on an album one or two songs intended for release as singles, with the rest of the songs being "throwaway" cuts.

In part because of these changes, rock music began to take on a more artistic identity and became a central component of the larger youth movement that was going on at that time. Groups like the Beatles, the Who, and Pink Floyd experimented with entire albums of complex, interwoven songs. Thus, the FCC regulations that first discouraged and then encouraged a new technology eventually made possible a new type of creativity within popular music.

Regulating Content

Most FCC activity is concerned with regulating the structure of the industry and impacts only indirectly on content. However, sometimes the FCC is encouraged to more directly regulate the content of the mass media. For example, at one time, the FCC believed that unsponsored (meaning no advertisements) and local live programming were more in the public interest than sponsored and recorded programs. The Commission attempted to encourage the former and discourage the latter. Another example is the **Prime Time Access Rule,** formulated during the 1970s, which limited ABC, CBS, and NBC to three hours a day of self-produced prime-time entertainment programming, Monday through Saturday. In this case, on the assumption that too many productions emanating from the three networks would have a negative effect on diversity, the FCC directly limited the amount of programs the networks could provide. As noted earlier, the prime time access rule has since been recinded with the effect of "freezing out" many independent producers.

Obscenity and Morally Offensive Content

Obscenity and other forms of what might be called morally offensive media content create particular problems for regulatory bodies in the United States. This is because of the First Amendment's guarantee of freedom of speech. The Supreme Court has struck down many attempts by the government to regulate the content of communication. However, it has ruled that obscenity is *not* protected by the First Amendment. Of course, defining what is obscene is not always easy. The Supreme Court attempted to define *obscenity* in *Miller v. California* (413 U.S. 15 1973), mandating a local rather than a national definition. The Court declared that for material to be declared obscene it must:

1. Be seen by the average person, applying contemporary community standards, as appealing directly to prurient (obscene) interest;
2. Depict or describe in a patently offensive way, sexual conduct specifically defined by the applicable state law;
3. Lack serious literary, artistic, political, or scientific value.

If any symbolic product—a book, movie, television or radio program, painting, or song—fits all three of the above criteria, it is legally obscene. None of the criteria, however, is sufficiently clear to avoid controversy in the labeling of material.

Where program content is clearly obscene, broadcasting is legally treated like any other area medium or forum. However, broadcasting is subject to stricter regulations regarding nudity, language, and sex where there is not a clear indication of obscenity. These stricter standards are rooted in the idea that the airways belong to the public and the concept of "the public good" discussed earlier.

Political concern about the content of the mass media comes and goes in cycles. In the 1960s, a major social concern was increased drug use among young people. The FCC mandated that radio broadcasters screen songs for references to illegal drugs. The U.S. Army provided a list of what were labeled as 22 drug-oriented songs. These included the Beatles's "Lucy in the Sky with Diamonds," the Grateful Dead's "Truckin'," and the Byrds's "Eight Miles High." Whether the songs actually were about drugs did not seem to matter. John Lennon of the Beatles has said that "Lucy in the Sky With Diamonds" was inspired by a drawing made by his young son Julian. Roger McQuinn, member of the Byrds and writer of "Eight Miles High," has remarked that, rather than being about a drug experience, the song was actually inspired by the group's flight to London for the beginning of their 1965 British tour. Nevertheless, the songs were banned.

Because of the changing membership of the Commission and the changing social climate, the ban against these songs is no longer enforced. For example, a song by Tom Petty, "You Don't Know How It Feels," received widespread radio airplay despite the fact that the song's character sings "…let's roll another joint." However, MTV, not the FCC, did alter the lyrics for the video version.

Content again became an issue for the FCC in the 1970s when a number of radio stations across the country developed call-in programs focusing on sexual issues. The broadcast of comedian George Carlin's "seven words you can't say on television" on one station attracted considerable public attention. Meanwhile, Congress was becoming increasingly concerned about what it considered to be an overabundance of sex and violence on television. Backed by the courts, the FCC in the 1970s acted to limit indecent (programming that describes, in terms patently offensive to community standards, sexual or excretory activities or organs) radio programs to the time period after 10 PM (later moved to midnight) and before 6 AM. It also instituted, in cooperation with the television networks, a "family viewing hour" at the beginning of primetime each evening.

Broadcasters and First Amendment advocates were not happy with the FCC's decision and in 1993 a lower federal court struck down the restriction of indecent material to the period between midnight and 6 AM. The FCC then loosened its rules to ban indecent material in the period before 8 PM. However, in 1995, a Federal Appeals Court reversed the earlier ruling, arguing that restricting indecent material in broadcasting is not a violation of the First Amendment. The Court reinstated the original ban on indecent material before 10 PM. In doing so the judge argued that it was simply unrealistic that parents could regulate children's access to indecent material before 10 P.M. without help from government regulation.

The controversy surrounding any government regulation of free speech is illustrated by the fact that this latest ruling has been severely criticized by civil liberties and civil-rights groups, broadcasters, authors and even Action for Children's television—an advocacy group which has pushed for quality children's television. Other groups applaud the regulations and have asked for even stronger measures. For example, when radio talk show host Howard Stern reacted to the murder of Grammy Award winning singer Selena by playing her music with added gunshot sounds and disparaging comments, the National Hispanic Media Coalition called for the FCC to revoke the license of the radio station from which Stern's program originates, or to move his program to a time period after 10 PM and before 6 AM (McConnell 1995a). The FCC rejected the request.

It is not only radio and television that have been scrutinized for content. In the early days of the motion picture industry there were numerous attempts to control content. In the 1920s many states and even cities had censorship boards. Threats of government regulation ultimately resulted in a voluntary ratings system. Similarly, there have been ongoing attempts to mandate a ratings system for recorded music.

Most recently, there has arisen considerable concern over the availability of obscene or pornographic material on the Internet. Both the Congress and the Senate, despite protests from civil rights groups and privacy advocates, added a subsection to the 1996 Telecommunications Act dealing with Internet content. Known as the Communications Decency Act, the regulations would have forbidden anyone from displaying "indecent" materials on the Internet and online services without first setting up an age-screening mechanism to keep minors out of the area. The law provided for prison terms of two years and a $250,000 fine if indecent material were transmitted to minors.

In response, a coalition including the American Library Association, the ACLU, the U.S. Chamber of Commerce, the Society for Professional Journalists, and the Microsoft Corporation challenged the law as a violation of First Amendment protection for the Internet. The opponents of the law argued that the Internet is more like newspapers than it is like TV. Hence the Internet is more controllable and voluntary and less legally susceptible to restrictive censorship. In June 1997 the U.S. Supreme Court supported this position, unanimously ruling the Communication Decency Act unconstitutional. The Court's finding ensured that the Internet will have the same free speech rights as newspapers and books do, rather than the limited rights afforded to cable television and broadcasters. Nevertheless, to avoid future government regulation, Internet providers have begun discussions with parents' groups, law enforcement, and other governmental officials concerning the establishment of self-policing guidelines and education for parents in the use of content-blocking software.

As highlighted by the Internet Decency Act, more than anywhere else it is in the area of children's exposure to the mass media that the real dilemma of freedom of speech versus the public good arises. In the next section we look in greater detail at some of the efforts to resolve this dilemma.

Children's Television

Dale Kunkel (1998) has outlined the various attempts by the FCC to influence the content of children's television. Concerns have been raised over the amount of children's programming available, the quality of that programming, especially the amount of violence it contains, and the effects of advertising on children.

One criticism of children's television is that there is so little of it available on the major networks. A problem with programming for children is that, except on Saturday mornings, children are a relatively small proportion of the viewing audience. At the same time, they lack direct purchasing power. Thus, there are limited economic incentives for broadcasters to program children's shows. Cable networks and public television, which do no have the same need to attract large audiences, have been more interested in children's television than have the broadcasters.

Of greater concern has been the amount of violence in children's programs. Beginning in the 1960s, research, particularly the Bandura studies (Bandura, Ross, and Ross 1963) seemed to indicate that TV had negative effects on children. These studies, especially those seeming to show the negative effects of violence, attracted the interest of Congress. By the early 1970s, the problem of the effects of violence in children's television had become an important issue. The U.S. Surgeon General's office commissioned a number of studies that were interpreted as showing a cause-and-effect relationship between televised violence and antisocial behavior on the part of children. Meanwhile a group of mothers concerned about the quantity and quality of children's television banded together to form Action for Children's Television (ACT). One of the activities of ACT was to begin lobbying in 1970 for the FCC to mandate no less than 14 hours of children's programming per week, and to eliminate commercial advertising from children's television. Thus, the FCC was being pushed toward regulation by a combination of research findings, congressional interest, public concern, and social activism.

In 1974, the FCC issued the *Children's Television Report and Policy Statement* (FCC, 1974). The FCC offered guidelines suggesting that children's programming be increased, without specifying by what amount. The Commission also said that broadcasters needed to take into account the differing cognitive abilities of children of various ages by providing for some age-specific programming content. The Commission responded to concern about the effects of advertising by demanding that broadcasters discontinue the practice of "host selling," in which a program character promotes products. It also set an upper limit on the amount of advertising time attached to children's programs.

While the networks did temporarily take steps to reduce the amount of advertising, and to more clearly separate advertisements from programs, studies indicated that by 1980 no significant progress had been made in increasing the *amount* of children's television. However, in an era of broadcast deregulation, the FCC chose not to pursue this issue.

Toy-Based Programming

Congress, however, *has* chosen to pursue it. In the 1980s, concern over children's television was heightened by a proliferation of "toy-based programming." Toy-based programs are a form of program-length commercial in which representations of the main characters are available as toys sold commercially. The products and the programs are developed simultaneously, with the program serving as a showcase for the toys. The producers of these programs work out deals in which the toy manufacturer picks up part of the production costs in return for advertising time. Another approach is to give the broadcaster a portion of the toy profits in return for carrying the program. These arrangements make such types of programming more lucrative than non-toy-based children's programs, and raise questions concerning the ability of children to distinguish the advertisements from the programs.

Concern over these issues led to a long legislative battle to add the educational and informational needs of children to the mandate of broadcasting in the public interest. One such attempt was passed by Congress but vetoed by former President Reagan. Though the final version of similar legislation was left unsigned by former President Bush, it became law in 1990. Among the provisions of the bill is the requirement that broadcasters provide at least three hours of children's educational programming per week. In addition it sets advertising limits of 10.5 minutes per hour on weekends, and 12 minutes per hour on weekdays in programs directly aimed at children up to age 12. The bill also disallows commercials for a product featured in the same program, and continues the prohibition against host selling. Toy-based programming remained untouched by the legislation.

Concern over children's television has not abated. The FCC has been an advocate of the minimum requirements of three hours per week of educational children's television. However, the four broadcasting networks have resisted. The networks have claimed that children's television increased 100 percent between 1990 and 1994—to over four hours per week—and therefore, the requirements are not needed (McConnell 1995). However, a more scientific study (Kunkel and Canepa 1994) called into question the amount of educational programming alleged by the networks. It was pointed out, for example, that the networks included such programs as the *Mighty Morphin Power Rangers, The Jetsons, Yogi Bear,* and *America's Funniest Home Videos* as educational programs. It was also found that, contrary to network claims, the amount of educational television for children had not increased. In 1996, the FCC acted to more clearly define educational programming to prevent such abuses.

The V-chip
One of the most discussed attempts at regulating children's television has been the incorporation into the 1996 Telecommunications Act of the requirement that television manufacturers install the V-chip in new televisions, and that broadcasters develop a rating system for their programs. The industry has opposed both the ratings and the V-chip on the grounds that they violate First Amendment rights and that they may drive advertisers away from adult-oriented shows. Nevertheless, to avoid having a system externally imposed upon them, they have agreed to develop a ratings system in conjunction with the V-chip.

The V-chip, invented by Canadian Tim Collings, allows the TV audience to block out programs with sexual or violent content. The chip works by reading numerical rating codes inserted into the same area of the broadcast band used for closed-captioned signals for the hearing impaired. The chip can be programmed to allow only programs with certain codes to be viewed, thus allowing for regulation of content. Canada has already tested the V-chip and the device will be generally available here within five years—installed in new sets or as an add-on device to old sets.

Meanwhile, after much debate, a voluntary ratings system has been devised by the television industry. The original system provided age recommendations only. After complaints from various consumer groups, this system was modified to include a combination of age recommendations and program content designations (V=violence, S=sexual situations, L=coarse language, D=suggestive dialogue) (see Box 6.1). NBC, however, has thus far refused to go along with the content designations.

Ratings are displayed both in newspaper and television guide listings as well as at the beginning of each program. Various groups have complained that the ratings are too complex for parents to understand, and that they are no substitute for lessening violence and sex in programs. Another criticism is that the ratings may free programmers to use more violent and sexual programs. The fear is that programmers will feel less responsible for violent or sexual content if ratings are there to warn parents and other viewers away. Still another criticism is that it is dangerous to let the programmers apply the ratings to their own programs. To combat the latter complaint, the industry has set up a Monitoring Board of outside experts to evaluate whether ratings are being applied appropriately. This is still a far cry from the method used by the Motion Picture Association of America (MPAA) to rate movies. Movies are rated by an anonymous panel of parents in cooperation with the MPAA. Filmmakers have no control over the outcome of this process except to re-edit or re-shoot to obtain a different rating.

The networks must also deal with the concerns of their creative personnel in applying ratings. For example, ABC was accused of censorship by Ellen DeGeneres of *Ellen* when the network added an extra warning before an episode in which Ellen kissed another woman. ABC, in addition to rating the show as TV-14, added an extra message: "Due to adult content, parental discretion is advised." DeGeneres remarked, "Where will it stop? If you say 'Don't watch a show that has gay people on it,' who's to say they won't one day say, 'Don't watch a show that has black people on it, or Jews?'" (Johnson 1997b:3D)

Summary of FCC Influence

As mandated by Congress, the FCC controls the use of mass media technology, ownership of mass media outlets, and, to a lesser extent, mass media content. It does so in pursuit of "the public interest." But the definition of the public interest varies according to the political and social climate. Because of the power of the FCC over the broadcasting industry, it is not surprising that, over the years, broadcasters have resisted FCC regulation in the courts. However, in such landmark Supreme Court decisions as *NBC vs. United States* (319 U.S. 192 1943) and *Red Lion Broadcasting vs. FCC* (395 U.S. 367 1969), the Court upheld the Commission's right to regulate

BOX 6.1   Television Rating Codes

According to guidelines issued for parents by the National Association of Broadcasters, the Motion Picture Association of America, and the National Cable Television Association (http://www.tvguidelines.org) the current system contains the following rating categories.

For programs specifically designed for children:

TVY

All Children. This program is designed to be appropriate for all children. Whether animated or live action, the themes and elements in this program are specifically designed for a very young audience, including children from ages 2 to 6. This program is not expected to frighten younger children.

TVY7

Directed to Older Children. This program is designed for children age 7 and above. It may be more appropriate for children who have acquired the developmental skills needed to distinguish between make-believe and reality. Themes and elements in this program may include mild fantasy violence or comedic violence, or may frighten children under the age of 7. Therefore, parents may wish to consider the suitability of this program for their very young children. Note: For those programs where fantasy violence may be more intense or more combative than other programs in this category, such programs will be designated TV-Y7-FV.

The following categories apply to programs designed for the entire audience:

TVG

General Audience. Most parents would find this program suitable for all ages.

Although this rating does not signify a program designed specifically for children, most parents may let younger children watch this program unattended. It contains little or no violence, no strong language, and little or no sexual dialogue or situations.

TVPG

Parental Guidance Suggested. This program contains material that parents may find unsuitable for younger children. Many parents may want to watch it with their younger children. The theme itself may call for parental guidance and/or the program contains one or more of the following: moderate violence (**V**), some sexual situations (**S**), infrequent coarse language (**L**), or suggestive dialogue (**D**).

TV14

Parents Strongly Cautioned. This program contains some material that many parents would find unsuitable for children under 14 years of age. Parents are strongly urged to exercise greater care in monitoring this program and are cautioned against letting children under the age of 14 watch unattended. This program contains one or more of the following: intense violence (**V**), intense sexual situations (**S**), strong coarse language (**L**), or intensely suggestive dialogue (**D**).

TVMA

Mature Audience Only. This program is specifically designed to be viewed by adults and therefore may be unsuitable for children under 17. This program contains one or more of the following: graphic violence (**V**), explicit sexual activity (**S**), or crude indecent language (**L**).

broadcasting over the broadcaster's rights to protection under the First Amendment. Nevertheless, changing technology and political climates have continued to make broadcast regulation a controversial issue.

Copyright Law

Less obvious than FCC regulations, but absolutely essential to the existence of cultural industries, is copyright law. Copyright law is the foundation on which our mass media industries are built. Without copyright law, it would be less possible to make a profit from books, television programs, CDs, and movies. When copyrighted works are copied without permission, the costs can be enormous. For example, it has been estimated that unauthorized copying in China has cost U.S. firms $400 million annually, $300 million of that amount in copying of software (Goldberg and Feder 1991). And the Motion Picture Association of America (MPAA) estimates that video piracy in Russia has led to losses of $312 million in a single year. The MPAA reports that, in 1996, there were 1,536 raids in the United States alone, confiscating 579,489 pirated videos (Motion Picture Association of America 1997).

Copyright law transforms creative activity into private property in much the same way that patents protect technological innovations. This private property can then be bought and sold like any other commodity. Just as patent law forms the basis of manufacturing industries, copyright law translates the creative works of authors, playwrights, screenwriters, moviemakers, artists, and songwriters into the multibillion-dollar culture industry. Thus, copyright law makes possible the financial survival of the artistic community as well as creating support for thousands of ancillary personnel: publishers, technicians, executives, accountants, secretaries and, of course, attorneys.

This means that copyright law is a matter of intense financial concern to many individuals and businesses and this translates into political concern as well—not just on the part of culture creators and the organizations they may work for, but for consumers. When battles over copyright law develop, the fate of entire industries may hang in the balance. For example, when the SONY Corporation began distributing a consumer version of the videotape recorder in the mid-1970s, Hollywood studios immediately felt threatened. In 1976, Universal Studios (owned by MCA) and Walt Disney studios sued SONY. It was their belief that allowing people to copy material off the air for free was a form of copyright infringement that would decrease the value of their products. Universal, backed by MCA, was further motivated because it had invested money in the development of the videodisc system and felt that sales of this system would be hurt by the competing technology. The Motion Picture Association of America, while not a formal plaintiff in the case, joined the fight against video recorders. When the case first came to trial in 1979, the chairman of Walt Disney Productions said that his fear of home taping had actually led him to cancel showings of *Mary Poppins* and *The Jungle Book* on cable television.

In October 1979, the U.S. Circuit Court ruled that home taping did not constitute copyright infringement. SONY was free to manufacture and sell its video recorders. However, in a surprise decision, the Ninth Circuit U.S. Court of Appeals overturned the ruling in October 1981. The new ruling called into question not only the legitimacy of the VCR, but also tape recorders, and computers capable of copying software. But, in 1984, the Supreme Court, by a narrow five to four margin, overturned the appeals court decision. The Court ruled that home copying of copyrighted broadcasts for later viewing was not, in fact, copyright infringement.

The Universal–SONY battle is an example of the importance of copyright to mass media industries. What at that time were two largely separate industries—entertainment "software" (recordings, movies, television programs) and entertainment hardware (sound and video recorders and computers)—locked into a long and expensive battle to protect their profits. At the heart of this battle was copyright law. In this case the dire predictions of the software makers did not come to pass—VCRs have turned into a multimillion dollar bonanza for entertainment producers. Video sales now account for 57 percent of studio revenue.

Copyright is the foundation of entertainment industries. This fact was dramatically illustrated when author Barbara Chase-Riboud brought a $10 million copyright infringement suit against Steven Spielberg's DreamWorks production company over the 1997 film *Amistad.* Chase-Riboud contended that the script for the movie plagiarized her 1989 novel, *Echo of Lions,* as well as a previous screenplay taken from that novel. In response, DreamWorks attorneys accused Chase-Riboud of plagiarizing a 1953 novel, *Black Mutiny,* in her novel. Such conflicts are not unusual in Hollywood, but this one gained national attention when lawyers asked a judge to stop the opening of the film. At the time of the request, DreamWorks had $75 million tied up in production, promotion, and distribution of the film (Puig and Seiler 1997). Fortunately for the producers, the judge refused the request and the film opened as scheduled, while the legal issues were still being sorted out

Effects on Creators

Copyright law can be used by mass media businesses in ways that may increase their profits but may be detrimental to individual creators. For example, the entertainment industry has developed a reputation for finding creative ways to reap profits without always paying the actual creators their due. The new synergies among mass media companies and technologies have raised new problems in this regard. As companies scramble to learn what form the mass media of the future will take, they have been amassing collections of copyrighted material. They have been doing so in order to insure a sufficient supply of the raw material of media content. According to at least one analyst (Jaquet 1997a), creative writers are increasingly being pressured to give up all future rights to their work. That is, producing organizations want to be free to use the creative material in new forms, perhaps combined with material from other creators, without paying the writers. This is already the case for writers of movie and television scripts where most contracts are on a "work made for hire" basis. This means the writer is paid a one-time flat fee for his or her work. Thus, writers receive no extra income if, for example, a television series goes into syndication. Newspapers and magazines are increasingly making similar arrangements with writers.

Copyright and the Public Interest

However, providing profits for corporations and individual creators is not necessarily the intended function of copyright law. From a societal point of view, copyright law is intended to accomplish two things:

1. The encouragement of the creation of literary, dramatic, musical, and artistic work, and
2. The encouragement of the distribution of these works to members of society.

The overall goal is to stimulate communication and learning—which are viewed as being in the public interest. An important point is that copyright is intended to promote the *public* interest, not necessarily *private* interests. At times, encouraging creativity and dissemination can be conflicting goals. For example, at one time recording industry spokespersons complained that the practice of home taping— **copying records** or CDs onto cassette tapes—costs the industry $1.5 billion a year. Consumers sometimes make tapes so that they can play a recording that they have purchased on another medium, perhaps copying a CD to cassette for play on an automobile cassette player. However, it is also true that cassettes are sometimes made to give to friends so that these friends can avoid the expense of buying the recording. While the arguments on each side of the issue are complex, it is true that, in either case, the record company, the publisher, and the recording artist receive no compensation for the copied version. Yet, the dissemination of their creative efforts is improved by the practice. Thus, it is not clear whether the public interest would be served by placing a tax on blank tapes as has been proposed.

The Battle over Copyright Extension

Even the length of the copyright period can be an issue for public concern. Current copyright law stipulates that the term of copyright on works copyrighted after 1977 lasts for 50 years beyond the death of the author, or for 75 years in the case of works made for hire (e.g., motion pictures). Copyright on works published before 1978 lasts for 75 years from publication. Pre-1978 unpublished copyrighted works remain under copyright for those same periods, but at least until 2003, whichever is longer. This type of copyright is significant because it often exists for potentially important historical documents (e.g., letters and diaries) in private hands. If the work is published before 2003, the copyright continues until 2028.

Proposed legislation to extend these copyrights has proven to be quite controversial. The legislation would extend the terms of all copyrights, including copyrights on existing works, by 20 years: 70 years after the death of the author for individual works, 95 years for corporate authors, and so on. Criticism revolves around the issue of the public good. The extensions of copyright would, in many cases, not profit the long-deceased creators or their families but rather profit corporations who had nothing to do with the creation of the original work. Because of the money at stake, the mass media industry has lobbied heavily for the extensions. However, opponents claim that copyright extensions could limit the public use of these works. For example, the 1990s saw an explosion of media adaptations of Jane Austin books. This was due in part to the fact that the Austin works had passed into the public domain, so there was no cost in acquiring them.

New Technologies

As with home taping, new technologies complicate the relationship between protecting creators and allowing for the dissemination of information. One recent example of this conflict was the Motion Picture Licensing Corporation's notification to daycare center operators that they must pay royalties when they show commercial videos to children. Another is the requirement by record companies that on-line services compensate them when subscribers to the services download copyrighted songs. While the ownership of creative works now seems to be a normal and essential part of doing business, the idea of owning intellectual or symbolic works is actually relatively new. Ploman and Hamilton (1980) point out that, for much of history, intellectual creations were seen as belonging to society rather than to the individual. The problem for culture creators was not the dissemination of their work without profit but, rather, getting their work disseminated in the first place. For example, when books were laboriously copied by hand, the central problem for the author was to get enough copies into the hands of readers. Under that system, patronage was the primary source of income for culture creators, so profit was not an issue. The advent of the printing press in the 15th century changed all of that in three ways. First, copies could now be made comparatively easily and, therefore, the control of copying became more difficult. Second, the printer had an economic investment in the press, type, and paper, as well as labor, which needed to be recouped somehow. Ownership was crucial to that recoupment. Third, the printing press made possible the spread of ideas and information that were not necessarily in the interests of the ruling elite, thus increasing their desire to control the medium. For these reasons, we can see that copyright law was not originally designed to protect authors as much as publishers and printers. It also often served as a form of censorship. For example, in the 16th century, copyright law was used in England to protect a printing monopoly as well as to censor Puritan tracts.

The idea of authors' rights really did not take hold until the 18th century with the passage of the "Act of Anne," the first English Parliamentary copyright act. With the passage of the Act, for the first time authors could own more than the original manuscript and the right to sell it directly to a publisher. Now they had some say in the use of their work even after it was published.

Copyright law has meant different things during different historical periods, but at the center is an attempt to stimulate and disseminate creative ideas. Exactly how a society attempts to accomplish these things can have important implications for the process of culture creation and communication. This is illustrated by two examples: one from the work of sociologist Wendy Griswold (1981) on the development of the American novel, and the other from the work of one of the authors of this text on the development of the American music industry (Ryan 1985).

Copyright and Literary Content

According to Griswold (1981), literary critics have long noted the difference in style and content of 19th century British and American novels. The British novels tended to focus more on love, marriage, and middle-class domestic life. The American novels focus more on a rugged male protagonist combating nature, the supernatural, or organized society. The most common explanation of these differences has focused on differences in the American and British national character. However, Griswold shows how copyright law may have played a part.

Prior to 1891, the U.S. copyright law did not protect foreign authors. Because American publishers did not have to pay royalties to foreign authors, it was actually more profitable for them to publish books by these foreign authors. In order to compete, American authors had to provide publishers with a quite different product from that of their English counterparts. In other words, because of copyright rules, the American authors could not easily compete in the same market as the British authors. Instead they produced novels quite different from those of the British authors.

If Griswold is correct, this should have changed beginning in 1891, when the United States signed the international copyright agreement giving protection to foreign authors. If copyright law had been at least partially responsible for the diverging content, then themes should begin to converge after this point in time. Griswold's extensive content analysis shows that this was indeed the case. After 1891, American authors began to produce novels with themes similar to those of the British authors. From this example, Griswold shows that the nature of copyright law in the 19th century had an important influence on the careers of American authors and on the content of American literature.

Copyright and Performance Rights

A second example, from the American music industry, also points out the importance of copyright law in shaping cultural products. This example begins with the passage of the first truly American copyright law in 1909. One section of this law stated that the copyright owner had "...the exclusive right to perform the copyrighted work for profit..." (Act of March 4, 1909, Ch. 320, 35 U.S. Stat. 1075, sec 1(e)). While there is evidence that this provision was not intended as such (see Ryan 1985), it came to be interpreted by publishers, songwriters, and, ultimately the courts, as meaning that any time music is played in public for profit a royalty must be paid to the songwriter and the publisher.

It appeared at the time that such an interpretation was unenforceable. How could individual composers keep track of when and where their works were performed? In order to solve this problem, a group of publishers and composers, with the aid of their attorneys, formed the American Society of Composers, Authors and Publishers (ASCAP) in 1914. The strategy was for the members, who owned the copyrights to the most popular songs of the day, to pool their songs into a single catalog. Music users—cabarets, restaurants, and, later, radio and television—would have to buy a license for the whole catalog or have access to none of this music. The money collected would be put into one pot, and members would be paid according to some measure of the popularity of their work.

The users were not happy to be paying now for what they had previously received for free. They challenged ASCAP in the courts and through legislation, but eventually ASCAP was victorious. The courts ruled that anyone who used the music of an ASCAP member for profit had to pay a royalty or be guilty of copyright infringement. These royalties became the primary source of income for songwriters and publishers, replacing royalties from the sale of sheet music. This turned out to be fortuitous when sales of sheet music dropped significantly with the rise of radio broadcasting. Thus, what appeared to be a minor provision of copyright law created new ways of making a living for culture creators, and made the contemporary music industry possible.

New technologies of culture creation always challenge existing definitions of copyright. For example, the performance rights clause of the 1909 Copyright Act, enforced by ASCAP, enabled songwriters and publishers to adapt to the rise of recorded performances, radio, and sound motion pictures and television. Currently, the principles of copyright are being challenged by the piracy of software and audio and video recording as well as by the rapid growth of the Internet.

Copyright and the Internet

On September 16, 1997, country music legend Johnny Cash spoke before the House Judiciary Courts and Intellectual Property Subcommittee about the Internet. At first this may seem like a strange topic for a country music singer. But Johnny Cash was there to tell members of Congress how his songs were being stolen on the Internet, available from a Web site in Slovenia to download for free. Cash is not the only musical artist to be affected by Internet piracy. Sites making popular songs available for downloading have been proliferating on the Internet. The industry considers such violations of copyright law serious enough that The Recording Industry Association of America (RIAA) has begun the process of successfully suing and closing down such sites.

The Internet is changing the way we think about intellectual property. Depending on your point of view, the digitalized songs, pictures, graphical icons, and newspaper and magazine articles that travel across the Internet are either the fulfilled promise of the information age or highway robbery. The question is, "What is fair use of intellectual property on the Internet?" In 1995 the Lehman Commission (National Infrastructure Task Force's Working Group on Intellectual Property Rights) released a report attempting to answer that question. Recommending a legislative package to tighten controls on digital works, the commission's basic proposal is to expand the use of licensing works for dissemination over the Internet. Copyright owners have breathed a sigh of relief but libraries, educational organizations, on-line services, and other interest groups fear that the balance has been tipped in favor of private rights over the public interest (Okerson 1996). In December of 1997, President Clinton signed into law the No Electronic Theft Act, making it a crime to possess or distribute multiple copies of copyrighted online material whether or not the distribution is for profit. This closed a loophole in criminal law which exempted not-for-profit copying. The new law allows for fines of up to $250,000 and five years in prison for unlawful copying. Lobbying continues on the issue of Internet copyright, but it is all but assured that information on the Internet is going to become more expensive.

Already the National Writers Union has formed the Publication Rights Clearinghouse, a licensing agency (modeled on ASCAP) to collect royalties on materials disseminated over the Internet as well as those disseminated by other media.

The problems of digital reproduction and commerce are further illustrated by the practice of downloading and copying software. On the Internet one can find software for almost any application. Known as "shareware," this software is made available free to anyone with the equipment to download it. In the past, creators of such software have attempted to either convince their customers to pay for the software through various types of pleading or threat in start-up messages, or have crippled the software in hopes that customers would be intrigued enough with its potential to purchase a fully operational copy. However, the first tactic was rarely successful and the second has become increasingly unworkable with the proliferation of alternative products on the Net. Even commercial software makers are almost guaranteed to have their products copied. And, unlike the copying of books with the printing press, or illegal pressings of vinyl records, copies of virtually any creative product can now be made by individuals with a comparatively small investment in equipment.

In the software industry, one solution that is just being tried is called "metering." Metering takes the form of devices that attach to a computer or a chip integrated into

---

BOX 6.2

PRC represents a major victory for our Operations Magazine Index campaign, which is fighting "information superhighway robbery." By setting up a royalty system to put money directly into the pockets of working writers, PRC hopes to do for you what organizations like the American Society of Composers, Authors and Publishers (ASCAP) has done for creators in the music industry.

(Letter to members January 1996. Used by permission, National Writers Union UAW Local 1981.)

the computer. These devices then charge the user for material downloaded and even the number of times a program is used. A major drawback to this method is that it will require the participation of large numbers of computer and software manufacturers who will run the risk of alienating customers who are used to receiving software for free and/or having unlimited use. Nevertheless, this is the approach that has some federal government support. There is a good chance that consumers will one day pay for material downloaded from the Internet. This may apply not just to software, but to *any* material downloaded, including documents, video clips, and music.

Dyson (1997) offers a different solution. She argues that the best strategy is for companies to concentrate on service and support rather than charging for the actual software. This is because, not only are products easy to copy, but the functions of most software are fairly easy to duplicate. According to Dyson:

> *Software is becoming a way to advertise other services and products. For example, Netscape gives away its browser in the hope of encouraging users to select its homepages as a "portal" to the Internet.*

This is an entirely new approach to handling digital products. Technology is, therefore, once again transforming the way in which we think about intellectual property. However, exactly how these issues will be resolved is still unclear.

Lobbying and the Legal Environment

In this chapter we have discussed how the mass media must operate in a complex legal and regulatory environment. Given the huge amounts of dollars involved, it should not be surprising that media organizations take an active part in attempting to control this environment. That is, media organizations do not sit passively waiting to be regulated. A 1997 report (*Wired* August 1997) from the nonprofit citizen's lobbying group, Common Cause, outlines just how active the media are.

The report makes clear that media organizations comprise one of the largest lobbying groups in Washington. According to the data compiled by Common Cause, the political action committees (PACs) of the four major networks' corporate owners, along with that of the National Association of Broadcasters, donated more than $6 million to Democratic and Republican congressional campaigns between January 1987 and November 1996. In the period January 1, 1996, through June 30, 1996, as the Telecommunications Act was being finalized, broadcasters, their parent companies, and the NAB spent over $4 million in various lobbying efforts, targeting members of congress who sat on important committees influencing telecommunications policy, the FCC, and the Clinton administration. The outcome of these lobbying efforts was the giveaway of valuable spectrum space for the development of HDTV and a telecommunications bill that allowed for lucrative mergers and partnerships among firms. Nevertheless, because of the importance of the mass media as a societal institution, the regulatory environment continues to be turbulent. The FCC has a new chairman, William Kennard, and he has already expressed concern over beer and wine ads on TV and the effect of media mergers on diversity. At the same time, some members of Congress and the public still see spectrum space as a source of revenue for the national treasury rather than private profit. Some would like to see the notion of "the public interest" revived. And concern over the content of media messages remains high on the public agenda.

Summary

In this chapter we have examined the influence of legal and political institutions on the mass media and the production of culture. We have seen that special rules are enforced for the broadcasting media because of the premise that the broadcast spectrum is a scarce and valuable resource that belongs to the public. We have seen that most regulation is accomplished through rules set by the Federal Communications Commission and that these rules are intended to promote diversity of ownership on the assumption that this will lead to diversity of viewpoints and a more informed public. We have also seen that other regulations are made by the courts in the form of rules of censorship and by the courts and legislators in determining copyright law. The point needs to be made, however, that despite all of this regulation, because of our constitutionally based belief in freedom of speech, the U.S. media are among the least restricted in the world.

Our purpose here is not to provide detailed information about every complicated nuance of media regulation. Even if we were to attempt that, the current volatile environment of media regulation would ensure that the information would be out-of-date by the time you read this. No matter what the exact nature of regulation turns out to be, we can be sure that:

1. Communication is always regulated,
2. These regulations are somewhat arbitrary, based on subjective interpretations of concepts like "the public interest," and
3. These regulations have powerful effects on the form and content of mass communication.

7

Industry Structure

The chairman of Apple Computer stared at the arugula, shiitake mushrooms, and unrecognizable leaves on his salad plate in the subdued, swanky dining room of the St.Regis Hotel in New York. This was November 1992. Sculley barely paused to eat, between the words and sentences and insights that just kept coming out of him. He spilled forth a whole vision of the world like an intense but carefully calibrated preacher. Sculley was talking about technological convergence. He described how the computer, telephone, wireless services, television, information, and entertainment industries were all flowing together—the very concept behind megamedia. But nobody else of Sculley's stature was talking about it, at least not so publicly, and not with such conviction (MANEY, 1995:13).

The mass media are big business. In 1996, consumers in the United States spent about $142.9 million on media products (Lieberman 1997b). That figure is expected to grow to $238 million in 2001 and to over $319 million by 2006. In fact, some analysts suggest that media spending is growing at twice the rate of the rest of the economy. The average American consumes some 2000 hours just of radio and television programming alone each year.

The last 20 years have seen a tremendous increase in modes of media access for the average American. Twenty years ago most people had access to three commercial broadcasting networks and, perhaps, a public broadcasting station. They had radio, a newspaper or two, some mostly general-interest magazines, and the movie theater. There were no 70-channel cable systems and 100-channel direct broadcast systems. No VCRs and video stores, no personal computers, and no Internet access.

Today all of this is changing rapidly. In just over 10 years, the broadcasters' share of viewers has slipped from 69 percent to 42 percent and is still dropping while cable's has risen proportionately. There have been major changes in technology and major changes in the way media industries are structured. As noted in the previous chapter, in 1995 two of the largest media acquisitions in U.S. history were announced just one day apart. On July 31, Walt Disney Company announced a takeover of the ABC television network and, on August 1, The Westinghouse Corporation announced its takeover of CBS. Mergers of this size and scope have not been confined to the United States. In May 1997, it was announced that Aamulehti Corporation, a Finnish newspaper group, would merge with MTV Oy, the leading commercial television company in Finland. This merger would result in a company that controlled not only newspapers, but books, radio, TV, and multimedia outlets as well. In this chapter we will look at the reasons behind such mergers and the possible effects on what we, as consumers, have available to us as mass media products.

Understanding Industry Structure

Industry Structure

Industry structure refers to the number and size of firms within an industry. Undoubtedly you have heard the term *monopoly*—an industry structure in which one dominant company controls the market. Because of antitrust laws in the United States, monopolies are rare, although some (including the Justice Department) would argue that Microsoft's domination in the computer industry comes pretty close. More common is an industry structure known as **oligopoly,** the domination of an industry by a few large firms. The automobile industry would be an example of an oligopoly, and most mass media industries follow that pattern as well. In this chapter we will look at the structure of mass media industries and how structure may influence the way business is done and, ultimately, the content available to the consumer.

Resource Dependency Theory

A major trend in media organizations today is the forming of large conglomerates through mergers and acquisitions. **Resource dependency theory** (Thompson 1967) helps to explain the logic behind organizational mergers and acquisitions. The basic idea is that organizations exist within environments that are made up of, in part, other organizations. Organizations need resources in order to survive. Resources include raw materials, personnel, permission to do business, technology, distribution channels, and cash. To the extent that one organization controls resources needed by another organization, it has power over that organization. Thus there are reasons, beyond simply removing a competitor from the market or making an investment to increase revenues, why one media organization might want to acquire another.

Creative products or information are both the raw materials and the output of many media organizations. Because creative personnel who can successfully produce cultural products are often in short supply, one organization may acquire another in order to gain access to these individuals. Or, it might be that one firm has developed technology that another needs, has a catalog of popular creative works, or possesses needed distribution channels such as cable or broadcast networks. Under certain conditions, for example, when markets are turbulent and uncertain, and when the regulatory environment is favorable, companies are likely to take action to reduce resource dependency. The later half of the 1990s has been characterized by conditions such as these.

Organizational strategies to reduce resource dependency may involve **vertical** or **horizontal integration.** Vertical integration takes place in order to gain control over various links in the supply, production, distribution chain. Such integration can occur forward or backward in the chain. For example, a hamburger chain may decide to acquire its beef supplier in order to insure quality and pricing, or a furniture company may acquire showrooms for its products. Horizontal integration occurs when an organization merges with another organization performing a similar function in order to increase the scale of its operation, or to offer a broader range of products. For example, the hamburger chain may acquire another hamburger chain in order to become larger and reach more markets, or it may acquire a chain of pizza parlors in an attempt to diversify.

Changes in structure such as these are often associated with regulatory changes. Since 1990 there has been an upward trend in mergers and acquisitions in industry in general, but mergers and acquisitions in mass media industries have outpaced this upward trend. The media industry was strongly affected by the FCC's decision in 1993 to relax rules that had prohibited the broadcast networks from producing their own programming. This was followed by the comprehensive Communications Act of 1996 which, as we have seen, greatly reduced restrictions on media ownership, leading to a wave of industry acquisition and merger activity. Among the changes made possible by the Act, cable companies can now enter into telecommunications, telephone companies may enter into video services, and broadcasters may enter into digital services. Because of regulatory changes and new technology, it seems certain that various media will be delivering new and different types of information in new ways in the years to come. To cite just one example, companies are already moving quickly to combine television, telephone services, and the Internet on personal computers.

Other changes brought about by the 1996 Communications Act involve the lifting of limits on the number of radio and television stations a single company may own, and allow for ownership of multiple stations in a single city. Remaining from the previous Communications Act are prohibitions against a company owning a daily newspaper and broadcasting station in the same city, and common ownership of a broadcasting and cable outlet in the same city, although lobbying continues in an attempt to remove these restrictions.

Meanwhile, rapid advances in technology, including digitalization of information, data compression, interactivity, and multimedia capability have also destabilized organizational environments, creating both vulnerabilities and opportunities. One of the driving forces in the changing structure of media industries is that these new technologies have blurred the distinction among discrete cultural products. Music, video, photographs, data, and computer software have all begun to merge together, as has the distinction between creator and consumer (where there is greater interactivity). These changes are mirrored at the organizational level as companies that once specialized in a particular medium or product merge with or acquire other companies, while, at the same time, totally new companies are formed to take advantage of a particular niche in the industry. On the distribution side, we have watched as long-distance telephone companies, local phone companies, and cable and broadcasting networks have rushed to get into each other's business. No one is sure which technology will emerge as dominant and no wants to be left with outdated technology.

Not all arrangements involve mergers and acquisitions. Joint ventures are increasingly common as organizations pool resources for particular projects. An example of this trend in action is the joint cable venture between NBC and Microsoft (MSNBC). All of this is taking place at a global level as the economic and cultural boundaries between countries blur as well.

While concentration has increased across the entire economy, it is viewed with greater concern when it occurs in mass media industries. This is because here, unlike, for example, in the manufacture of automobiles or microwave ovens, the consequences may affect the amount and type of information relevant to the public agenda. In the following sections we examine those consequences for the mass media and for society. The key focus is on the relationship between industry structure and the nature and diversity of cultural products available to consumers.

Competition and Diversity

A basic argument from economic theory is that the level of competition in an industry affects the diversity of the products available, although the nature of that relationship is not always clear. On the one hand it could be argued that when only one or a few firms control the market, the lack of competition allows them to experiment freely. Conversely, it could also be argued that the more concentrated (fewer firms controlling the market) an industry is, the less diverse the products produced. The rationale goes like this. A highly concentrated industry is a stable industry. At most, a few firms are competing for customers. Under these conditions the simplest strategy is to try to produce products that appeal to the majority of people and not to alienate any significant portion of the market. Because all of the firms are trying to do the same thing, they typically produce similar products but with sufficient superficial differences to maintain market share. Most competition that does exist is in the realm of advertising these products. This strategy has the added benefit of lowering costs by reducing investments in fundamental technological innovation. Thus, in an attempt to gain a mass market, large firms are conservative in their approach, appealing to the majority. At a microlevel, this traditional view suggests that managers in large firms are less likely to take risks for fear of hurting their careers and, at the same time, the complicated decision structure of these organizations makes it difficult to innovate.

It would seem that under conditions like these, change would rarely or never occur. However, while all of this is going on, segments of the market become bored and alienated bit by bit, dissatisfied with products that appeal to the majority. When a critical mass of these disaffected consumers is reached, small firms come into the market in an attempt to attract those consumers. These firms offer new and different products. Competition increases and so does diversity. In time, if the new firms begin to hurt the larger firms, the big firms react and buy up the small firms, incorporating their innovations and then, eventually, returning to their conservative approach and the cycle begins again.

A classic test of the relationship between competition and diversity in a cultural industry was published by Peterson and Berger (1975). The researchers examined changes in the number of different artists having records in the top ten of the Billboard "Hot 100" music charts. Their study showed that during periods of greater competition, diversity increased, as measured by the number of different artists reaching the charts. Conversely, during periods of industry concentration, fewer artists reached the charts, the music was more homogenized. Replicated by Rothenbuhler and Dimmick in 1982, the association between greater competition and more diversity was again supported. Similar results have been found across the entire range of cultural industries, including book publishing, motion pictures, television, and even opera (Peterson and Berger 1996). Likewise, Ryan (1985) showed how the competition between two music licensing firms, ASCAP and BMI, increased the diversity of popular music in the 1940s and 1950s and set the stage for the birth of rock 'n' roll.

More recent studies (Burnett 1992, Lopes 1992) suggest a refinement in the relationship between competition and diversity. While it is difficult to compare the measures used in these studies with the earlier studies, they suggest that considerable diversity now occurs in the music industry even during periods of concentration. This may be the result of a new corporate strategy, in which large firms buy up smaller independent firms, but with the important innovation of leaving their day-to-day operations relatively autonomous. This allows the larger firms to benefit from the innovations of the smaller firms while undertaking relatively little risk, because each small label is such a small part of the overall company.

Peterson and Bergen (1994) and White (1997) offer a different explanation of what is going on. They say that there is no doubt that many different acts now cycle on and off the various music charts. However, they argue that this is more the result of aesthetic bankruptcy than true diversity as the major companies flounder in their attempts to find the next "big thing." In either case, the structure of the industry is now such that companies cannot sit complacently and attempt to allow a few big stars to dominate the charts.

We now turn our attention toward examining the structure of various media industries. We will do so with an eye on the level of competition in each particular industry, as well as across industries, and the potential effects on product diversity.

Industry Structure and Effects

Overall Concentration

Perhaps more than any other social scientist, Ben Bagdikian has tracked and commented on changing patterns of media ownership in the United States. His most important work, *The Media Monopoly* (1997), now in its fifth edition, traces the dramatic changes in media ownership in the United States over time. Since the first edition of his book in 1983, media concentration has increased greatly. By Bagdikian's measures, in 1984 there were 50 corporations that controlled the U.S. media. By 1990 the number had shrunk to 23, and he estimates that today there are only about 10 corporations that control the media in the United States (Bagdikian 1997:xiii). For Bagdikian this concentration of ownership puts unprecedented political, economic, and social power in the hands of media owners. The Telecommunications Act of 1996, heralded by industry as opening the door to competition, he argues, is reflective of media owners' power to influence the political process to reduce competition and produce private gain.

There is no doubt that media power is increasingly in the hands of the relative few. But what does concentration mean for the consumer? We begin our examination with the newspaper industry.

Newspapers

The newspaper business has seen a large growth in industry concentration in the last 25 years. Waterman (1991) shows that over the period 1977–1989, the eight largest newspaper publishing firms increased their market share from 32 percent to 36 percent. An example of the scale of mergers and acquisitions in the industry is the $1.3 billion purchase of Cowles Media by McClatchy Newspapers, moving McClatchy from the thirteenth to the eighth largest chain as measured by circulation (see Table 7.1).

Although the increase in the market share of the top eight companies is a significant change, Waterman points out that it is really the continuation of a long trend. Head-to-head competition between local newspapers was already rare by the late 1970s.

For the most part, increasing concentration of newspaper ownership has been driven by the attempt to create a better economy of scale and higher profits. However, even subtle legal issues can have an effect, for example, the way the IRS applies rules regarding estate taxes to newspapers when the owner dies. A trend in the newspaper industry has been for family-run papers to be bought up by large corporations. This is due at least in part to the fact that the IRS has ruled that when a newspaper is sold, estate taxes are computed on the basis of the current market price of the

TABLE 7.1   Top Eight Newspaper Companies by Circulation (in millions)

Gannett	5.84
Knight-Ridder	4.05
Newhouse	2.81
Dow Jones	2.36
Times Mirror	2.31
The New York Times	2.28
Hearst	1.74
McClatchy	1.35

(Source: Lieberman 1997c, Copyright USA TODAY. Reprinted by permission.)

paper, rather than against annual income. The problem is that current market value has been driven quite high by large corporations willing to pay top dollar to acquire papers. With newspapers being taxed at current market value, many family owners have been unable or unwilling to pay the large estate taxes without selling the paper. This, in turn, accelerates the trend away from family ownership.

As Bagdikian (1997:xv) points out, of the 1,500 daily newspapers in the United States, 99 percent are the only daily paper in town. The twelve largest chains control nearly half of all circulation and the trend toward concentration is continuing. Data gathered for the period 1994 to1996 indicate a high volume of merger and acquisition activity on the part of newspaper publishers. During that period approximately 140 newspapers changed hands, with the majors actually selling more than they bought. However, the pattern clearly was one of increasing circulation by selling smaller papers and buying larger ones (Table 7.2). In 1996, the pace of buying and selling increased even faster, with 84 daily newspapers changing hands (*Editor & Publisher* 1997).

Effects of Concentration

Some argue that the rise of large publically owned newspaper chains has lead to a greater focus on increasing profits. This is due to the need to recoup the high costs of acquiring the newspapers, the (sometimes) high cost of newsprint, the need for expensive new technology, and increased competition from other media for advertising dollars. Typical solutions have been to increase profit margins by reducing the number of reporters, shortening stories, and increasing the amount of "soft" news. A survey conducted by Martha Matthews (1996) supports the existence of this increased focus on profit. Matthews surveyed publishers from the five largest publically held newspaper chains and the five largest privately held newspapers. The publishers employed by the publically owned newspapers reported that their companies placed greater emphasis on generating revenue than did publishers of privately

TABLE 7.2   Daily Newspapers Bought and Sold by Number and Circulation, 1994 to 1996

Companies	Number Bought	Circulation Bought	Number Sold	Circulation Sold
New York Times Co.	1	504,869	4	59,300
Knight-Ridder	4	185,100	1	21,000
Gannett	3	145,700	1	88,000
MediaNews Group, Inc.	5	116,220	0	0
Cox Enterprises	2	36,300	0	0
Dow Jones & Co., Inc.	1	30,000	0	0
Times Mirror Co.	2	18,942	1	10,800
Thomson	1	7,100	32	367,878
Capital Cities/ABC	0	0	1	6,500
E. W. Scripps Co.	0	0	1	11,000
Totals	19	1,044,231	41	564,476

(Data compiled from various industry sources.)

owned companies. The public company publishers also reported that overall they had less autonomy, especially on staffing and content matters.

Increased focus on profit may lead to more advertising and less hard news. A study by Christopher (1985) suggests this may be true. This study showed that independent newspapers had 23 percent more local and national news than papers owned by large media conglomerates.

Critics have argued that another effect of concentration has been to dilute the local character of papers as editors move from paper to paper within the corporation. Allegedly it is the policy of one major chain to keep editors in place for no more than five years at a time.

One analyst (McManus 1995) believes that one consequence of concentration in newspaper ownership has been an increased focus on keeping constituents— investors, advertisers, sources and consumers—happy. This, the author argues, is not necessarily a good thing as such pressures may serve to distort the news in undesirable ways. It is interesting that journalists themselves believe that competition produces higher quality news reporting (Coulson and Lacy 1996). However, a study by Entman (1989) found few differences in content in newspapers whether they existed in competitive environments or not.

Radio

Since the passage of the Telecommunications Act in 1996, concentration in radio has proceeded rapidly. Once the most fragmented of the major media, with nearly

11,000 stations nationally, the relaxation in FCC regulations has allowed for new levels of concentration. In the first two years after the passage of the Act, approximately 4000 stations changed hands. During the same period, the top ten radio-owning groups increased their holdings from 652 to 1,134 stations. The deal which has attracted the most attention has been Westinghouse's $4.4 billion purchase of Infinity Broadcasting. This acquisition resulted in Westinghouse, which was already the number one company in terms of revenue, owning 83 stations nationally, and, more importantly, between 20 and 50 percent of each of the 10 largest markets in the country.

With that kind of market penetration, it is not surprising that Westinghouse is first in total station revenue. However, even with its 83 stations, Westinghouse is not the largest player in the market in terms of number of stations. A company named Hicks Muse Tate & Furst, Inc., owns Capstar Broadcasting, which, at the time of this writing, has 243 stations nationally. In the fall of 1997, Hicks Muse Tate & Furst announced its intention to purchase SFX Broadcasting, a company with 71 stations nationally, including one AM and three FM stations in one city alone. This is an unprecedented amount of concentration in the modern radio industry.

According to industry observers, such high levels of concentration are likely to affect advertising rates. Already there has been evidence of "package deals" in which, in order for advertisers to buy access to an important station, they have to buy time on lesser stations as well. Such concentration in single areas also allows radio to better compete with television and newspaper by delivering a larger audience to the advertiser. A final benefit is that savings occur in the centralization of administrative functions.

Effects on content are unclear. Adler (1996) argues that, similar to what is happening with newspapers, these mergers have increased pressure on radio stations to make larger profits. One way of doing this has been to cut back on news staffs and news programming in some markets (McKean and Stone 1991). However, in large markets with high levels of competition, an alternative has been for some stations to specialize in news programming. In fact, in 1997, the number one format in audience share was News/Talk with 16.6 percent of national listeners. The number two format was adult contemporary with 14.8 percent of listeners (Rathbun 1997).

Another possible effect is the standardization of radio formats across the country. Most radio stations are already locked into specific formats; nearly 64 percent of all stations utilize either country, adult contemporary, news/talk, or religious programming formats (Lazick 1997). It is unclear whether combining these stations into larger chains is likely to have much of an effect. It is certainly true, however, that nonmainstream music is most likely to be heard on public stations or small independent stations, a dying breed in the industry.

One clear correlation with the changing ownership rules has been a drop in minority ownership of radio stations from 3.1 percent to 2.8 percent (a 10 percent drop). This change has been enough to raise the concern of FCC Chairman William Kennard. Meanwhile, perhaps because of these effects, unlicensed, low-power, "pirate" community radio stations have been proliferating.

Television

There have been dramatic changes in television as well, although concentration has not proceeded as rapidly as in radio. This is largely due to the continuation of the duopoly rule that limits TV broadcasters to one station per market. Television was once dominated by the "big three," ABC, CBS, and NBC. The seeds that were to end this dominance were sown by the beginning of consumer cable in 1980. Later in the 1980s, added competition was created as Fox emerged as a fourth network. In 1998 the new network was attracting about 7 percent of prime-time viewers. The year 1995 saw the development of two more networks, UPN and Warner Brothers (WB). The two new networks, UPN with 2.8 percent of prime-time viewers in 1998 and WB with 3.1 percent, are vying with each other to claim the status of the fifth network. UPN has had its most success with the *Star Trek Voyager* series, while WB has made an impact with the popular program *Buffy the Vampire Slayer.* The two new networks not only are representative of increased competition for the major networks, they also reflect the vertical integration taking place in the industry. WB is owned by Time Warner and Tribune Broadcasting, while UPN is owned by Viacom, which also owns Paramount Studios and BHC Communications. The competition between these networks has resulted in several attempts to steal each other's affiliates, which are always a scarce resource for new networks. Currently, WB has 99 affiliates, reaching about 87 percent of the U.S. market. UPN has 167 stations, reaching 94 percent. Meanwhile, entertainment giant Seagram has announced an alliance with the Home Shopping Network, with the intention of creating a seventh broadcast network.

Consolidation has proceeded rapidly among cable delivery systems as well. In 1996 alone, trades and acquisitions in the cable industry totaled $23.1 billion (Coleman 1997:20). At that time the largest deals were US West's acquisition of Continental Cablevision for $11.5 billion, Tele-Communications' $2.7 billion purchase of Viacom, and Comcasts's purchase of Scripps Howard Cable for $1.58 billion.

Despite the relative concentration in the television industry, a high level of competition exists among the various broadcast networks and cable and satellite services. This is in contrast to the time prior to the early 1980s when there were only three networks. Then, the high cost of production, the relatively stable market shares with virtually guaranteed high profits, and lack of information about consumer preferences led to fairly standard programming formats across the three networks. The addition of the Fox network led to some immediate diversity as the network pursued the relatively untapped youth and young adult markets. It is obvious that the introduction of cable and satellite systems has led to an explosion of diversity in television programming. While some argue that this does not carry over into the important news programming aspects of television, the presence of C-Span and politically oriented talk shows certainly indicates greater diversity than had existed previously. One available cable channel even carries foreign language news broadcasts from Germany, France, and South America.

However, some disturbing trends in news content exist. Television networks have never been known for challenging business interests, and current ownership patterns may have heightened this tendency, as illustrated by the dramatic case of CBS and an interview with a tobacco executive.

The 60 **Minutes** *Controversy*

In 1995, *60 Minutes* dropped a scheduled broadcast of an interview with a former executive of Brown and Williamson Tobacco, the first tobacco executive ever to reveal the inside secrets of the industry. The executive charged in the interview that the company purposely manipulated nicotine levels in order to enhance the addictive quality of cigarettes. In a July 1997 speech before the Commonwealth Club of California, San Francisco (rebroadcast on C-Span), Lowell Bergman, the award-winning *60 Minutes* producer who had secured the interview, spoke about his attempts to get the story on the air. Bergman described how Brown and Williamson, the employer of the executive, had already won a $3 million award against CBS because of remarks made by a commentator at a CBS Chicago affiliate. This may explain why the General Counsel of CBS made the unprecedented move of coming from corporate headquarters to the news division instead of going through channels. The producers of *60 Minutes* were told that they had put the whole company in danger because the executive had a confidentiality agreement with his company that prevented him from revealing company secrets unless indicted by a federal agency. The CBS council believed that there was risk of a $10 billion judgment against CBS that would bankrupt the company. Another possible factor in the pressure not to broadcast the interview was that large tobacco companies, such as RJR Nabisco and Phillip Morris, have massive holdings in the food and beverage industries, and are among the biggest television advertisers. In his speech, Bergman charged that he was told that the corporation would not risk its assets on the case, but asserted that conflicts of interest were even deeper than that.

Lawrence Tisch assumed control of CBS in 1986. Through his ownership of another company, Tisch also owned a tobacco company. This company was, according to Bergman, Tisch's biggest moneymaker, and Tisch's son, Andrew, was chief executive officer of the company. In that capacity, Tisch's son testified before Congress that he did not believe that tobacco was addictive. In the interview with *60 Minutes,* the industry executive was accusing the industry CEOs, including Tisch's son, of lying. The executive was also about to become a witness against the other CEOs in the Justice Department investigation of the industry. Thus, *60 Minutes* was intending to broadcast an interview with a man who would end up testifying against the son of the network owner.

Problems with the story did not end there. By August of 1995, Tisch had announced that he intended to sell CBS to Westinghouse. According to Bergman, concerns were raised that a potential lawsuit from the tobacco industry over the interview might interfere with Westinghouse's desire to purchase the network. This was a valid business concern that arose from clear precedent. Bergman alleges that ABC had previously caved in on a multimillion-dollar lawsuit brought by Philip Morris for fear that it would taint their merger with Disney. In his speech Bergman states that a number of corporate officers and executives of CBS, including the general counsel and the president of the news division, were about to make millions if the deal with Westinghouse went through. Thus, through a complex network of both personal and corporate conflicts of interest, the story was killed. This would seem to be a clear case of the negative effects of media ownership by large conglomerates.

But it is not that simple. As this corporate intrigue leaked to the outside world, the story took a new turn. As we have seen, much of the concern over media ownership has been the movement from ownership by relatively small, family-run companies to ownership by large conglomerates. Yet, CBS under Tisch was a private, family-owned business, small in comparison to some of today's conglomerates. When Westinghouse, a much larger corporation, took over CBS, it installed new leadership for the news division. The new head of the news division, in the face of considerable lobbying by news professionals, decided to run the story. It has since been broadcast and rebroadcast. Bergman believes that, in part because of revelations in the interview, the tobacco companies changed their position and agreed to a settlement with the states.

What we can glean from this story is that the construction of news is a complicated matter. As suggested by the *60 Minutes* story, Wolzien (1996) argues that the prospect of large libel awards may be as much of a factor in the way some stories are covered as are conflicts of interest. His argument is that the not very profitable news divisions are anxious to prove their worth to their bottom-line oriented corporate owners. Thus, they work to avoid lawsuits by staying away from controversial stories.

Other Conflicts of Interest

One obvious point is that the larger the company that controls media-related companies, the more opportunities there are for internal conflicts of interest. To cite just one example, General Electric, which owns NBC, is a major player in the nuclear power industry and the defense industry. At the same time it has been the leader in receiving fines for improper corporate activities (Gunther 1995). Some critics have argued that such ownership will hamper NBC News's willingness to cover related issues. For example, Gunther (1995) charges that in 1989 the *Today* show failed to implicate GE in a story on defective bolts, even though GE used the bolts in its nuclear reactor. Likewise, another *Today* show segment on consumer boycotts failed to mention an ongoing boycott against GE. However, the researcher claims that since 1990 NBC news has covered GE more like other corporations, so the evidence here is mixed. Yet, even the *New York Times* has reported that "it is now common for publishing executives to press journalists to cooperate with their newspapers' "business side," breaching separations that were said in the past to be essential for journalistic integrity" (Glaberson, 1995:1). All of this, as pointed out by *60 Minutes* producer Bergman, makes it easier in the United States to report on government abuses than on corporate abuses.

An added concern is that the nonmedia companies moving into the media industry will not share a corporate culture that values news over entertainment. At the same time, these firms and their owners possess large amounts of cash that they may not hesitate to use to influence the political process. Such a potential conflict came to light when Rupert Murdoch's Fox TV franchises were receiving congressional scrutiny because of concerns over foreign ownership. At about the same time, House Speaker Newt Gingrich received a $4.5 million book advance from the publisher HarperCollins, a firm owned by Rupert Murdoch. Under much pressure from the press, Gingrich later returned the advance for fear of seeming bought off by Murdoch.

The Motion Picture Industry

The film industry is also highly concentrated. In 1996, seven firms controlled 88 percent of the market (Table 7.3). As can be seen from the table, Disney is by far the largest in market share.

Concentration is not confined to the production side. Disney's Buena Vista International, Inc., is the largest film distributor, with 19 percent of the market. A mere six firms, Buena Vista, together with Warner Bros., Sony, Universal, Paramount, and Fox, control 80 percent of U.S. film distribution.

In looking at the table of top film producers, not only is concentration evident but so is the large scale of conglomeration, as firms with major holdings in television and music are also active in the motion picture business. Indeed, some have argued that, because of the rapidly increasing cost of motion pictures and small profit margins,

TABLE 7.3   Film Producers and Market Share, 1996

Walt Disney	21.4%
Warner Bros.	15.4%
Fox	13.7%
Universal	10.9%
Paramount	10.4%
Sony	09.1%
MGM/UA	07.2%
Other	11.9%

(Reprinted from the August 26, 1996 issue of *Business Week* by special permission, copyright 1996 by McGraw-Hill Companies.)

A trend in the motion picture exhibition industry has been toward mergers of theater chains and the development of large "multiplex" theaters.

it is nearly impossible to be active in the motion picture business without other entertainment holdings (Roberts 1997).

Motion Picture Exhibition

The motion picture exhibition (theater) business also underwent considerable consolidation during the 1980s. Waterman (1991) reports that the share of the market
controlled by the eight largest firms increased from 20.6 percent in 1977 to 42.6 percent in 1989. Data from 1995 suggest that the top eight companies control 46 percent
of theater screens. In 1997, two of the largest theater chains, Sony's Loews Theaters
Exhibition Group and Cineplex Odeon, announced that, pending the approval of
antitrust officials, they would merge. If approved, the new company will have 2,600
movie screens in 460 locations. This would make it the second largest theater chain,
behind Carmike Cinemas, which has 2,700 screens. However, other mergers are
pending, including a merger between Regal Cinemas, Kohlberg, Kravis Roberts and
Hicks, Muse, Tate & Furst, which would create the largest theater chain in North
America.

The exhibition sector of the movie business has experienced both horizontal
integration, theater chains buying theater chains, and vertical integration, distributors

becoming involved in exhibition and producers involved in distribution. This latter form of industry structure had been illegal, but the relaxing of antitrust laws in the 1980s made such vertical integration again possible. The vertical integration process is driven by the fact that theater owners are in a power-dependent relationship with producers: They need products to put on their screens. At the same time, producers have been dependent on exhibitors to show their films (Guback 1987). Thus, both groups have been motivated to vertically integrate.

Effects of Concentration

Some argue that the concentration in Hollywood has made studio executives more conservative, thus reducing diversity. Not because they feel they have the market locked up and do not need to innovate, but because pictures are now so expensive and companies more bottom line than artistically oriented. At the same time, overseas sales are a major factor in the success or failure of a film. Because it is widely believed that large-scale, action-oriented films travel cross-culturally best, there has been a growth in the production of this type of film. However, there seems to be plenty of evidence that concentration is not complete and diversity still exists. The strategy for the motion picture industry seems to be the same as that followed in the music industry, large companies buying up independents, but granting them considerable production freedom. In this way the smaller companies act as R&D (research and development) units. For example, the large independent producer Miramax has spawned Dimension Films. Miramax has been quite successful with small films and now seems to be going for the mass market by producing new horror films through Dimension. Other indications of diversity are the success of such independent films as *The Madness of King George, Hoop Dreams, Bullets Over Broadway,* and *The Full Monty.*

The Recording Industry

To the casual observer, the recording industry must look highly diverse. There are recordings from literally hundreds of separate labels available in music stores. However, counting individual labels is deceptive. In reality, since the 1970s, the recording industry has been dominated by only six firms. Since that time these six powerful players have been absorbed into even larger firms, mirroring the process of vertical and horizontal integration and conglomeration that we have seen in other segments of media industries. CBS records has been purchased by Sony of Japan, RCA by the German company Bertelsmann, Polygram is owned by the Dutch company Phillips, MCA was purchased by Seagram of Canada, Warner is part of Time Warner, and Capital is part of EMI Music, a subsidiary of the British firm Thorn EMI. In 1995, these six firms controlled nearly 81 percent of the market in prerecorded music sales (Lazich 1997), with Warner being the largest at 22 percent of the market. Not surprisingly, the majors also control the bulk of recorded music distribution. The Warner–Elektra–Atlantic Corporation alone controls over 22 percent of distribution.

Counting recording labels is deceiving—the music industry is dominated by only a few large firms.

In the summer of 1998, Seagram moved to consolidate the industry even further with the announcement of its intention to purchase PolyGram from Philips. If successful, this reported $10.5 billion deal would make Seagram/PolyGram the largest music company in the world (with a combined music revenue of $6.8 billion in 1997), surpassing Sony.

In a market so dominated by a few firms, it is difficult to understand why there are so many labels. The explanation has to do with simultaneous strategies developed by the majors and by recording artists. As noted in our discussion of the motion picture industry, the majors use independent labels as research and development units. Under the assumption that smaller labels may be in better touch with emerging music acts, the majors will sometimes provide a significant portion of the funding for "independents." If the label is successful enough, the major company may actually buy the label. Ideally, the label will retain autonomy in choosing and recording acts, but the reality is that when it comes to distribution, the majors carry the most clout.

However, there is a countervailing trend to centralization in the industry. Advances in digital technology and microelectronics have enabled the development of relatively cheap digital recording devices and sound processors. More than any other single genre, Rap music has used these advances to remain somewhat independent of the music industry. Rap music is concerned with lyrics. These lyrics often do not match the sensibilities of the mainstream (Ryan, Calhoun, and Wentworth 1996). Thus, the driving force behind this independence is often the attempt to maintain creative control (Jaquet 1997a). However, a consistent problem with remaining independent is in the area of distribution. To accommodate the distribution of not only rap music, but various forms of alternative, singer/songwriter, and other music recorded on small labels, various alternative distribution systems have sprung up utilizing the Internet, mail order, and local music shops. However, these alternative forms of distribution are rarely able to produce national reputations and true careers as understood by the mainstream industry.

The forces of new technology and changing consumer demand have affected the retail side of the industry as well. Large retailers have felt the pinch of relatively flat sales since the temporary boom caused by the transition from vinyl to CDs. Now that many people have finished replacing their vinyl recordings, sales have slowed. At the same time, traditional retail music stores have seen a 20 percent decline in sales as consumer electronic stores, discount retail chains, and music clubs have garnered increasing shares of the market (*The Nation*, August 25/September 1, 1997:27).

A rapidly emerging form of distribution is the Internet. Sales over the Net were about $18 million in 1996 and are expected to jump to $1.6 billion by 2002 (Turner 1997b). But, as large as these numbers seem, they still only account for about 6 percent of all music sales. However, there may be some real competition lurking for the majors. For example, Turner (1997b) points out that the band *The Tragically Hip*, the most popular rock band in Canada, has already decided to distribute an album over the Internet. M. C. Hammer and Duran Duran are selling singles over the Net, David Bowie has made a single available for downloading for free, and Capital Records has formed a partnership with America Online to deliver music directly to consumers.

Faster computers, quicker Internet connections, and ever-improving storage mediums are rapidly expanding the capability for downloading music. Home CD recording units are now available for about $300, and blank CDs cost a mere $4. At the same time, new techniques allow for music to be encrypted and digitally marked to prevent copying. What this means is that the potential exists for musical artists to make their own albums, promote them on the Internet, and distribute them directly to the consumer for downloading. Obviously this is something that neither the majors nor retailers want to see happen. Digital technology carries the potential for bypassing music stores, and, ultimately, the music industry altogether. As Lou Mann, senior vice president of Capitol Records, has remarked in reference to changes in the industry, "I think there's no question that five years from now the whole universe will change" (Haring 1997:10D).

Book Publishing

A wave of mergers in the 1980s has led to a high level of concentration in book publishing as well. For example, in hardcover book publishing, five publishers (Random House, Inc., Bantom Doubleday Dell, Simon & Schuster, Time Warner, and Harper Collins) control 77 percent of the market (Lazick 1997). If we look at all of book publishing, eight firms control most of the market (Miller 1997). The horizontal and vertical integration that has taken place is obvious when we find Simon & Schuster is owned by Viacom, which counts among its publishing holdings The Free Press, Pocket Books, MTV Books, and Scribner's. Vertical integration is evident when we see that Viacom also owns movie theaters, numerous cable services, television syndication and production companies, TV and radio stations, theme parks, and Blockbuster Entertainment. Likewise, HarperCollins is now owned by News Corporation, a Rupert Murdoch company involved in newspapers, magazines, and broadcasting and satellite television. In fact, mergers and acquisitions have left only two major independent publishers, Houghton Mifflin and W. W. Norton.

The strongest evidence of consolidation in book publishing came in the spring of 1998 when German media conglomerate Bertelsmann announced a deal worth between $1.2 and 1.4 billion to purchase Random House, long regarded as the "crown jewel" of publishing (Giles and Sawhill 1998:39). With the acquisition of Random House, Bertelsmann, which already owns Bantam Doubleday Dell, will become the largest publisher in the world, more than twice as large as it nearest competitor, Simon & Schuster, and controlling 26 percent of the U.S. market.

The consolidation of publishers seems to be having some negative effects on the diversity of available content. The publishing world was shaken up by HarperCollins disassembling of its subsidiary Basic Books, a longtime publisher of serious fiction. HarperCollins did so in an attempt to focus on mass market fiction, which constitutes 52 percent of all books sold, compared to 9 percent for general nonfiction (*USA Today,* September 3, 1997). Not surprisingly, if profit is the major motivator, the major publishers have begun to steer away from biography, history, and current events books. University presses are trying to adapt by publishing such books, as well as serious fiction, but they do not have the distribution capabilities or the financial resources available to compensate authors that the major publishers do.

Distribution and Sales

Meanwhile, distribution is controlled by just two firms. Chain bookstores such as Borders and Barnes & Noble have consolidated bookselling, driving out many "mom and pop" local bookstores. This phenomenon is dramatically illustrated by the plight of San Francisco's famed bookstore, City Lights. The store was founded in 1952 by Lawrence Ferlinghetti and Paul Mason as the country's first all-paperback bookstore catering to beat poets and writers. As a relatively small store, City Lights is faced with competition from two megastores that are within walking distance. One is a 30,000-square-foot Barnes & Noble store, and the other a 40,000-square-foot Borders bookstore, each with well over 100,000 titles in stock (Brainard 1995).

Not only are the independents squeezed by the sheer size of the chains, but the chains are also given special pricing deals from the publishers. They even receive payments for simply displaying books in the "power aisles," an industry term for prime locations. However, the independents have held on by specializing in such areas as theater books, women's books, mystery books, and new age and metaphysical books, as well as by streamlining operations and improving customer service.

Nevertheless, the rise of the megastores has been devastating to the independent stores which, according to industry statistics, have dropped from 32.5 percent of adult book buying in 1991 to 18.6 percent in 1997. In response to these challenges, the American Booksellers Association (ABA) filed suit in 1994 against major publishers, charging them with discriminatory pricing practices. In response, the publishers agreed to change their policies. Subsequently, the ABA won a $25 million settlement from Penguin Putnam for violations of that agreement. The conflict between the major chains and independent booksellers intensified when, in the spring of 1998, the ABA and 24 independent stores filed an antitrust suit against Barnes & Noble and Borders Books. The suit challenged the special privileges exacted by the big stores from publishers.

The big chain stores have hurt independent publishers as well. It is standard practice to order large quantities of books and then return the ones that they could not sell as payment for the ones that they did sell. Small publishers have difficulty absorbing this type of cost.

The megastores continue to extend their reach within the publishing industry. Barnes & Noble even publishes its own books, about 350 titles a year. The important new competitive battles are for dominance in the on-line book market. Barnes & Noble and Amazon.com are just two of the companies vying for a share of that growing market. Despite all of this, overall book sales have remained relatively flat. This has increased the pressure for projects that involve synergy among various media in order to produce titles with enormous sales.

Concentration and Content

There have been some powerful effects of changes in structure in the publishing industry. Since the buying up of independent publishers by major conglomerates began in the 1980s, the focus has been more and more on "blockbuster" books. With large cash reserves on hand, large companies have been able to offer huge cash advances to writers. Authors' advances have so escalated in the industry that author Stephen King was able to turn down a $17 million advance from his publisher as he searched for better offers. The effect of these huge advances is that smaller independent publishers have been increasingly unable to compete for big name talent. These independent publishers have traditionally used a few big names to support lesser known writers and important, but not necessarily popular, older works. At the same time, the larger firms are not interested in those types of works either. They are more intent on recovering their large investments in mergers and authors' advances. Traditionally, the publishing industry expected after-tax profits of about 4 percent. However, the new media conglomerates have come to expect profits of 12 to 15 percent from movie and TV ventures and want the same from publishing (Miller 1997). Also in an attempt to increase profits, the focus has been increasingly on books that can be easily turned into motion pictures and other multimedia products. Typically this means books with relatively simple plots and high action.

Added pressure on the industry has come from an unlikely source, the Internal Revenue Service. In 1979 the IRS decreed that books stockpiled in warehouses were taxable assets. This meant that there was a real cost to publishers with large inventories of unsold books. The result was that many publishers dropped books that they felt would have small or modest sales and concentrated on blockbuster titles. Hurt in the process were academic and classic works. Here is a case of tax policy shaping culture production. The change in tax laws helped drive publishers to pursuit of sales on the popular Internet, and created a reluctance to print and keep in stock books with slow sales.

Finally, as with television news, the ownership of publishing firms by large conglomerates opens up more opportunities for conflicts of interest. For example, Miller (1997) shows that publishing houses sometimes steer away from books critical of their parent companies and owners.

The New Media Giants

We have been looking at the patterns of ownership in each medium individually and have noticed considerable movement toward concentration in each media domain. There is a more encompassing trend. More than ever before, media companies are crossing the boundaries of individual media types (e.g., TV, publishing, newspapers, radio, recordings, etc.) and becoming active in a diverse range of media and media-related activities. As noted earlier in this chapter, part of what is driving this structural change is the desire to reduce resource dependency, making sure that the company is involved in everything from creation to distribution. Another factor is the industry buzzword *synergy. Synergy* refers to the prospect of taking a single creative product, a song or a movie for example, and marketing across a number of different mediums. For example, a book can be made into a movie, the movie can be marketed in theaters and sold on videotape, the musical soundtrack can be sold separately, the film and soundtrack can provide story content for conglomerate-owned media magazines, and logos, T-shirts, posters, action figures, and computer games may all multiply the value of the original book. A third and related factor driving the move toward conglomeration is the increasing potential for multimedia (a single product combining various media elements) products.

Much of the merger activity has been made possible by alterations in FCC regulations. For example, when the FCC lifted the prohibition on a major television production studio owning one of the big three broadcasting networks, this allowed for the merger of Disney and Capital Cities/ABC. Sometimes described as the "perfect media merger," Disney's acquisition of ABC is an excellent example of vertical integration. The merger provides Disney with another outlet for distribution, while ABC receives a steady supply of programming, including the always problematic children's shows. What is attractive to advertisers is the possibility of taking advantage of such integrated media marketing packages as ABC, Disney Channel, a product placement in a DreamWorks production, and a series of ads in a Disney-owned magazine.

Another dramatic move toward conglomeration was Westinghouse's acquisition of CBS, announced just one day after the Disney deal. The merger made Westinghouse/CBS the number one television station group in 1996 as measured by the number of homes reached (Sandin and Jessell, July 8, 1996:12, 7). The newly merged company owns stations reaching 31 percent of U.S. homes. Other media holdings include CBS Radio Network, CBS Television Network, 82 radio stations, Eyemark, Maxam Entertainment, Group W Productions, Group W Satellite Communications, and Westinghouse Broadcasting International. Table 7.4 summarizes the holdings of the top five television station–owning companies at the end of 1996 and gives a good indication of the wide range of media holdings of these companies.

By the time you read this, the exact configuration of these companies will undoubtedly have changed but we can expect that as long as the legal, marketing, and technical environments remain turbulent, the process will be the same. From examining the table, we can see that the three networks have been replaced by conglomerates that contain within them broadcasting, production, magazines, motion picture companies, newspapers, and so on—illustrative of both vertical and horizontal integration. Of course, conglomeration is not restricted to these companies that are dominant in television. Companies like Time Warner, Sony, Philips Electronics, Seagram, and Bertelsmann, with revenues in the billions of dollars, are active in music, motion picture publishing, television, and even theme parks and retail sales.

As noted above, the a driving force behind conglomeration is **synergy,** or the combining of forces into something greater than the sum of their parts. In his analysis of Turner Broadcasting's marketing of the 1998 Goodwill Games, Burgi (1997) shows how this might work. Turner, which includes among its many media holdings the TBS Superstation, Turner Network Television (the number one prime-time cable network), The Cartoon Network, and Turner Classic Movies, is now a subsidiary of Time Warner, a worldwide leader in publishing, entertainment, cable networks, and cable systems. Time Warner currently operates in more than 100 countries with the combined revenues of Time Warner, Inc. and Time Warner Entertainment, L. P., approaching $21 billion in 1996. Truly an international company, 33 percent of Time Warner's revenues from Time Inc., Warner Music Group, Turner Broadcasting, and Warner Bros. come from markets outside the United States. For the first time, The Goodwill Games, which have never made money, will have at their disposal the incredible resources of Time Warner. Burgi reports that, according to the president of the games, over 25 divisions of Time Warner will be involved in the support and promotion of the games. Among the promotions planned, Warner Music Group recording artists will perform in concerts tied to promotion of the games, Time, Inc.'s *Sports Illustrated* will provide extensive print coverage, and Time Warner's book publishing unit will produce a coffee table book about the games. Turner Broadcasting is expected to spend over $40 million to promote the games, much of that money going to other Time Warner units.

Another example of the integrated marketing strategy now prevalent in the industry is Warner Brothers's handling of its production *Batman & Robin.* The film

TABLE 7.4   Market Share and Holdings of Top Five TV Station–Owning Companies

Company	% Market	Media Holdings
Westinghouse/ CBS	31	CBS Radio Network, CBS Television Network, 82 Radio Stations, Eyemark, Maxam Entertainment, Group W Productions, Group W Satellite Communications, Westinghouse Broadcasting International
Tribune	25	CLTV News, Tribune Entertainment Co., 5 radio stations, Tribune Radio Networks, Farm Journal Inc., 4 newspapers (including *Chicago Tribune*), Tribune Media Services, 14 niche publications, Chicago Online, Orlando Sentinel Online, 33% of Qwest Broadcasting (TV stations in Atlanta & New Orleans), 31% of Food Network, 11.125 % of The WB TV Network, 5% America Online, 8.1% of Excite, 15.1% of Softkey, 4.4% Peapod (interactive online shopping), 54% of PNI
NBC	25	NBC Television Network, CNBC, MSNBC, A&E, and the History Channel (joint venture with Hearst and Disney/ABC), American Movie Classics (joint venture with TCI and Cablevision), interest in Court TV, Bravo, and Independent Film Channel (joint ventures with TCI and Cablevision), NewSport and Prime Sports Channel Networks (joint ventures with Liberty Media and Rainbow Holdings), NBC SuperChannel Europe, NBC Asia, CNBC Europe
Disney/ABC	24	ABC Radio Networks, ABC Television Network, Walt Disney Pictures, Touchstone Pictures, Hollywood Pictures, Caravan Pictures, Miramax Films, Walt Disney Television, Buena Vista Television, Touchstone Television, The Disney Channel, 21 Radio stations, 14% Young Broadcasting (14th largest holder of TV stations), 80% of ESPN/ESPN2 (which owns Creative Sports marketing, 80% of SportsTicker, 33% of Eurosport, and 20% of Japan Sports Network), 37.5% of A&E and The History Channel (joint venture with Hearst and NBC), Hearst-ABC Video services (joint venture with Hearst), 50% of Lifetime TV (joint venture with Hearst and Viacom), Disney Interactive, Disney Televentures, Rainbow Holdings (joint venture with TCI and Cablevision), 7 daily newspapers (including *Kansas City Star* and *Fort Worth Star-Telegram*), Diversified Publishing Group (more than 100 periodicals) weekly newspapers in Illinois, Michigan, Oregon, Pennsylvania, Fairchild Publications (14 periodicals), Institutional Investor (4 publications), International Medical News Group (6 publications), Chilton Enterprises, interests in German Tele-Munchen (50%) and RTL-2 (23%), French Hamster Productions and TV Sports of France, Tesauro of Spain, Scandinavian Broadcasting System (23%)
Fox	22	Parent Company News Corp owns Fox Broadcasting Company, Fox Filmed Entertainment (20th Century Fox, Fox 2000, Fox Searchlight, Fox Family Films, Fox Animation Studios, Twentieth Century Fox Television, Twentieth Century Television), fX Networks, (Fox, fXM: Movies from Fox), 40% of BskyB, UK, Canal Fox, and News Corp/Globo joint venture, Latin America, 49.9% of Zee TV, Asia, *New York Post*, 5 newspapers in the UK (including *The Times,* the *Sunday Times* and *The Sun*), 127 newspapers in Australia and the Pacific Basin (including *The Australian*), magazines and inserts in North America, Europe, Australia, and the Pacific Basin (including *TV Guide),* HarperCollins U.S./UK/Australia, numerous printing plants, 71% of Sky radio UK, 50% of Delphi Internet services, News Datacom, and other media technology providers, interests in New World and Blackstar Communications

(Source: *Broadcasting & Cable* 126, 29 (July 8, 1996), 12; reprinted by permission.)

...pported by one of the studio's largest promotional campaigns ever. This campaign included partnerships with Taco Bell, Kellogg's, Amoco, Apple Computer, and Frito-Lay. The film even had its own Internet site, an increasingly common promotional practice for movie producers. In addition, the studio arranged for over 250 licenses and tie-ins with such major outlets as Toys 'R' Us, Kmart, Wal-Mart, Target, and J. C. Penney, as well as over 130 exclusive products featured at Warner Bros. Studio Stores worldwide.

In summary, synergy refers both to integrated marketing and to the opportunity for a company like Disney or Warner Brothers to use the same story line for a movie script, a book, a magazine article, an audio recording, a CD-Rom, a theme park ride, and cable rerun without ever having to go outside of its own subsidiaries.

Public Ownership

Even in public radio and television, ownership can matter. This was made evident by the controversial decision of the University of the District of Columbia to sell its public radio station (WDCU) to a company that owns a chain of religious radio stations and a syndicate that provides programming such as the Oliver North talk show to several hundred radio stations (Soloman 1997). WDCU was Washington D.C.'s only full-time jazz radio station, one of just a handful of stations in the country that program all jazz music, and one of only three public radio stations in the country to have a large black audience. Assuming that the new owners follow their usual format, the effect of this sale will be to reduce programming diversity in the Washington market. Soloman (1997) believes that the sale of public stations to religious and for-profit organizations may be a growing trend. For example, a public television station in Pittsburgh is also in the process of being sold to an evangelical broadcasting group. Many public radio and television stations are licensed to universities and nonprofit groups that are in financial difficulty. At the same time, other organizations have plenty of cash, and are hungry for spectrum space and broadcast licenses that are in short supply. Solomon points out that the public has no formal power to prevent such transactions.

Even when it is not being transferred to the private sector, ownership of public airwaves still matters. In her fascinating analysis of the effects of political administration changes on the Corporation for Public Broadcasting (CPB), Lashley (1992) explains that executive and legislative turnover is for public television somewhat akin to ownership change in private broadcasting. Of course there are a number of important differences between public and private broadcasting. A key difference is that the success or failure of public broadcasting is linked more to the policy preferences of particular administrations than to economics. Lashley shows how, with changes in presidential administrations, funding, decision hierarchies, boards of directors, and broadcasting goals are changed. Under various administrations from Johnson to Reagan, changes were made: (1) to either increase bureaucracy or reduce bureaucracy; (2) to set national programming objectives or to turn programming back to the local level; and (3) to fund centralized program production or to fund independent program production. A constant theme was to load the CPB board with partisan political appointees.

Lashley shows how particular presidential policies had direct program impact. For example, under President Nixon, programs critical of the government or deemed "anti-administration" were canceled or their tone moderated, and, under the Reagan administration, budget cuts led to severe cutbacks in children's programming, including the temporary cancellation of *Sesame Street*. Another change during the Reagan years was a decline in news and public affairs programming, and a rise in instructional and skill-learning types of programs, programs that are relatively cheap to produce. The bottom line for public television is that political interference, either through direct intervention, imposed organizational changes, or imposed fiscal crises, has resulted in less diversity, less controversy, and less innovation. So, even here—perhaps especially here—ownership is an important factor in determining content.

The Internet and Industry Structure

Some have argued that the solution to media conglomeration is the Internet. However, studying Internet use has turned out to be problematic. Some data suggest that nearly 21.4 percent of the 102.1 million U.S. households have Internet access and estimate that by 2001 that number will grow to 37.9 percent (Thomas 1997). But other studies have actually suggested a decline in Internet use and linkages from home (Snider 1997). Even if that is true, Internet traffic continues to become heavier. Most experts predict long-term growth in the medium. At the same time, there is considerable interest on the part of major corporations to harness the Net for commercial purposes, a fact that may lead to similar conditions that exist in other media. The announcement by America Online of its intent to purchase Compuserve and WorldCom's proposal to buy MCI suggest that horizontal integration is at work in this medium as well.

Consequences of Industry Structure

We have seen that there are at least two logics behind the changes in industry structure that we have presented in this chapter. One is termed "economy of scale." By integrating horizontally, companies can often increase capacity with minimal increases in administrative overhead and technology. The second strategy is the reduction in resource dependency or the power of other organizations in the production–distribution chain. Producers and distributors are dependent on each other. We have seen that one strategy of distributors is to integrate horizontally to increase buying power. The larger the theater chain, cable system, radio chain, the more power one has over producers. At the same time, producers are motivated to buy distributors in order to keep that from happening.

These organizational logics make sense from a business point of view. However, they have consequences for what media content we as consumers have available to us. Some observers such as Bagdikian (1985, 1997) believe that the concentration of media ownership in the United States should be a matter of public concern. Bagdikian (1985:97) writes that:

> *The proper measure of a country's mass media is whether...they increase understanding of important realities, and whether, through the presentation of the widest possible spectrum of thought and analysis, they create an adequate reservoir of insights into the social process.*

We have seen that there is concern that our media are not performing these two functions, particularly in the area of news programming. While the United States has a vast array of media outlets, the argument is that centralization of ownership prevents true diversity of perspectives from occurring. For example, some believe that news is increasingly being packaged as entertainment, with a subsequent loss of quality. Such claims are difficult to measure and at times seem to glorify a past that never existed. But CBS news anchor Dan Rather has observed, "We are all Hollywood now."

Owners and advertisers have always interfered with content in one form or another. However, the levels of concentration and the sheer scope of contemporary media activities add a new dimension to such interference. There is no doubt that if our goal is a truly independent media—independent of both government and economic constraints—we have not achieved it. The media, as currently structured, are far from perfect watchdogs of the public interest. We have seen that, at times, they seem to have their own agenda of interests or to be more of guard dogs of corporate interests.

Other Cultures, Other Systems

Despite the seriousness of the consequences of media ownership discussed in this chapter, it is important to keep these changes in perspective. In much of the world the very concepts of private media ownership, multiple media access, and a free press are unheard of. For example, Scott (1996) points out that while Africa has 12 percent of the world's population, it has only 2 percent of the telephone lines. In developing nations in general, most media information comes from state-controlled entities. Scott reminds us that, in these nations, the main media concerns may be obtaining paper for a printing press, locating windup radios, and finding extra car batteries to run televisions. In these countries, because of infrastructure problems and local government regulations, there has been understandably little interest or opportunity for the large-scale multinational media companies to enter such a market. Yet, Scott tells us, an indigenous media conglomerate, M-Net, has sprung up in South Africa and has begun programming across Africa. Although this effort is largely funded by newspapers, there are no outcries of cross-medium ownership. In Africa, the problem is to establish a private mass medium, not to worry about who owns it.

Brazilian Television

In contrast, Margolis (1996) describes how, in South America, highly sophisticated media systems have developed. In Brazil, television is hot. Three-quarters of the nation's population are reached by television, compared to approximately 5 percent reached by newspapers. Brazilian television is dominated by TV Globo, which developed and prospered under a military regime. It did so sometimes with government support, sometimes by evading or bending rules. The end result was that Brazil developed a sophisticated television system.

Since the late 1980s, when Brazil made the transition to civilian rule, competition has increased in the form of cable and satellite networks, many formed in partnerships with multinational firms. A strong tradition of local programming in Brazil makes it unlikely that entanglements with foreign investors will necessarily lead to the domination of programming produced elsewhere. Margolis's description shows that it is possible for developing nations to acquire sophisticated media given the right combination of government policy, entrepreneurship, and technology.

Asia

Finally, unlike in Africa, where there appears to be little interest on the part of media conglomerates in establishing a presence, in Asia the opposite condition exists. Large companies such as Dow Jones, NBC, CNN, the BBC, and the Pearson Group have a strong interest in establishing a presence in Asia (Vines 1996). However, unlike in Brazil, strong government hostility to outside media influences has hindered their entrance into these markets. For example, Rupert Murdoch's Star TV satellite television conflicted with the Chinese government over BBC reporting about a biography of Chairman Mao, and, as a result, dropped the BBC from its service.

An important factor in media development in parts of Asia is that Hong Kong has become the de facto media hub of the region. It is unclear what its return to Chinese rule will mean for the future of the media in the region.

Summary

What these examples illustrate is that mass media mergers, cross-media ownership, and concentration are not necessarily irresistible forces. Conditions in different parts of the world and in different countries allow these forces to play out in different ways. It is also true that concerns over media ownership are, in many ways, the luxury of highly developed industrial economies. This is not to say that these are trivial concerns, but they need to be kept in perspective. Our long tradition of democracy and citizenship has thrived on the free flow of enlightening and critical information. Compared to most of our fellow world inhabitants, we in the United States still have more and more varied media outlets than can even be imagined.

8

*Media Organizations
and Occupations*

*Managing creative people isn't like managing an accounting
department where all the numbers add up at the end of the
day. You are talking about a group of people who are being
judged primarily on the strengths of their personal visions
and ideas. Creatives can be temperamental, ego-driven,
and tortured. But what you can't forget is that their
pain buys them beautiful accomplishments.*
—ADVERTISING EXECUTIVE PHIL DUSENBERRY (1997)

*The odds against "making it" are enormous. Promoter–
manager Bill Graham asserts that the chance of succeeding in
the music business is approximately "a thousand to one." With
odds so monumental, it is not surprising to find a good deal
of misinformation and superstition surrounding the making
of a star. Success almost becomes a product of luck, time,
divine intervention, or some other* deus ex machina.
(DENISOFF 1986:38–39)

*Imagine having to publish a story the way films are made. The
publisher does the outline, then turns it over to you, the
"writer," and says, "OK, write the story." You write it, but once
you've written there's no such thing as being able to take words
out and change them around. Then you turn it over to me, the
editor. The editor says, "Now, I'm going to put it into my word-
processor. I'm going to move everything around," and he does.
You get to check in once in a while and say,"No, no, that's not
what I meant. I meant this." "Oh really, I had no idea that's
what you were talking about. OK, I'll put that in." And then
you turn it over to the printer, the printer retypes it however
he wants, and then prints it that way. Then you say, "But
you can't do that!" That is the way it's done in movies.*
—GEORGE LUCAS ON THE COLLABORATIVE PROCESS IN
FILMMAKING (QUOTED IN KELLY AND PARISI 1997: 162)

Creating cultural products, whether a television sitcom, newscast, compact disk, or novel, is a peculiar sort of process. It's really not at all like making other consumer products such as microwaves or cars. This chapter will cover the ways in which mass media and other cultural organizations actually operate as they attempt to turn creative activity into marketable products. We will also examine some of the key occupations in culture production, and show how changes in those occupations affect the nature and content of cultural products.

Cultural Products

Types of Cultural Products

Not all cultural products are the same, and the differences between them help to explain some of the different ways that cultural organizations behave. B. Ryan (1992) distinguishes among several types of cultural products.

Private Goods

These are goods primarily intended for private, individual use. The main examples are books, musical recordings, and, more recently, video games and CD-ROMs. Video versions of motion pictures are also a private good, but, as we shall see below, are produced more as what B. Ryan (1992) calls "quasi-private goods."

Cultural organizations producing these private goods employ some of the normal ways of attracting attention: attractive packaging, placing products prominently in retail space, and so on. But, because there are so many products to choose from (the problem of overproduction), reaching the desired levels of sales requires much more. Media campaigns, critical reviews, guest appearances, and artist tours are all used to bring the product to public attention.

A peculiar aspect of recorded music production is the symbiosis between music-producing organizations and radio and music video networks. While most manufactured products from soap to soups cannot normally be tried without purchasing the product, the music buying public is often unwilling to purchase an album from any but the biggest stars without first hearing the music. Thus, radio airplay and music videos become essential to the promotion process. This leads to the unusual situation in which music-producing organizations literally give their product away for free to another industry in the hope of reaping larger rewards from increased sales. The other industries, radio and music video networks, in turn, make money by using the products they have obtained for free to attract advertisers.

Quasi-Private Goods

These are plays, concerts, exhibitions, other types of live performances, and movies. The idea here is that, while people consuming these products are in close physical proximity, they are expected to maintain their private space. Thus, with some special exceptions (e.g., showings of the *Rocky Horror Picture Show*), it is not correct behavior to turn to a stranger sitting next to you in a theater and comment on the movie. At the same time, access to the performance is limited in that each ticket sold excludes someone else from that particular performance. This is unlike the situation with CDs and videos, which are available to everyone willing to pay the price. In performance situations such as these, where ticket sales are the primary source of income, the cost must be in line with what the public is willing or able to pay. In some cases prices have been rising to a point that extends beyond these levels. The motion picture industry has handled the problem of increasing production costs and relatively fixed ticket prices by increasing the number of available screens and seats as well as by expanding into private goods such as video rentals and sales. In comparison, the performing arts have suffered greatly in recent years from the circumstance that the cost of productions continues to increase, by inflation, union demands, and so on, while seating remains relatively fixed. One strategy of performing arts agencies has been to supplement ticket income by seeking public subsidies, creating another set of dependencies on organizations such as the National Endowment for the Arts.

Live performances, such as plays and concerts, are particularly expensive to produce because the performance must be repeated in its entirety for each new audience. The invention of motion pictures, however, made possible the reproduction of live performances for mass audiences. The basic problem this new industry faced was the development of sites for exhibition. In the late 19th century these were Vaudeville, penney arcades, nickelodeons, and storefront theaters, but, by 1917, motion picture exhibition had evolved into elaborate specialized venues (Sklar 1975). The requirement for specialized exhibition arenas on a large scale created the dependency relationship between motion picture producers, distributors, and exhibitors outlined in the previous chapter.

Like the music industry, the film industry depends heavily on marketing to attract audiences to its products. However, the film industry has less ability than music producers to involve the public in its products beforehand. This is a major difference between media. The audience experience of a film requires more time, attention, and bulky supportive equipment than that necessary to experience recorded music. So the film industry relies more heavily on promotion by mass advertising campaigns. An important part of the promotion is the drawing power and celebrity status of the film's lead actors. Like music, there is heavy reliance on "hot" stars, but in motion pictures the number of stars is much more limited.

Thanks to VCRs and laser disks, the movie industry now has a backup system in place that makes movies more of a true private good. At first it was expected that video rentals would drive exhibitors out of business, but that has not been the case. Instead, while people still attend motion pictures, video rentals and sales have blossomed into a major revenue source for producers. For example, in the first eight months of 1996, Warner Brothers alone brought in over $642 million in sales from the video rental market.

Quasi-Public Goods

Television and radio programming make up what B. Ryan (1992) calls quasi-public goods. What makes these products special is that they are, in a sense, free to the public. That is, most television programming, and, until very recently, all of radio programming, cannot be sold in the normal sense. Broadcast television must by law be free, and cable television is, with the exception of a few speciality networks, unable to recoup its production costs solely through subscriber fees. The solution to creating value in quasi-public products depends on relationships with advertisers. As with radio, the goal of nonsubscription television and radio is to attract an audience that can then be "sold" to advertisers. The basic format is that of an old-time medicine show. Performances take place in order to attract an audience so that the real business can begin, the business of selling products.

Art Worlds

When we think of most artistic creation, whether it is painting, songwriting, scriptwriting, or some other creative activity, we often think of the lone creator working in relative isolation from the rest of society. This romanticized image greatly underestimates the degree to which all forms of artistic production, not just those associated with the mass media, are collaborative activities. Even creators that we would consider to be "fine" artists carry out their work in networks of social relations. Becker (1982) refers to these networks of relations as **art worlds.** For example, painters need certain materials—paint, canvas, brushes—to carry out their work. For the professional artist, training is increasingly carried out in an art school where conventions are developed and shared throughout the network. Dealers first filter and then distribute the work, and peers, critics, museum curators, and the art public evaluate it. Exceptions to some of these network relations are creators engaged in naive or "outsider" art. This is work done by untrained artists operating outside of the conventions of the art world. However, as works by such artists have become popular, the creators have increasingly become enveloped in the same network of relations as that of traditional artists.

Becker (1982) shows how there are major differences in art worlds, depending on the medium and the location. Some art is created in a context that is almost entirely freelance, while other activities are tied to large-scale organizations with relatively permanent relationships. Further, a major difference between fine art and the forms of popular culture distributed by the mass media is that the latter are, by definition, intended for large-scale mass production. As a result the sheer scale of the enterprise is larger, the roles more rigid, and the organizational structure more elaborate. However, because of the nature of creative work, even in large-scale cultural industries, some networks of relations are relatively fluid and temporary.

The Problem of Creative Production

The Role of the Artist

The conventional view of the creative product is that it springs from the imagination and the talents of especially gifted and unique individuals who must be allowed considerable freedom for the process to occur. This view of the creative person is undoubtedly a social construction. There clearly has been an evolution of the perception of creative artists and their role. This has occurred in a fairly unilinear direction, but at different rates in different places. It begins with the idea in antiquity of the relatively uneducated but technically trained craftsman. This person is of modest social standing and income, with few distinctively ascribed personality traits or behaviors other than a certain lighthearted deviance. By the end of the 19th century, there existed a perception of the artist as broadly educated, divinely inspired or otherwise possessing services, capable of achieving an elite social status and high income, outside the restrictions of normative rules, and with such personal characteristics as procrastination, egotism, moodiness, obsession, and self-neglect.

Two Tracks

Looking specifically at visual artists, poets, and writers, by the end of the 19th century the role of the artist was splitting along two tracks. On one was the waning image of the artist as academy-trained, chronicler of history through portrait and history painting, representative of classical education, arbiter of good taste, professional, wealthy (or at least middle-class), and largely serving an integrative function in society.

The other emerging track, represented by the Romantics and members of the Paris avant-garde, imagined the artist as intuitive, unconventional, outside and above society, and nonmaterialistic. This view also labeled the artist with such traits as moodiness, self-neglect, and obsession, traits sometimes present in the other track as well (Shapiro 1976).

It took some time for the romantic view of the artist to take hold in popular culture production. In the early days of motion pictures and the popular music industry, creative personnel were typically treated as industrial wage laborers or as the equivalent of track one described above. Witness for example, the songwriting mills of Tin Pan Alley where there was a division of labor between musical composers and lyricists, and in which writers sometimes had daily writing quotas imposed on them (Ryan 1985). The Hollywood studio system likewise took a semi-industrial form. Only the biggest stars in either system could afford to adopt the artistic temperament. Increasingly, however, mass media creative personnel have adopted the role of creative genius. This has coincided with the elevation in status of popular culture and the blurring of the distinction between popular and fine art.

The Artistic Personality

In the modern era, the artistic personality is thought to include: irrationality, intensity, impulsiveness, and sensitivity (Pelles 1963); loneliness (Tuchman 1965); individualism, extravagance, and peculiarity (Sorokin 1957); the seer and eccentric genius (Crane 1987); and effeminacy, homosexuality, hypersexuality, shallowness, cynicism, bizarreness, dirtiness, all summed into images of the "wild man," and the "dissolute wastrel" (Rosenberg and Fliegal 1979:67). While the mix of attributed characteristics may vary, the point is always that creative artists are viewed as being different.

Rosenberg and Fliegal (1979), in their study of successful visual artists in New York, found that the artists themselves did not believe themselves to be very different from other people. They did, however, believe a number of qualities were necessary to become an "authentic artist." These included personal responsibility, intelligence, sensitivity, freedom at work, ability to accept and withstand solitude and isolation, discipline and perseverance, courage to face rejection and to break with tradition, strong ego and self-confidence, and innocence. These traits do not correspond completely with the stereotype of the creative genius. But many of them are not typically associated with industrial work. This image of what creativity requires, to the extent that it is internalized by creators and their employers, has important consequences for culture-producing organizations.

Consequences of the Artistic Role

Whether or not creative personnel are really different from other workers, the fact that they are perceived to be this way, and, just as importantly, perceive themselves this way, creates a problem for culture-producing organizations like the mass media. The basic problem is how to integrate creative work into the industrial capitalist enterprise. Certainly this cannot be done by following the trends that have characterized the rest of industrial work. In the workforce in general, the trend has generally been an evolution through the following stages:

1. The preindustrial individual craftsperson;
2. Craftspersons grouped together in a shop supervised by the owner;
3. Groups of craftspeople under the supervision of a foreman operating as independent contractors within factories;
4. The breaking down of work into specialized tasks and standardized production procedures;
5. Machine production.

Culture production is basically stuck at phases 1 and 2, mirroring work conditions closer to that of 200 years ago than the modern factory system. In other words, no one thus far has been able to gain control of or automate the creative aspects of culture production.

According to organizational theorist Charles Perrow (1970), the production of any product is either relatively analyzable or unanalyzable, and contains either relatively few exceptions or many exceptions. This is another way of saying that for the creation of some products the process is very well understood and for others it is much less well understood. Perrow would argue, for example, that we understand very well how to make a quality microwave oven, but we understand much less well how to create a hit song. Similarly, each microwave oven of a given model is the same, so there are no exceptions in the process. By contrast, each hit song must be relatively different from all other songs and, therefore, each one is an exception. Thus, cultural products are both unanalyzable and contain many exceptions within the production process. The fact is that producers don't really understand what makes a good movie, a good piece of art, a good song, a good TV sitcom, or even a good news program, although most will say they know one when they see it (or hear it). If they did understand the process better, producers would move to routinize it, just as the process of manufacturing microwave ovens or automobiles has been routinized.

It is not for lack of trying. Numerous software programs are available for the development of screenplays and even novels. While they may help someone develop one of these cultural forms, they cannot guarantee that it will be good. And even if it is good, they cannot guarantee that it will be successful. This problem is compounded by the fact that each product must be different (many exceptions); even if it is accomplished once, there is no guarantee that it will happen again.

Organizational Forms

Perrow links the analyzable and exceptional aspects of the production process to the forms that organizations take. Where tasks are analyzable and there are few exceptions, organizations can afford to concentrate power in the hands of decision makers at the top of the organizational hierarchy, have lots of rules regulating production, and perhaps even employ machinery to perform many production tasks. A typical example of this type of arrangement would be automobile manufacturing. However, the less analyzable the process, and the more exceptions required, the more power that must be left in the hands of the workers. Organization takes on a more "organic" form, with more independence allowed. This type of arrangement is often seen in the skilled trades and craft work, such as in the building industry, engineering, science, academic work, and the arts. However, the trend has been to attempt to bring this type of work arrangement into large bureaucracies. This creates the problem of maintaining the autonomy of these workers while at the same time integrating them into the requirements of the bureaucracy. The research and development (R&D) units of large corporations are a case in point. These units employ scientists and engineers whose ties to their professions and peers may be as strong as or stronger than their ties to their employing organization. In an attempt to spur their creativity, such workers are often granted considerable autonomy and flexibility that other workers do not enjoy.

Known Authorship

Like these R&D workers, the creative personnel in culture industries are given considerable freedom. This is not just because creative work is not well understood. There is also the fact that it is part of the ideology of creativity that creative works must have an identifiable author. That is, creators expect to have their names linked to their creative product and the audience expects to know who the director of the movie is, who the actors are, who the singer and (sometimes) the songwriter are, and who painted the painting. Thus, creative production has not dissolved into the anonymity of industrial production: We do not really care which person or persons made our car or microwave.

Authenticity

In addition to known authorship, a certain degree of authenticity is required in much of culture production. While hard to explicitly define, *authenticity* refers to a sense that the work is true to its genre, and that the creator has the proper credentials, "roots," or commitment. For example, Peterson (1997) has shown how a sense of authenticity has always been central in defining good country music. However, he shows that the specific meaning of *authenticity* has changed over the years. In the 1920s, for example, the fiddle represented the sound of authentic country music and the steel guitar was an exotic pop music import from Hawaii. But by the 1960s the fiddle was often absent and the wailing steel guitar was the signature of a country rendition. In the 1950s, being southern, uneducated, and rural were important to making it as a country artist, but now, in the era of college-educated performers (e.g., Garth Brooks, Mary Chapin Carpenter), it is references to such images and the artists that made them that are essential marks of authenticity.

You may remember the public outrage when it was learned that the two members of the group Milli Vanili had been lip-synching their material in live performance and were not the real voices behind their music. It may have been rational, from an industrial standpoint, to match attractive faces with better voices, but such tinkering is not often allowed in culture work. Of course, this was a deception from the beginning and, as noted above, notions of authenticity change over time. For example, in Japan, the Netherlands, and a few other countries, one of the most popular recording artists is Kyoko Date, who has had several dance–pop hits. On her Web page you can find the usual celebrity information, height, weight, favorite foods, hobbies, hopes, and dreams. The only difference from other celebrities is that Kyoko doesn't exist in the real world. She has been created by a computer graphics team. Not surprisingly, given our definitions of authenticity, no U.S. company has thus far agreed to release her records here.

Notions of the artistic personality, known authorship, and authenticity are associated with creative freedom for some culture workers. However, the requirement for creative freedom is also accepted for culture workers whose job it is to transcribe the creative work: camera crews, recording engineers, and so on, while those responsible for reproduction (CD manufacture, videotape manufacture) are completely industrialized.

Organizational Requirements

Like research and development workers in large organizations, culture creators are typically allowed considerable freedom. But this does not mean that creative workers in cultural industries are given *complete* freedom. From the perspective of the producing organization, the stakes are too high for that. Creative freedoms must be corralled to meet organizational requirements. As B. Ryan (1992) notes, these requirements include:

1. The need for product that takes the correct form. For example, songs that are intended for radio airplay must be relatively short, television programs and movies are restricted in length, pieces of art intended for museums must be able to fit in the gallery.
2. The creative pieces must be produced at the correct time or rate in order to avoid too much downtime in reproduction and loss of market. This is the result of the industrialization of the reproduction side of the process. For example, it would not make sense for a compact disk manufacturing plant to manufacture one run of CDs and then shut down for an extended period of time until someone gets inspired again. There needs to be a flow of product in the production pipeline in order for the production system to work efficiently.
3. The creative products must be potentially marketable. As we shall see in this and the next chapter, this is a very problematic area of culture production. But producers carry some definite ideas of what is marketable, and some things would appear to be fairly obviously not marketable, for example, a sitcom about life in a hospice where all of the characters are there to die.

Star Power

As we shall see, while requiring these conditions, culture-producing organizations find that achieving them is often difficult. A rule of thumb is that the bigger the star, the greater the freedom that star must be given and the more difficult it is to impose organizational requirements. The "star" in this case need not be a single individual. As we shall see, success in culture production is most often the result of the efforts of a combination of personnel. In television, some shows revolve around a single star but others have more of an ensemble quality. In the latter case the show itself becomes the "star" and power accrues to the production company. Thus, *ER* producer Warner Bros. TV was able to command $13 million an episode from NBC based on the successful "star power" of the program itself.

Supply of New Material

Another problem faced by cultural industries is their voracious appetite for new creative products. Unlike fine art creations, whose value may increase over time, most mass media products have a limited "shelf-life." Shelf-life is also limited when compared to industrial products in general. A refrigerator will, hopefully, go on cooling for years, but a newspaper edition is old within a few hours. Songs, movies, and entertainment television programs last longer, but, with the exception of a few classics, their economic value greatly declines once the novelty wears off.

Formula and Overproduction

Sometimes a new product needs to be similar to what is already being produced. Because culture producers do not know what will work, the most rational thing to do is to produce works similar to what has worked before. Cultural works with this family resemblance are said to fall with a "school," "genre," or "style." But when entire genres fade, something new and different must be found. The supply problem is compounded by the uncertainty of producers about what will sell. Part of their solution is an "overproduction" strategy. They produce a larger range of products than can possibly be successful, hoping that some will "take off." Referring to this process as the "buckshot" approach to production, Denisoff (1986) reports that only about two out of every ten recordings released are profitable. This approach is most evident when the creative product is relatively inexpensive to produce, for example, in the areas of book publishing and recorded music. Compared to most areas of manufacturing, in which only one or two new products may be launched each year, cultural industries literally may launch hundreds of new products annually. Television and movie production is simply too expensive for such an approach. But in broadcast television several new series are launched each season by each network, knowing that only a small percentage will be successful.

Not only does the "buckshot" approach have implications for the way the culture-producing organizations do business, it has important effects on artists' careers as well. Because companies cannot afford to promote all of the products they produce, only those products that quickly begin to show promise receive the full weight of the company's marketing and promotion resources. Again, using the recording industry as an example, for a band to sign a record deal is an important but small part of the overall process. Many bands have learned the hard lesson that simply recording an album does not mean that it will be released, and, if released, that the company will promote it. Without promotion it has virtually no chance for commercial radio airplay, and will likely quickly disappear into the bargain bin, perhaps along with the careers of the band members.

There is, then, a basic tension in culture-producing organizations between the needs of the creative personnel and the needs of the organization. Creativity needs to be encouraged, but must be disciplined. Much of the burden of managing this tension falls on individuals occupying a particular set of occupations that have evolved to mediate between the creator and the organization. We will examine these mediating occupations in the next section.

Organizations and Occupations

The nature of cultural products outlined above results in particular organizational forms and occupations. In the move from folk culture to mass-mediated culture, there has been an increasing division of labor between producing and performing. For example, the separation between a music composer and performer, and a choreographer and a dancer. However, this is not a simple trend. In popular music, for example, singer–songwriters were once extremely rare, but now this is a common form of artistic creation. This is partly due to changes in copyright law making such a combination of functions more profitable (Ryan 1985). Likewise the number of musical genres has proliferated, resulting in increased specialization. For example, popular music is fragmented into pop, rock, alternative rock, dance, industrial, rap, bluegrass, country, blues, jazz, and so on. Few musicians cross these boundaries.

Organizational imperatives, as well as the occupations involved, differ according to the stage of the production process. Our focus here is primarily on the creative phase. In the next section we examine how organizations attempt to control this phase of production.

Creative Management

As noted earlier, the creative phase of culture production has been extremely resistant to rational management. That is, no one has yet figured out how to program a person or a computer to write a hit song, a successful novel, or a screenplay. As a result, culture creators retain considerable control over their labor in the production process. Mediating between these creators and the organization are the creative managers: editors, directors, producers, music publishers, A&R (artist and repertoire) personnel, art dealers, talent agents, and so on. The roles may differ somewhat according to the status of the creator and the particular art world involved, but the underlying dynamic is always the same. The creative manager must, as the title suggests, manage creativity. That is, the creative manager must help to facilitate creativity, but facilitate it in such a way that it meets the organizational requirements discussed earlier.

The creative manager's job is a difficult one. Because of the mystique of the artist, the opportunity to give direct orders, "Write me a novel about..." or "Write a song by Friday," are rare. The general mode has to be management through negotiation and collaboration as the creative manager tries to cajole artists into producing the needed products. The greater the status of the creative artist, the less power the manager has, and, of course, the opposite is true as well.

The business dealings of country music artist Garth Brooks provide an excellent example of star power in action. Brooks is the most successful country artist of all time with over 67 million albums sold and 15 No. 1 hits. In 1997, Brooks, unhappy with the way his previous album had been marketed by his label, Capitol Nashville (it sold 4 million copies), withheld his new album rather than entrust it to the same personnel (Schoemer 1998). As a result, Capitol's president and four other key executives were fired and a new president and ally of Brooks was installed. Brooks then agreed to release the album.

Creative Managers as Stars

Successful culture creation is so mystifying that some executives rise to star status of their own, and some creative stars become executives. This has been the case for movie director Steven Spielberg and industry executives David Geffen and Jeffrey Katzenberg. With much media fanfare, these three individuals have formed Dream-Works, a motion picture, television, and music production company. While Spielberg's primary status is still that of creative artist, all three are typically described as wildly creative. Spielberg's talents are in directing film, while Geffen and Katzenberg have received almost as much attention for their track records in putting money behind, and overseeing, the creative efforts of others. Similarly, the late NBC programmer Brandon Tartikoff elevated the role of programmer to celebrity status as he managed to add such shows as *The Cosby Show, Miami Vice, L. A. Law, Family Ties,* and *Cheers* to the NBC lineup. These programs took the network from last to first place in the 1980s (Seiler 1997). Some of these shows were conceived of by Tartikoff, but his true role was in drawing creative personnel into producing programming for the network, deciding which projects would likely be hits, and championing them. Commenting on Tartikoff's death in 1997, the co-president of Sony Pictures Entertainment said, "...talent gravitated toward him: In his heart he was one of them" (Seiler 1997:2D).

Showdown at Heaven's Gate

Tartikoff was a very successful creative manager. An example of just how *badly* creative management can go has been outlined in the fascinating book *Final Cut* by Stephen Bach (1985). This book deals with the making of the film, *Heaven's Gate,* and is worth an extended discussion because it so nicely illustrates the interplay between the requirements of the organization and the requirements of the artist. Bach, one-time senior vice president in charge of worldwide production for United Artists, tells the story of the virtual destruction of the studio as an independent film company by a single director, Michael Cimino, and his film *Heaven's Gate.*

In the book Bach describes a showdown with Cimino, an academy award-winning director for his film *The Deerhunter,* in a Montana Inn aptly named the "Outlaw Inn." The showdown focused on cost overruns on the film. These overruns had escalated from the original budget of $7.5 million to $10 million and this was before shooting had even started. The actual shooting of the film was not going well. After six days of filming, Cimino was five days behind schedule. Reportedly, because of a decision to house the cast and crew members some distance away, half of each work day was spent traveling back and forth to location. Bach also vividly describes how Cimino kept crews on hold for hours, waiting for just the right light. The director was such a perfectionist that each day he shot the equivalent of enough film to make a two-hour movie. By the time Bach arrived in Montana to try to corral his director—six weeks after shooting was supposed to have finished—it was predicted that five more months of shooting would be required.

Adding in postproduction costs and interest, the breakeven point for the $10 million movie was now being estimated at $125 million. Even by today's standards these are large numbers, and *Heaven's Gate* was becoming one of the most expensive films ever made, certainly the most expensive film that United Artists had ever made.

According to Bach, the main problem was Cimino's now legendary artistic ego. Even the filmmaker's own agent suggested that, "You have to understand that the only thing he understands is force." For example, early on he insisted on casting a relatively unknown French actress, Isabelle Huppert, rather than a star such as Diane Keaton or Jane Fonda, actresses favored by the producers. Now Cimino refused to allow Bach to see anything of the film except for a few unedited minutes from the day's shooting. There was simply no way for Bach, as the organizational representative, to judge the market potential of the film in which United Artists had already invested so much. But the company needed a film in order to make up its investment. There is no partial product, no limited production run in the movie business. Either you have a movie or you don't. United Artists needed to continue to fund Cimino in order to have a movie.

In an attempt to harness Cimino to the needs of United Artists, Bach describes how he offered him a number of ultimatums. He offered $9 million to finish shooting, and capped expenditures at $25 million. Bach threatened that if Cimino exceeded the cap, and if he failed to deliver a director's cut of less than three hours in length, final editing would be taken away from him. From an artistic point of view, this was a potentially severe sanction. In addition, Cimino had wanted to shoot a prologue and epilogue to the film, but if he did not conform to Bach's demands, those funds would be denied as well.

For a while, Bach seemed to have regained control of the project, and shooting proceeded more or less on schedule. But then Cimino became obsessed with the climactic battle scene. By the time he was finished, that scene alone ran for an hour and a half, and Cimino had spent all of the rest of the money. The film he brought to United Artists in return for their money was an amazing five hours and twenty-five minutes long! This made it the longest film ever intended for release to theaters in the United States.

The rest of the story is about United Artists' creative manager's attempts at molding the product into a usable form. The story of the battle between Bach and Cimino got into the press where it was alternately framed as "art versus commerce" or as an "egotistic, self-indulgent artist" story. United Artists, desperate to recoup its money, insisted that Cimino recut the film to under three hours, a restriction Cimino ignored.

The film opened in 1980 to highly negative reviews. United Artists demanded another edit. This brought the film down to two hours twenty-eight minutes for general release, still a long film by current standards. *Heaven's Gate* eventually lost United Artists $44 million. Nearly all of the company executives, including Bach, lost their jobs and the company, founded by Charlie Chaplin, Douglas Fairbanks, Mary Pickford, and D. W. Griffith as a haven for artists, was sold. Truly this was an extraordinary disaster. But, while unusual in it scope, the explanation for the *Heaven's Gate* debacle lies in some of the basic dynamics of culture industries.

Unanalyzability

First of all there is the problem of not having a good idea of what will work and what will not work with the audience. Cultural choices and aesthetic reactions are predictable only within a very general range. There is no simple formula for a successful film, either aesthetically, or in terms of audience reaction. Thus, we have a situation in which management cannot manage an "unanalyzable" product. As a result, cultural industries find that their best guess of future success is past success. That is why we see so many sequels and copycat versions of movies (e.g., "disaster flicks") and television programs (e.g., *The Visitor* as a sort of *X-Files* and *Independence Day*).

Track Record

Not only do culture-producing organizations copy previously successful formulas, they also want previously successful personnel. The relevance of this to creative personnel is that "track record" becomes the single most valuable currency for career success. The industry knows that audiences too like to "play it safe" by following performers with track records. In the case of *Heaven's Gate,* Michael Cimino's academy awards for "Best Director" and "Best Picture" for the much acclaimed *Deer Hunter* made him a hot property within Hollywood, despite the fact that he had exceeded his budget by 100 percent on that picture. Big names almost always provide the greatest hope of big profit. A director without Cimino's artistic reputation would never have been allowed so much freedom. Likewise, to change directors would have confused the critics and the public and placed the film in even more jeopardy. It was highly unlikely that a well-known director would have been willing to take over another director's project. This dilemma has much to do with the evolution of the occupation of directors into studio executives.

Director as Auteur

Once the salaried employees of studio owners, directors have transformed into the primary "authors" of motion pictures. We discussed earlier that cultural products are expected to have known authors. Films, more than many other cultural products, are complex productions requiring large-scale collaborations of professional personnel: writers, actors, and a myriad of technicians. However, in the search for a place to lay praise or blame, the director has largely become the "auteur" or author, and often the most powerful person in the chain, providing he or she has the proper track record. This evolution has been enhanced by the takeover of the studios by conglomerates, insulating studio personnel from distant owners who do not understand the business (Powers et al. 1996). Creative power that once resided in the hands of studio moguls has shifted to production executives and directors.

Interdependence

The *Heaven's Gate* story also illustrates another mass media lesson: the interdependence of culture-producing organizations. Why was it so important that the film be under two-and-a-half hours? There was a time when audiences would routinely go to see two full-length double features, plus a number of "shorts" (e.g., cartoons and newsreels), in a given evening. This has changed partly due to altered lifestyles and competition from television. But it has also changed because of the requirements of theater owners. When television began to steal away audiences, the motion picture industry responded with smaller, less centrally located theaters. In order to continue to make money, theater owners need to have several successive audiences each evening. A three- or four-hour movie allows for only one audience in a given evening, but a 90-minute film might allow for squeezing in as many as three separate audiences.

Likewise, *Heaven's Gate* is a story about the dependence of filmmakers on movie critics and the press, an important form of advertising and cultural gatekeeping. As noted above, the story of cost overruns for *Heaven's Gate* made it into the press with two competing frames. The one most destructive to the movie, the "self-indulgent artist" frame, became dominant in the United States. This insured that the movie had virtually no chance. No matter how good the movie was, and it has since been evaluated more positively by a few critics, it was prejudged as a symbol of artistic excess and organizational bumbling. This is not the kind of image likely to draw audiences. Seventeen years after the film was originally released, the film was shown on the TNT cable channel. The running time, with commercials, was four hours and thirty minutes. The listing in the December 5, 1997 (195), issue of *TV Guide,* read: "Michael Cimino's overbudgeted, overlong picture about cattle wars in the 1890s." Interestingly, from the beginning, the film was reviewed more positively in Europe, where the dominant frame was one of organizational interference with the work of an artist. Perhaps as a result, in Europe, the film was much more successful.

Creating Jaws

Of course the story of *Heaven's Gate* is unusual in the magnitude of the film's problems. Most productions do not go nearly so wrong. It is a clear illustration of the power of the artist wielded by an artist who has reached star status. By comparison, the creative manager has much more power and influence in dealing with beginning artists. Ted Morgan (1974) outlines how the then-beginning author, Peter Benchley, worked with his editor and other publishing house personnel to produce the best-seller *Jaws*. In doing so, Morgan shows the complex process of negotiating a creative project from inception through the various layers of bureaucracy in the modern culture-producing organization.

Peter Benchley had relatively easy access to the publishing world. He had a very limited personal track record, but his grandfather Robert and his father Nathaniel Benchley were both well-respected authors. Granting the uncertainty about who is capable of producing a popular book, the publishers were hoping that the abilities and fame of the elder Benchleys had somehow rubbed off on or been inherited by Peter. Some magazine articles he had written showed promise. In 1971, Peter Benchley met with Tom Congdon, a senior editor at Doubleday publishing. During lunch Benchley described an idea for a novel about a great white shark that terrorizes a Long Island resort. The editor asked the author to write a single-page description, which was then taken to a board of nine editors for approval along with a proposal for a $1,000 advance. The material presented by Congdon included the description of the book, a list of the author's previous work and experience, an estimate of the break-even point (the number of sales after which Doubleday would start earning money), and the sales point at which the author would earn back his advance. With the project approved by the editorial board, it was next taken to the publishing board, made up of members of the various business and advertising departments. The book was given the go-ahead for a trial four chapters, on the condition that half the advance be returned if the chapters were not acceptable. Benchley's agent resisted this provision, and, after a number of days, the board relented.

Morgan reports that Congdon was disappointed by the four chapters. The shark was convincing, the main characters were not. He found Benchley's attempt to blend humor and horror unsuccessful. The shark scenes were well-written but repetitive. The editor did not feel the chapters were good enough to show the board, and asked for a rewrite. During the rewriting period Benchley was sent numerous suggestions from Congdon and another editor. Morgan (1974:126) reports Benchley as saying, "When they insisted, I gave in. They've been in business a long time and I'd never written a novel." Finally, nine months after the beginning of the project, the four chapters were deemed good enough to continue the project, and Benchley was given a contract. The money was minuscule by today's standards, a $7,500 advance.

The editor continued to send comments to Benchley who continued to accept them. A sex scene between the police chief character and his wife had to be changed to meet the editor's sensibilities. In all, there were two complete rewrites and a partial rewrite of the book before Congdon was satisfied. In a small, family-run publishing house that may have been enough, but in a bureaucratic organization like Doubleday the process was far from finished. Congdon now had to begin the process of selling the book to the other editors. At the same time, Benchley's suggested title,

A Stillness in the Water, was not deemed acceptable. Another suggestion was *Summer of the Shark* but Benchley worried that this title would place the book on the nature shelves. In all, 237 different titles were tried before the final title, *Jaws,* was suggested by the author. It is interesting to speculate whether the book or the movie would have been as successful with some of the other suggested titles such as *Why Us?* or *The Year They Closed the Beaches.*

The next stage in the process was to win the support of the sales staff. Congdon sent the dramatic first five pages of the book to every salesman on the staff and asked for their reactions. The comments were very positive and the editor felt positive that the sales staff would work hard to place the books in stores. Next, Congdon made a dramatic presentation in an attempt to sell the book to the regional sales managers. The reception was generally warm. But some did not care for the book jacket, which showed a resort town through the bleached jaws of a shark. The sales managers then met to decide their best estimate of how many copies of the book they could place in stores. They decided on a comparatively large advance printing of 25,000 copies (normally the advance printing of a first novel for Doubleday was 4,000 copies) and an advertising budget of a dollar per book or $25,000.

The book was also being pushed by Doubleday's head of subsidiary rights. Bantam quickly bid $200,000 for the paperback rights, at that time a very high figure for a first novel. The book was sent to eight other paperback publishers in hopes of getting a higher offer. Two rejected it. In hindsight, this was a major mistake indicative of the fact that even professionals cannot always recognize potentially successful cultural products. The highest offer turned out to be $375,000, an astronomical amount for any book in those days, and especially for a first novel that had not even been published yet. The book was also taken by The Book of the Month Club and two other clubs, another potentially enormous source of sales. The clubs advanced $85,000 for rights to include the book in their club selections.

Another part of the process was to get some praise for the book from some well-known Doubleday authors. According to Morgan, authors are in a bind in that they feel obligated to their publisher, but really don't want to be quoted praising another author's book. Leon Uris agreed to contribute a quote. His wife later said that her husband had not actually read the book, but that she had read it and didn't like it.

Morgan reports that just as *Jaws* seemed to be ready for publication, a controversy developed over the book's jacket which, because of earlier criticism, now simply had the title in stark lettering against a black background. Thirty-thousand versions of the jacket had been printed. However, when the Bantam editors saw the cover, they did not like it. They wanted an image. The problem was that any image of a shark alone would seem small. The art department then came up with the famous image of the enormous head of a shark rising through the waters toward a swimmer on the surface—the image that would become the poster for the movie as well. Bantam was satisfied.

Next, the publicity campaign kicked into gear. The head of publicity lunched with reviewers and critics. They pushed the book and the author's pedigree as a third-generation Benchley. Letters and complimentary copies were sent to the media and Benchley was scheduled to appear on the *Today* show.

The book was now in the hands of Doubleday's merchandising offices, whose job it was to control the number of copies printed. If too many copies were printed, that would result in costly returns. If too few, the book would not be available when people wanted it. Meanwhile, the movie rights to the novel had been sold for $150,000, and Benchley had a $25,000 deal to write the screenplay.

Publishers Weekly heralded the financial if not critical success of the book. Doubleday and Benchley made huge sums of money from the book and movie, although Benchley was never to see such success again. As a creative manager, Congdon did not participate directly in the profits of the book. However, unlike United Artists' Stephen Bach, whose career was virtually destroyed by the artist he was attempting to manage for *Heaven's Gate,* Tom Congdon improved his "track record," and his stature in the industry was enhanced. The result was he was appointed an editor-in-chief at E. P. Dutton & Co. As an effective creative manager he had succeeded in developing a successful project from idea to product. He had made sure that the product met the needs of various other players within his organization and without: editorial boards, salespeople, designers, bookstores, paperback publishers, and motion picture producers were all involved. The author "merely" produced the idea and the writing (with help from the editor); the creative manager and the rest of the production team produced the product available to the audience.

Lessons Learned

What we have seen is that in culture production, creative work is carried out in a complex web of authority relationships. The better the track record of the creator, the more power he or she has. But it is important to remember that, even in the best of circumstances, culture creators are dependent on the capital, technology, and the promotion and distribution systems of the large-scale organizations that contract for their services. Because of the collaborative nature of much cultural work, even artists with excellent track records can, in fact, push the limits too far in their attempts to control their labor. When they do, they risk a loss of support from powers within the industry and can do serious damage to their careers.

The Decision Chain

The case of the making of *Jaws* illustrates what Ryan and Peterson (1982) refer to as the "decision chain" in the production of cultural products. As noted earlier, cultural products are the result of systems of collaborative production. This is especially true of mass-mediated products produced by large-scale complex organizations. Ryan and Peterson outline the decision chain for one particular cultural form, country music recording (see Figure 8.1).

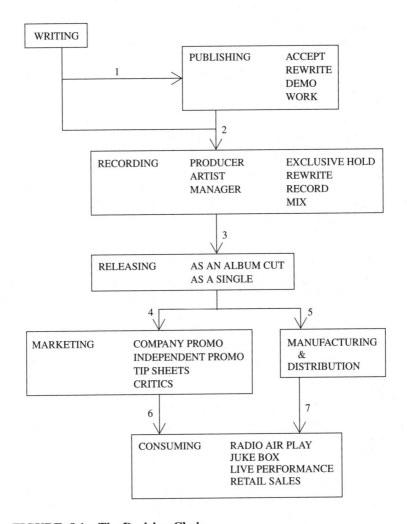

FIGURE 8.1   The Decision Chain

(Source, Ryan and Peterson, 1985, p. 14. Copyright Sage Publications 1985, reprinted by permission.)

Most popular music passes through a chain very similar to this one, with the exception that the publishing stage in country music is much more important than in some of popular music. In rock, for example, it is much more common for performers to write their own songs.

What is clear from looking at the chain is that there are several "filters" through which creative material must pass. Songs may be screened out or altered at several points along the way, with only about 1 in 1000 songs making it though the process. These filters are embodied in creative managers such as publishers, record producers, and artists' managers, as well as in organizational representatives from marketing and distribution.

The Product Image

What Ryan and Peterson found was that these organizational and occupational factors are so strong that they alter what might be considered the normal way of thinking about one's creative product. You might expect that songwriters would be primarily concerned with how the audience might react to a song. While this may be true in an abstract way, the practical day-to-day reality for the professional writer is getting the song through the next stage in the decision chain. The same is true for each member of the chain. For example, the primary task of the writer is to please the publisher. The publisher, in turn, must please the recording artist, his or her manager, or both. The performer must please the record producer, who must please record company executives in order to get the song placed on an album, or more importantly, released as a single. The process does not stop there. The writer, publisher, artists, and producer all have a stake in convincing the promotion department to throw enough resources behind the record to get radio airplay. Notice that, in this process, the notion of "audience" changes from the consuming public to the next person in the decision chain. Thus, the **audience image** is converted into what Ryan and Peterson call the **product image.**

Production based on a "product image" is a common way of working in cultural industries. For example, Kapsis (1987) shows how the film *Halloween II* was shaped by the writers, the cinematographer, the director, and the producers in the process of making the film. The true audience for most of them was John Carpenter, director of the original *Halloween* film. The production team was constantly judging its performance against what Carpenter might think of the work. This idea of "product image," or focusing on other members of the decision chain, constitutes a major shift away from the audience-oriented focus of folk production, and is characteristic of the collaborative nature of mass media production.

Gatekeepers

Some occupations within cultural industries serve gatekeeping functions. Because many more people want to write books or screenplays, write and record songs, and paint pictures than are needed, every cultural industry employs a variety of individuals in gatekeeping roles. Gatekeeping can happen at various points along the decision chain, as well as after the product is finished. For example, music publishers not only try to move songs along to the next stage of the decision chain, but also select from the thousands of songs they receive those that they believe will be salable to recording artists and producers. As we have seen with the decision chain in country music, creative works are filtered out at nearly every step of the process.

In the music industry, when there is a recorded song that the company is willing to promote and distribute, gatekeeping continues to take place as radio stations select from the overabundance of product available to them. Ahlkvist and Faulkner (1997) have shown that, despite a trend toward subsuming individual stations within large corporate chains and standardized formats, the way in which individual radio programmers view their occupation can have important implications for the ways in which they serve the gatekeeping function. For example, some programmers see themselves as guardians of good music and may be less concerned about listeners' tastes than are those who see their jobs as delivering specific demographic groups to advertisers.

Other gatekeepers include theater owners, bookstore owners, music store managers, and critics. Uncertainty about the decisions of gatekeepers has led cultural producers to engage in a number of strategies. One is to employ specialized personnel to deal with gatekeepers. For example, in the record business, "promo" people visit various radio stations to "push" recordings. A second strategy is for companies to provide incentives to gatekeepers. These may take the form of gifts to radio programmers and music store owners. Illegal incentives, such as cash rewards, are known in the music business as **payola.** A third strategy is to provide free publicity materials to music stores, but only if they sell recorded material at a price deemed acceptable to the producers. If stores overly discount their product, the promotional materials are withheld. This practice is being looked into by the FTC as a possible form of price-fixing. A fourth strategy is vertical integration, whereby culture producers take over organizations that serve a gatekeeping function, for example, when the same company owns movie production and distribution units as well as chains of theaters. This seemed to be the strategy when Sony and Cineplex Odeon announced the merger of their theater chains.

Gatekeeping is used to weed out both creators and creative products. This does not mean that gatekeepers know with certainty what they are doing. Cultural industries are brimming with stories of creations that were initially turned down by gatekeepers and then went on to be enormously successful. And of course there are many stories about "sure bets" that turned out to be flops. Nevertheless, gatekeepers have a powerful influence on which cultural products come before the consuming public. Owners of local bars screen performers, gallery owners screen artists, theater directors and agents screen actors, news directors screen reporters and anchors, and so on. Because of the attractiveness of mass media occupations to so many people, these are extremely difficult careers to enter and, once entered, they are difficult careers in which to be successful.

The point here is that as each gatekeeper is passed, there is a filtering and shaping of talents and artistic sensibilities, a "professionalization" that, in part, can mean a shaping to fit prevailing conventions. The trick for successful commercial culture creation is to know the conventions while having the ability to bend them sufficiently to produce a product that is just unique enough not to be "the same old thing."

The Project Team

The decision chain in country music is representative of the "project team," the characteristic form of production in the mass media. We have seen that the creative portion of culture production has resisted industrialization because culture creators are seen as possessing rare talents that cannot be understood and must be nurtured. The decision chain described above typically involves a loose coalition of personnel centered around a particular project. In country music production the most stable relationship is between the writer and publisher. But publishers will "pitch" songs to a relatively large number of artists, artists' managers, and record producers. Producers may work with a particular artist over the artists' entire career—as George Martin did with the Beatles—but most do not. Likewise, producers increasingly are independent of the record company itself, and some may fund and complete an entire project before bringing it to the company for distribution. Publishers sometimes do this as well. Thus, the configuration of personnel will change from project to project.

The Simplex

Peterson and White (1979, 1981) have shown this process at work among studio musicians in Nashville. These session musicians make up an informal, but nevertheless structured, set of arrangements with each other and with other recording industry personnel. Peterson and White call this type of organization a "simplex." Simplexes are informal groups that function without the normal elements of titles, offices, written rules, and other arrangements that characterize formal organizations. With mention of the simplex we are referring to the process whereby some people are called to participate and others are not, where some people are able to "break in" and others are excluded.

The degree to which a simplex is involved in production depends on one's function for the project team and the particular industry involved. For example, in movie production, the assembling of writers, directors, and actors is very fluid and changeable. Sound and light personnel, set and costume design, and other technical personnel tend to be more closely associated with specific production companies. Cinematography and special effects are somewhere in between these levels of formalization. The music and motion picture industries typically employ very fluid project teams. In contrast, television entertainment and news teams often center around ongoing projects and therefore are relatively stable over time. However, in contemporary culture production, the core group of creative personnel is almost always assembled around specific projects and in a temporary way.

Breaking In

"Breaking in" is the real barrier to entrance into the creative aspects of culture production. In these industries there is no orderly career line based on academic credentials. We have already seen that one's track record is the most important factor in success, but one cannot gain a track record without experience.

Breaking in to the culture-creation occupations is not only about what you know or what you can do. It is also about who you know. Peterson and White (1979, 1981) show how musicians must be talented and must also hang out with the right people. Musicians must spend time to establish their talent and their correct attitude in the eyes of the insiders. They must be willing to work for free or nearly free and to be appropriately humble. Availability is a major issue even with established studio musicians. Project teams are often assembled at the last minute and if one is not available for the gig the chance is passed on to the next person.

Each cultural industry has its own particular requirements for breaking in, and its own type of simplex structure. For example, Peterson and Ryan (1983) describe how, in order to break in to country music songwriting, it is normally imperative for new writers to cowrite with established writers, even if the latter contribute little more than their names to the composition. Every cultural industry has its own form of "paying dues."

Discrimination

Added barriers to breaking in are created by rampant gender and race discrimination in various industries, especially where production costs are high, for example, in feature films (Bielby and Bielby, 1992, 1996). Only 20 percent of directors and 24 percent of writers in Hollywood are women. Only 3 percent of writers and 2 percent of directors are black. Even after breaking in, opportunities are less available for minorities. For example, Bielby and Bielby (1992) show that, while a few women have become powerful writer–producers in television, in general, women earn 11 to 25 percent less throughout their careers. They also tend to be segregated into female-typed genres, for example, children's and daytime programming. In motion pictures opportunities for minorities are even more limited.

The point is that "breaking in" to creative roles in cultural industries is a process of entering in to the simplex, or the informal network of relationships that characterize artistic production. Once in, the process of competing for particular projects continues in the same informal way. Many culture creators are, in essence, fired after each project. There is no career path other than creating a track record that can lead to long-term contracts. Even that can be a problem when creators become trapped within past successes as, for example, when actors become typecast or when musical artists are expected to follow a certain formula.

Technology and Occupations

Before there were microphones, singers had to sing loudly and from the chest. After the invention of the microphone, singers with different types of voices, crooners such as Bing Crosby and Perry Como, were able to have careers. Just as in other industries, technology in cultural industries provides the tools and shapes the context within which work is performed. Some occupations are enhanced or even created by new technologies, others are diminished or disappear, and still others just become different. There are many examples of this process in action. For example, originally, sound engineers were charged with the task of faithfully reproducing the sounds of live performance. However, as we shall see below, changes in technology and aesthetics have led to the attempt to produce records which are "better than live." Another occupation that has been transformed is that of motion picture special effects designers. Special effects were once created by self-educated entrepreneurs and theatrical set designers. Today this occupation relies on highly technically trained personnel. For example, Disney employs some of the world's foremost computer scientists as part of a staff of "imagineers" working on movie special effects and theme park rides.

Likewise, new technologies employed in the context of industry mergers and the internationalization of the mass media industry have shaped occupations. These developments have led to increased cross-fertilization among books and movies as well as a push toward multimedia and interactive entertainment products. A result is that authors are now selected on their ability to produce work that is easily transferable across media and across cultures. In the next sections we show how occupations are shaped by changing technology and provide some examples from the music, television, and motion picture industries.

Technology and Occupations in the Music Industry

Microphones were just one of a long line of new technologies for aiding musical performance. One of the most influential was the application of the multitrack recorder to music production by jazz guitarist Les Paul in the 1950s. These recorders allow musical parts (e.g., rhythm guitar, lead guitar, bass, drums, lead and backing vocals) to be layered separately onto a final recording, one "track" at a time. There are a number of consequences of this technology for occupations within the music industry.

The multitrack recorder allows each part to be worked on, recorded, and edited separately rather than assembling a band to act as an ensemble. If a musician or vocalist makes a mistake or simply is not happy with a performance, he or she can go back and, with the aid of a recording engineer, "punch in" a note, a musical phrase, or entire sections to get the best performance. An alternative method is to record several "takes" of a performance and then splice together elements from each into a composite version that is better than any of the individual performances. In either case, what this means is that musicians and vocalists are now able to create studio performances that may surpass their own abilities to play the material live. The studio, rather than being a place to use technology to faithfully recreate live performances, has become a site of creative experimentation. In this sense, studio

Beatles' producer George Martin (second from right) helped elevate
the role of record producer.

equipment has changed in function from mechanical reproduction to an essential element in the artist's tool kit.

This change has, in turn, two contradictory consequences. On the one hand,
less musical skill and more technical recording skill are required to produce a quality recording. Other types of sound-enhancing devices, such as reverbs, choruses,
delays, and pitch shifters, all contribute to this process. However, this creates a
problem if the musicians are unable to reproduce their performances in a live setting. On the other hand, because young musicians, particularly in popular music,
learn their instruments primarily by listening and imitating recordings, they are, in
some ways, pulled by those recordings to higher levels of technical expertise than
their predecessors.

Ryan and Peterson (1993) have shown how the advent of digital reproduction
in music has had a number of effects in the same way that multitrack recording has.
At the simplest level, digitalization of sound has made many of the processes noted
above easier and, most would argue, has improved sound quality. However, it has
also had the effect of requiring greater computer literacy among musicians and
recording personnel, and potentially threatens the occupations of some musicians.
Multitrack recording, whether analog or digital, allowed for the use of a large variety
of sounds on a particular cut. In the analog era, these sounds, for example, the use
of a string section, were too expensive to reproduce in live performance. One reason
often cited for the Beatles' decision to end touring was that they could no longer
reproduce in a live concert the sound textures of their studio recordings. However,
digital technology has made it ever more possible to make convincing reproductions

of the sounds of a wide variety of instruments. Digital sound modules, controlled by a midi keyboard, guitar, wind controller, or even a computer, can reproduce these sounds either in live concert or in the studio. Because digital sound modules are cheaper than real musicians, some jobs are threatened. As one member of the English group Ozric Tentacles remarked, "Why bother to learn the guitar when you can program a sequencer to do it for you?" (Farber 1994). However, the previously mentioned requirement of authenticity has slowed this process. A good example is the role of the drummer in rock music. There are now quality drum machines that can do as good a job or, in some cases, a better job of providing rhythm than can a real drummer. Yet there is a large mythology in the industry that the "feel" is not as good with the machine, although, in fact, most listeners cannot tell the difference if the machine is programmed well. In fact, one of the expanded roles of the drummer has been to program drum tracks in the studio. The notion of authenticity is expressed by many audiences (but not all) of popular music who would not accept the use of a drum machine on stage in the place of a human drummer.

Home Studios

Another important consequence of digital reproduction as outlined by Ryan and Peterson (1993) is the democratization of the recording process. Relatively inexpensive digital recorders are now widely available and, combined with inexpensive effects boxes, allow for the creation of high-quality recordings in home studios. This equipment is as good as recording equipment that would have cost hundreds of thousands of dollars just a few years ago.

Home studios have given the modern musician the potential for creating a record of his or her work that simply was not available to earlier generations. Virtually any local band or singer–songwriter can now produce a tape of excellent recording quality, and even CDs are becoming more common. Graphics for album covers can be produced on home word processor equipment and the tapes and CDs manufactured in quantity for a few thousand dollars.

Sequencers

Likewise, digital sequencers, which are essentially word processors for music, can be programmed to "play" sound modules, allowing lone composers to hear full-blown versions of their work, whereas, in the past, ensembles of musicians had to be hired to achieve that end.

Television and Motion Picture Acting

Technology has also profoundly impacted the occupation of actor. The arrival of, first, motion pictures, then television, altered both the craft and social relations of acting. This is because the technical requirements of producing and disseminating a television program or film are greater and more complex than those for a stage pro-

The technical requirements of television and movie production have consequences for the way actors do their work.

duction. The technical requirements necessitate the coordination of a large number of artistic, technical, and administrative personnel. There is considerable time pressure as producers and directors seek to adhere to a strictly coordinated schedule. One result is that writers have less time to perfect their work, tend to stay with safe material (that which is similar to what has worked before), and actors are more limited in their ability to explore characters (Mast 1983).

Another difference brought about by the medium is in the role of the director/producer. In the theater, the definition of the actor as artist has a more solid tradition, and the actor often has greater power than the director. However, in television, and the same could be said for film, the large array of technology needed to translate performance into product reduces the autonomy of the actor. At the same time, the power of the director–producer to shape the performance is raised.

Film and TV performance are distinguished from theater performance by the emphasis on greater naturalism, discontinuous performance, and the technology that mediates between the actor and the audience (Barr 1982). The closeness of the filmed image of the actor's face requires greater naturalism than in the theater. Conversely, theater actors have to "act larger"—use larger gestures and facial expressions to convey information to the audience. At the same time, the detail that TV and film audiences can see on an actor's face increases the likelihood that the performer will be typecast in certain roles. This is because, as compared to the theater, it is easier to associate that face with a particular role.

Another difference between theater and television is **discontinuous performance.** Thanks to film and video editing capabilities, performances do not have to run continuously from beginning to end as in the theater. This gives the director much greater control. In theater, once the actor leaves the wings he is on his own. However, in film and TV the performance can be stopped and redone until the director and the actor are satisfied. In fact, often the director is the only one who truly has access to a view of how the scene actually looked, a factor increasing his or her power. The need for conventional over-the-shoulder shots of actors speaking to each other also requires stopping the performance and repositioning actors and cameras. Because of such requirements, the decision, in the fall of 1997, by the producers of the popular television drama *ER* to do a live telecast made national news. Because of the continuous nature of this performance, the over-the-shoulder shots could not be done. In order to deal with this constraint, the writers used the device of a storyline in which *ER* personnel were being filmed by a documentary film crew, thereby, creating a context for a less polished-looking production.

Similarly, scenes in television and movies do not have to be shot in sequence. For example, in order to simplify the jobs of technicians and reduce expenses, all outdoor scenes may be shot together. Because of this, actors in film and TV must often be prepared to involve themselves in scenes without the buildup in characterization and emotion from previous scenes.

Sharon Mast (1983) argues that technology also affects the social relationships between audience and actor and between actor and actor. In the theater actors are used to a certain amount of interaction with an audience, in a sense "playing to" the audience. This is not the case in motion pictures, although many television productions are now done in front of a live audience in order to help create this dynamic. However, even in those productions, there are major differences from the theater as audiences are "warmed up" before the performance by a professional announcer who serves as a sort of master of ceremonies. The announcer will also entertain and coach the audience during breaks in the shooting. Similarly, applause and laughter signs are used to cue the audience to the desired reactions during the performance.

The lack of an audience also affects the social relationships among actors. In the theater, the actor's power to shape his or her own performance independent of the director is coupled with the presence of the live audience. This coupling creates the possibility of actors trying to "upstage" the other actors, for example, by playing more directly to the audience, or attempting in other ways to undermine the performance of the other actors. To prevent this from happening, actors maintain social relationships with other actors and produce more of a team performance. In film and television, without the audience, and with the ability to reshoot and edit scenes, social relationships are less important. According to Mast, compared to theater actors, television and TV actors spend less time discussing how to play scenes with each other, and typically invest less time in social relationships with the other actors in a production.

In summary, the technical and organizational requirements of television and motion pictures have important consequences for the way actors do their work. TV and motion pictures, although far from a factory system, are more routinized and rationalized than is the theater.

Summary

In this chapter we have seen that turning creativity into cultural products requires some special organizational and occupational arrangements. These arrangements are necessary because:

1. The nature of creative work is such that it is unanalyzable;
2. Each cultural product must be different from the others so there are many exceptions;
3. Creative people are seen, and see themselves, as being different from other types of workers and therefore are treated differently.

We have seen that the problem for culture-producing organizations is meshing the needs of creativity with organizational requirements. Mass media organizations need a steady supply of products in the correct form. Solutions to these organizational problems include: overproduction, reliance on track records, the use of loosely organized production teams, and the utilization of creative managers who are closely aligned with creative artists

We have also seen that technology plays an important part in mass media occupations. Technology has eliminated some occupations, created others, and substantially changed still others. As occupations change in interaction with technology and organizational requirements, so do the cultural products that are the output of the mass media and other cultural industries.

9

"Show Me the Money":
Advertising and the
Mass Media

*The largest consumer group in history, baby
boomers, are no longer desired... They're wealthy.
They're powerful. And they're out of the loop.*
—ADVERTISING EXECUTIVE JERRY DELLA FEMINA ON THE
NETWORK TELEVISION ADVERTISING'S FOCUS ON 18-TO-
49-YEAR-OLDS (QUOTED IN LIEBERMAN, 1997A:1B)

In the last chapter we saw how the mass media and other cultural organizations deal
with the problems of creative production. Solutions such as relying on the track
record of creators, employing creative managers, and forming fluid project teams are
all intended to produce a regular supply of properly formatted creative products.
Once the products are created, they must be sold. Typically, this means for profit,
but even in state- or public-owned systems, products must be sold by attracting consumers for whatever purposes producers have in mind. Typical purposes include persuasion, education, and entertainment.

In this chapter we examine the relationship between marketing and the mass
media. There are three different aspects to this relationship:

1. Using the mass media to market commodities produced by other industries;
2. Particular problems associated with marketing products specifically designed
   for the mass media;
3. The ways in which media producers gather information about their market, and
   the impressions producers develop concerning audience preferences and behavior.

In this chapter we will focus on the first aspect, the relationship between the mass media and advertisers. We will cover the other two aspects in Chapter 10.

As we shall see in the first section below, marketing, as an activity central to industrial production, has driven the expansion of the mass media. That is, an important influence on the mass media is the fact that other industries use the mass media to sell their products.

The Rise of Marketing

In the 1950s the main focus of competition in American industry shifted from price to product differentiation and marketing. Capitalist production was evolving from a model in which products were mass-produced for a large homogenous group of consumers, and were differentiated largely on the basis of price, to a model in which products were targeted to meet the desires of specific groups of consumers. Henry Ford's Model T fits the first pattern. Ford's efficient production methods brought the price of the Model T down and resisted changes in his car so that it would remain affordable. Of the Model T he said, "You can have it in any color you want, as long as it is black." The second pattern is illustrated by the current vast array of automobiles from small two-seat sports cars to family sedans to sport utility vehicles, each model with an array of optional accessories and engine sizes, and each model conveying different images and statuses. It's not that price doesn't matter. Any product must appear to provide good value; it's just that price is often no longer the main arena of competition. This newer approach to marketing requires much more in the way of market research and effort in advertising, as the desires of specific demographic groups need to be shaped, created, or just discovered. Then existing products are linked with those desires, products are modified, or new products are created to appeal to public tastes in consumption. Entire industries of cultural workers have developed in order to perform the functions of market research and advertising, in essence to promote consumption.

Use Value

The goal of advertising is still to identify a product's purpose or usefulness. Use value can be fairly obvious, for example, a car's usefulness as a form of transportation. But it can also be more subtle, as when a car is also used as a form for representing one's status. Thus, needs and desires may not only be material or practical, but psychological and sociological as well. Increasingly products are sold as much for their indication of a particular lifestyle and social status as for more practical uses. It is the task of the marketer to package the product in such a way that it symbolizes that usefulness. Thus, a sports car must not only *perform* like a sports car, it must conform to our ideas about what a sports car should *look* like, and advertisers

Most sport utility vehicles never leave the pavement.

must place it in a context where its various use values are apparent, for example, by showing bystanders admiring the car and the person in it.

In recent years, advertising has seemed to focus as much or more on the latter aspect of products than on the former, that is, concentrating on symbolizing the product's place in a lifestyle more than on its practical utility. When a Chevy Tahoe is advertised by showing an individual, perhaps an Inuit, paddling a kayak across clear Alaskan water against a spectacular mountain background, while dolphins and whales break the water's surface, the point is not that most potential buyers need a vehicle that can take them into the Alaskan wilderness. The point is that people that purchase such vehicles like to think of themselves as in touch with the environment (at 8 miles to a gallon), the outdoors, and adventure. Research shows that most 4-wheel drive sport utility vehicles never leave the pavement. Similarly, ads such as those for Levis 501 jeans mainly create an atmosphere more than they give information about the product.

Advertising creates fantasies. The idea is to create a story in which a particular product shows its use in a context appealing to specific types of viewers. As seen with the sport utility vehicle ad, a typical strategy is to position the product amidst other objects and situations that create associations for the viewer. For example, a beer manufacturer may want to convey that the usefulness of its product is not simply its taste, but also that it provides "good times." A fantasy might be created in which a group of young, attractive, exuberant friends are sharing beer together and having a wonderful time. The idea is to link beer, happy attractive friends, and fun together in the consumer's mind. Sometimes such attempts reach ludicrous proportions, as in attempts to link cigarettes and waterfalls and mountain streams to create an image of "clean, fresh taste." Of course, as in other areas of culture production, advertisers are constrained in the types of uses they can declare and the fantasies they can create. We have yet to see an advertising campaign directly declaring that, in a drunken oblivion, beer can temporally help you forget your troubles.

Learning to Consume

It may seem unbelievable to modern consumers, but in the early days of capitalism the very idea of consumption had to be sold to the public. In agricultural societies, the term *consumption* had a negative connotation; it meant to "use up" or "deplete." In the 19th century, the Montgomery Ward and Sears and Roebuck companies, with their ubiquitous catalogs, had to work hard to convince rural customers that consumption could be enjoyable (Ewen and Ewen 1982). An advertising industry developed in order to push consumption beyond mere necessities. There were two reasons for this. In order to grow, capitalist industry needed to create expanded markets for industrial production. And, with the long hours, poor working conditions, and deadening labor of the early factory system, leisure and consumption provided a substitute for job satisfaction. The solution was to tie consumption of products to images of the "good life": youth, being up-to-date, personal liberation, and sexuality (Ewen 1976).

It was an effort to do no less than change our cultural self-conception. This was to be culture production on a large scale. Advertisers wanted us to shake off old boundaries. We had seen ourselves through the lens of an agricultural society: scarcity and hardship were common, frugality was a virtue, and success and the pursuit of profit were morally suspect. Industrial society offered the promise of surplus and wealth.

Advertising and Mass Media Content

Advertising as Content

Advertising can creep directly into content in several ways. First of all, advertising *is* content. This is nowhere more true than in the case of music videos, and, less subtly, in the case of infomercials. In both cases the advertisement and the content are one and the same. More generally, advertisements take up significant space and time in commercial media. For example, on prime-time network television in 1996, there were 15 minutes and 21 seconds of advertisements every hour. Daytime network television had more advertising with an average of 20 minutes and 15 seconds per hour (Katz 1997).

As the cost of obtaining rights to hit programs increases, the networks have compensated by expanding the amount of ad time in those programs. The amount spent on such ads can be staggering. In just the second quarter of 1997, broadcast television advertising amounted to $3.77 billion. During that three-month period, General Motors alone spent $399 million and Procter & Gamble spent $300 million (*Mediaweek,* 1997: 8,1). In 1996, $894 million is estimated to have been spent on children's television advertising alone (Crowe 1997), despite the fact that advertising on children's television is limited to 10.5 minutes per hour on weekends, and 12 minutes per hour on weekdays. It is amazing the market coverage that some ads can claim. For example, in the first week of September 1997, data collected by Nielsen Media Research showed that Burger King led all advertisers with 503.2 million households reached. Each household could have been exposed to Burger King several times.

Given those numbers, the stakes for both the advertiser and the medium can be huge. In broadcast television, how much advertisers pay per spot is dependent on the ratings promised by the networks. With new programs this is largely guesswork. In 1997, a 30-second spot on a new program cost as much as $400,000 and as little as $55,000. Of the 26 new shows premiering in the fall of 1997, 15 drew fewer viewers than predicted by the networks (Wells 1997:1B). When this happens, advertisers are compensated with free airtime. For example, when the ABC show *Hiller and Diller* failed to bring in the expected audience, ABC had to compensate each advertiser with $40,500 in free airtime for each 30-second spot. Similarly, when the 1998 Winter Olympics did not obtain the ratings guaranteed by CBS, the network compensated advertisers with free airtime, which lead to a glut of ads during the second week of coverage.

Product Placements

Advertising can also become content in the form of product placements, the practice of a company paying a movie producer to use its products on screen. Sometimes the products placed are simply those of another division of the same company. Miller (1990) has shown how, after Coca-Cola purchased 49 percent of Columbia Pictures in 1982, Coke products and slogans began to pop up in Columbia releases. Sometimes there were even direct references to Coke products in the dialogue. Miller provides many other examples of product placements in well-known movies, including Philip Morris's payment of $350,000 in return for James Bond smoking Larks in the movie *License to Kill.* More recently, BMW spent an estimated $10 to $12 million on advertisements linked to the James Bond Film, *Tomorrow Never Dies.* Only some of the time are brand products used to make scenes appear more realistic. Instead, Miller argues, the goal is actually to make the product stand out in an unrealistic way, to interrupt the dialogue or the images on the screen in order to call attention to the product. He sees such placements as an intrusion by marketers on the viewer, as well as an intrusion on the artistic autonomy of directors and producers.

It is now common practice to send scripts to marketing professionals who scan them scene by scene to determine where products might be placed.

Sponsorship

In the early days of radio and television, programs actually carried the name of the sponsor in the title, as in *Camel Caravan of Stars* or *U.S. Steel Hour.* This practice survives in the attachment of company names to sporting events and rock concerts. However, in the mass media, companies quickly learned that their ad money was better spent spread across a variety of programs. Today, the most common type of sponsorship is one in which a company simply buys advertising time to place commercials during breaks in the program. However, products are also "plugged" on talk shows and increasingly placed in entertainment programs or, as in the case of the sitcom *Friends,* the cast is recruited to perform in commercials in character (Savan 1996). Perhaps indicative of this trend is the fact that NBC transformed the function of its broadcast standards department from monitoring the acceptability of advertisements to searching out opportunities for product tie-ins to programming (Bogart 1995).

Style

Still another way that ads are becoming content is through a trend in which Hollywood directors are increasingly directing television ads and advertising directors are directing feature films. Miller believes that this is leading to a similarity in the two forms: movies like advertisements and advertisements that look like movies. Regarding the latter, some ads have taken on more complex story lines, as when one brand of instant coffee used a series of ads to explore the developing relationship of a man and a woman.

Advertising Shaping Content

In addition to *being* content, advertisements can shape the form of nonadvertising mass media content. Advertisers have the power to influence content because the media depend on it for survival. Advertising is where the money is and, in the words from the movie *Jerry McGuire,* mass media producers are saying, "Show me the money." Advertisers might easily reply, "Show me the audience" or, better yet, "Show me the audience I want to reach." Producers of commercial media will argue that, despite the volumes of criticism they receive about the quality of the content they provide, sufficient audience is *not* found watching the type of programming found on public television stations, or listening to classical music or news on public radio. Despite the official position of Congress and the FCC, mass media production in the United States is not, for the most part, about serving the public interest, if we take that to mean creating an informed citizenry. It is, more than anything, about the money. Sometimes the quest for the money coincides with the public interest, sometimes it does not. It probably does not when, for example, advertisers have clustered their ads only in the leading newspaper in an area, driving contenders out of business. It is probably not in the public interest when news divisions of broadcast and cable networks decide that in-depth coverage of national or foreign news is not something most Americans are interested in; it is probably not in the public interest to broadcast programs heavily laden with sex and violence. But these things are in the interest of profit-oriented media organizations.

There are no easy alternatives. State-run systems have their own dangers and would probably not be acceptable to most Americans. And, much of our subscription-driven content, such as that found on HBO and Showtime on television, or in the motion picture industry, are not known for necessarily serving the public interest (equated with creating an informed public) either.

Bogart (1995), in his comprehensive look at the effects of commercial media, lists numerous ways in which marketing products through the mass media can influence content.

1. Direct pressure on programmers;
2. Passing on interest-group pressure to media programmers;
3. Supporting some types of content over others;
4. Altering the formats of media content;
5. Targeting ads to specific demographic or lifestyle groups.
   In the sections that follow we will examine each of these influences.

Direct Pressure from Advertisers

Sometimes content is shaped when there is direct pressure to change programming by withholding ads or threatening to withhold them. This occasionally happens when the mass media attempt to carry stories unfavorable to specific industries or companies. Examples of such conflict include Coca-Cola's pulling of all its ads from NBC in 1970 when the company ran a documentary unfavorable to its Minute Maid subsidiary, and, in 1990, Nordstrom department stores' refusing to advertise in two Seattle newspapers that ran articles about allegedly unfair labor practices in the stores. Such direct pressure is rare, perhaps because editors and producers avoid content that may antagonize advertisers.

Public Television
Even public television is not immune to such pressure, not from advertisers but from corporate underwriters. In 1996, South Carolina Educational Television (ETV) refused to carry a historical documentary that was running nationally on the PBS network. The documentary, *The Uprising of '34,* chronicled a massive textile strike in the 1930s in which several strikers were killed by agents of the textile industry. Despite the fact that the deaths occurred in South Carolina and were part of South Carolina History, ETV used scheduling conflicts to explain its decision not to run the documentary, despite the fact that it had run other films in the series. The economic and

political influence of the South Carolina textile industry is still powerful in this small southern state. In one South Carolina city, local interest in the documentary was great enough that it was shown at 11 o'clock Sunday night on a commercial station, paid for by donations from private citizens. After a change of leadership at SCETV, the documentary was finally shown in the summer of 1998.

Interest Group Pressure

A second influence of advertising on content occurs when advertisers feel real or anticipated pressure from outside interest groups, and, in turn, pressure mass media producers. An example of this process in action is the Catholic protest against the Walt Disney/ABC program, *Nothing Sacred.* The central character of this program was a Catholic priest whose ideas on abortion, birth control, divorce, and homosexuality did not coincide with those of the church. After receiving complaints from the Catholic League for Religious and Civil Rights, several companies, including Kmart, du Pont, Electrasol, Red Lobster, Isuzu, and Weight Watchers withdrew their advertising (Ashkinaze 1997). Fortunately for this program, other advertisers were willing to step in. However, the program was cancelled at the end of the 1997–1998 season.

Type of Programming and Content

A third influence of advertisers on content stems from the fact that advertisers tend to stay away from media content that makes targeted viewers uncomfortable or produces negative emotions. The general belief among advertisers is that strong content in a program interferes with attention to and retention of advertising. Thus, there is pressure to provide programming that is entertaining and not too disturbing. Sex and violence within the bounds of public taste are OK with most advertisers. Stories about various sorts of atrocities, or about very controversial issues (e.g., partial birth abortions), are a harder sell with advertisers.

Newspapers and magazines too have made efforts to produce content that fits the needs of advertisers. The desire to create more advertising space either shrinks the amount of hard news in newspapers and features in magazines, or expands the number of pages and destroys trees. In newspapers, one strategy for attracting both readers and advertisers has been to expand "lifestyle" sections. These sections are useful in their ability to link stories and products. For example, articles containing recipes are designed to attract advertising from the food industry and articles about home computing are meant to attract ads from computer hardware and software manufacturers. Founding editor of *Ms.* magazine, Gloria Steinem (1990), has described how the magazine has had difficulty attracting advertisers. Steinem believes this is because *Ms.* does not run the kinds of stories advertisers believe will enhance sales of their products. She relates how advertisers have increasingly created official policies concerning the types of stories their ads can and cannot be linked to. Steinem cites, for example, Dow Cleaning Products, which demands that ads for bathroom cleaner be placed adjacent to home furnishing and family features. And The De Beers Diamond Company insists that its ads not be placed next to hard news or copy that is anti love or romance. Similarly, Baker (1997) alleges that a major advertiser approached *Time, Newsweek,* and *U.S. News,* and told them that their editorial content regarding the advertiser's industry was going to be closely monitored for a three-month period. At the end of that period, the advertiser would award all of its advertising to the one magazine that treated the industry most favorably.

Even television news is not immune to pressure to be more entertaining, attract audiences and advertisers, and make a profit. Local television news has always relied heavily on a mixture of sex, violence, and lifestyle pieces to attract audiences. Critics say that network news is increasingly adopting a similar format. They point to the fact that coverage of foreign news by the three major networks has dropped by more than half in the 1990s. Meanwhile, CBS news anchor Dan Rather, in a *Los Angeles Times* wire story, has accused NBC of "...doing news lite" (*The Greenville News,* December 8, 1997b: 8B). However, in an interview (Johnson 1997c) Don Hewitt, producer of the highly rated CBS news magazine *60 Minutes,* lashes out at his own (and other) network's attempts to make news profitable. In the interview Hewitt states, "It's not about reporting anymore, it's about promoting" (1D). One of Hewitt's biggest complaints is that, in the quest for advertising dollars, networks increasingly cross the line between news and entertainment. Hewitt says, "The fact that it happens now doesn't bother me as much as the fact that nobody gives a damn" (2D).

Hewitt's claims may help explain why, in 1997, CBS news executive Lane Vernardos, a 25-year veteran of the news division who led the network's coverage of Tiananmen Square and the Persian Gulf War, was demoted for failing to act quickly to provide live coverage of the car crash that killed Princess Diana (Johnson 1997c). Perhaps Vernardos was operating under an older set of journalism norms under which such live coverage was typically reserved for crises involving heads of state and other major political figures.

Shaping Formats

A fourth effect of advertising occurs when media create formats to fit the needs of advertisers. For example, songs on commercial radio are limited in length to insure the proper number of ads per hour, and television content flows in a discontinuous stream punctuated every 10 minutes or so by commercial messages. Likewise, sporting events have been changed to accommodate advertisers. "TV time outs" are now a part of televised basketball, and breaks in televised football and baseball games are extended to accommodate advertising. Sports have also been affected when, in order to attract viewers and advertising dollars, professional leagues have arranged for extended multilevel playoffs to determine league championships, or when baseball owners propose league realignment to maximize television revenues. Much controversy exists concerning such intrusions into the internal rhythms of sporting events, but the desire to expand revenue and profit is compelling.

The Family Viewing Hour

In entertainment television, watchdog groups have lamented the loss of the family viewing hour and decry the networks' placement of programs unacceptable for children as early as 8 o'clock. This change in format, like the others noted above, is advertiser-driven. The traditional strategy of the networks was to create an "audience flow" throughout the evening in order to hold viewers to the network. They began with programs ostensibly suitable for the whole family and moved toward more adult content later in the evening. However, in order to carve out a niche for itself, the Fox network began, in the 1980s, programming shows in the 8 o'clock time slot aimed at young adults without children, a group very attractive to advertisers. In an attempt to hold on to this twenty-something audience, the big three networks followed suit by programing shows like *Friends* and *Mad About You* in this time slot. One unintended result was to increase viewership for more family-oriented cable networks as parents sought more suitable content to watch with their children (Turow 1997b).

Summary

To summarize our discussion thus far, we have seen that, in addition to accounting for a significant portion of mass media content, advertising affects media content in these four ways:

1. Advertisers may be offended by media content that portrays them negatively and pressure the media to avoid such content;

Programs like *Friends* are aimed at capturing the twenty-something crowd for advertisers.

2. Advertisers pass on pressure from interest groups to producers;
3. Advertisers do not like to be associated with certain types of strong content;
4. The business of attracting advertisers alters media formats.

Taken together, these examples suggest that mass media producers and advertisers work together to shape content to fit the needs of advertising. We now turn our attention to an important new trend in this synergy between advertisers and culture producers, the complementary practices of target marketing and "narrowcasting."

Targeting Marketing and Narrowcasting

The fifth effect of advertising on content has to do with the trend toward target marketing and its companion process "narrowcasting." Together they refer to the practice of seeking to place specific kinds of ads for specific kinds of products before groups with the "right demographics" (gender, income, age, race, and region) and lifestyle. This practice has led the growth of specialized content designed to specifically appeal to the targeted group. For example, a trip to your local newsstand will show that there is now a type of magazine related to nearly every interest. The same specialization can be seen in cable and satellite television with their multitudes of narrowly focused channels. Even though the broadcast networks must still work to capture broader audiences, program content and scheduling nevertheless reflect attempts to capture certain types of audiences in certain time slots. Thus, early evening is typically filled with young, single, affluent characters, and Saturday evenings, when young people are typically doing other things than watching television, are more likely to contain programming aimed at older viewers or families.

Fragmentation

The implications of this trend toward target marketing and narrowcasting are far-reaching. In his book *Breaking Up America,* Turow (1997a) argues that advertising has both contributed to, and has been affected by, fragmentation in U.S. society. Whether or not such fragmentation has actually occurred is a matter of some debate. For example, DiMaggio et al. (1996), using General Social Survey and National Election Survey data, found little evidence of a polarization in U.S. attitudes on social issues (the primary exception to this was in the area of attitudes toward abortion). However, in the 1980s, most data seemed to show greater individualism and a decline in community. In addition, there appeared to be a shrinking of the middle class, the backbone of nonsegmented mass-marketing. Even the old categories of gender, race, education, and income did not seem to matter as much anymore. Ideas about the way society was changing, interest in subcultures that developed in the 1960s, new statistical tools, and more powerful computers all shifted the focus of marketers to determining "lifestyles" and marketing to them. Their hope was to pinpoint, with as much precision as possible, the buying habits of the public. Researchers gathered data on behavior and attitudes and attempted to identify lifestyles and link product choices to those classifications. An early attempt at such classification was the Values and Lifestyles (VALS) program at the Stanford Research Institute. Advertising their findings as "a significant sociological portrait of Americans," VALS researchers contended that, by using VALS analysis, everyone could be classified into one of four broad categories containing a total of nine lifestyles (Mitchell 1983).

By the early 1990s a new version of VALS was out (VALS2), and now U.S. consumers were classified into just eight categories as indicated by their self-identity and their resources. They range in affluence from "Actualizers" (upscale independent intellectuals) to "Strugglers" (mostly nostalgic, downscale elderly women). In between are the principle-oriented "Fulfilleds" and "Believers," the status-oriented "Achievers" and "Strivers," and the action-oriented "Experiencers" and "Makers" (Piirto 1991). Box 9.1 shows the characteristics of each type (can you locate yourself?) and Table 9.1 shows the percentage of the U.S. population that falls into each category.

There are now many such attempts at classification. A new field of market research, "geodemographics," has emerged in an attempt to characterize neighborhoods and communities according to lifestyle. For example, Weiss (1988) has developed a classification scheme that classifies neighborhoods into one of 40 types. Even

TABLE 9.1   Distribution of VALS Types in the U.S. Population

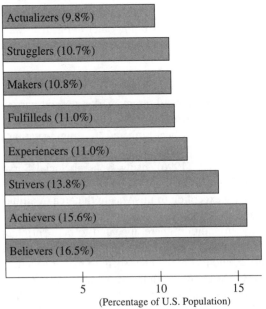

(Percentage of U.S. Population)

(Source: SRI International Consultants; used by permission.)

BOX 9.1   Short Descriptions of VALS Types

Actualizers are:

— Independent
— Leaders
— Risk Takers
— Fragmented
— Global
— Complex

Fulfilleds are:

— Organized
— Self-Assured
— Intellectual
— Well-Informed
— Content
— Open-Minded
— Curious

Achievers are:

— Conventional
— Brand Conscious
— Pragmatic
— Diligent
— Focused
— Enterprising

Experiencers are:

— Impatient
— Impulsive
— Spontaneous
— Creative
— Rebellious
— Trend Conscious

Believers are:

— Literal
— Respectful
— Loyal
— Consistent
— Traditional
— Dependable

Strivers are:

— Eager
— Social
— Trendy
— Approval-Seeking
— Image Conscious

Makers are:

— Self-Sufficient
— Practical
— Family-Oriented
— Physical
— Role Conscious

Strugglers are:

— Cautious
— Conservative
— Conformist
— Nostalgic
— Religious

(Source: SRI International Consultants; used by permission.)

though the validity and utility of such classifications have been sometimes questioned, this approach has exerted a powerful influence on the advertising industry.

Limits to Narrowcasting

There may be limits to how far narrowcasting can go. Already the available cable and broadcasting options have split the audience into what at one time would have been considered tiny fractions. Even such well-known cable channels as CNN and ESPN rarely capture more than one percent of the cable audience. As the field becomes more crowded, each channel must work to distinguish itself from the others.

Branded Formats
By the early 1990s media "narrowcasting" had evolved into the effort to create "branded formats" (Turow 1997b:92) as an attempt to deal with the identity problem. **Branded formats** refers to a package of distinctive content (e.g., television programs, music, magazine articles) that consumers associate with their own particular lifestyle. In television, "signature programs" (*Beavis and Butthead* on MTV, *Biography* on A&E, *Crossfire* on CNN)—designed to highlight the identity the channel is trying to create—are a component of branded formats that have become the norm.

New Technology
On the media consumption side of the production–consumption relationship, new technology may render ineffective this strategy of focusing an entire channel's programming on a particular group. Software is being developed that will search the broad spectrum of television programming for content a particular viewer is likely to be most interested in. In the same way that "push" technology scans the Internet for items of interest to the user and brings them to the user's computer, viewers will assemble their own media menu in specialized ways beyond what any single channel could do.

On the production side, new technologies are driving target marketing to new levels. The key words in advertising have become: *relationship, difference,* and *customization* (Turow 1997b:173). Advertisers now strive to engage the consumer in a dialogue. They want to accent the differences between consumers and deliver to them customized content and products. Insertion technology is becoming available, a way of targeting ads that are not associated with particular programming directly at viewers. That is, no matter what you are watching, if an advertiser believes that you possess the necessary characteristics that might indicate an interest in their product, a message could be inserted into whatever you are watching. Two blocks away, in a different household, a different message may be inserted into the advertising slots of the same program. Kraft Foods and TCI cable systems have formed an alliance to do just that. Kraft will use the multimillion dollar alliance to tailor ads for its products to specific neighborhoods and ultimately to specific types of consumers in the same household.

Fragmentation?
While, in some ways, all of this may reflect the triumph of individual cultural choice and a certain democratization of media, there may be hazards to catering to individual differences. As noted earlier, Turow (1997b) warns of increased fragmentation. If we think of the mass media as the central nervous system of a complex society, and if the mass media are individualized and no longer mass, then we may be losing

our means of producing and sharing a common core of culture. Technology, advertisers, and programmers have come together in an effort to cater to and exploit differences. Turow believes that what may result is the creation of "image tribes" in which we will be able to insulate ourselves from ideas we do not agree with and images we do not want to see.

Summary

This chapter has examined the relationship between advertising and mass media industries. We have seen that advertising is an important aspect of the mass media in the United States simply because so much of media content *is* advertising. We have also seen that mass media producers go to great lengths to shape programming to suit the needs of advertisers. This can happen with public as well as private media. Finally, we have examined the trend toward target marketing and narrowcasting. This breaking down of the mass audience is driven by both the desires of advertisers and the development of new technologies that make such targeting increasingly possible. Some believe that target marketing offers greater opportunity for consumers to get what they want. Others see it as a new and effective form of manipulation, as well as the cause of a fragmentation of our society. In either case, advertising and advertising dollars remain a central component of the mass media system in the United States.

10

The Mass Media Audience

Safety first is the network rule. There seems safety in numbers: in test results for new and revamped shows, in extrapolations from previous ratings in the case of returning shows. But in the end, the numbers don't suffice to make decisions. To build certainty, the "science" of numbers has to be joined to the "art" of hunches— consisting mainly of noting previous hits. The safest, easiest formula is that nothing succeeds like success (GITLIN 1983:63).

In the previous chapter we examined how advertising, as the life blood of commercial media, has major effects on the form and content of what is put before consumers. In this chapter we turn our attention to two more aspects of the relationship between marketing and the mass media: (1) Particular problems associated with marketing products specifically designed for the mass media, and (2) the ways in which media producers gather information about their market, and the impressions producers develop concerning audience preferences and behavior.

Special Problems of Culture Markets

We begin with the marketing of the cultural products themselves, the books, articles, television programs and music that make up much of cultural fare. As we saw in Chapter 8, such cultural commodities present some special problems for producers. In addition to the complexities of the creative process, there are massive overproduction, typically high levels of competition, and a very short "shelf life" for most products. Now we focus on the difficulty in predicting the behavior of the market and, therefore, the economic yield from any particular product. Market research is not of particular use because of the changeability of cultural choices and numerous other methodological problems in assessing audience desires and response. As we shall see, culture producers have a much better picture of where the audience has been than where it is going (although, as we shall see, even the latter can be problematic). In the sections below we examine some of the ways that cultural industries attempt to deal with particular problems in marketing cultural products. First there is the problem of establishing the equivalents of "brand names."

Creating Brands

In many areas of industrial production, "brand names" are an essential ingredient to marketing success. Successful brand names become symbols of trust and reliability. Companies work hard to establish "brand loyalty." In cultural industries company names are fairly worthless in this regard, because it is unlikely that anyone looks forward to, and purchases, "the latest musical release from Sony," or the latest NBC sitcom, because it *is* a release from Sony or scheduled on NBC. Culture producers must find other ways of establishing the equivalents of brand names. They do this in two ways: (1) genre and style, and (2) the "star" system. Together these strategies emphasize, simultaneously, product familiarity and uniqueness.

Genre

The first method to create something akin to a brand name is to employ the use of genres and styles within genres. Here the goal is to emphasize the sameness, or relationship, of one cultural product to another. In music, for example, recordings are marketed as alternative, classic rock, rap, or country, or as any one of a number of other genres. Some genres, like blues or bluegrass, are rather narrowly defined. Some, like pop or country, are rather broad. In movies there are romantic comedies, action films, slasher films, and so on. In television, programs fit into such categories as sitcoms, sports, sports information, crime drama, action drama, talk, news, and newsmagazines. The works are discussed as part of the genre, are critiqued by critics who may specialize in the genre, and graphics and other promotional materials may be developed to demonstrate the linkage with that style.

Styles typically emerge from the activities of culture creators. As we saw in the previous chapter, culture-producing organizations must give creators room to create, so innovations do occur. But it most often requires the conscious activities of cultural industries to take innovations and define them as a particular style. For example, musicians may develop local or regional ways of playing, but typically it is critics and publicists who will highlight the distinctive elements of that sound and give it a label. Thus, local ways of playing or making records become labeled as "The Nashville Sound" or "Mussel Shoals Sound." In the music industry, styles grow out of the work of musicians and a few record producers who may themselves achieve something akin to the status of "artist." Phil Spector's "wall of sound," Berry Gordy's "Motown sound," and Chet Atkins's "Countripolitan" sound are all examples of this phenomenon. In movies and television, styles emerge from the work of writers and directors, but typically are not labeled and marketed as such for the general public.

Fitting Categories

Establishing genres or styles allows marketers to target particular groups of consumers who tend to consume within a specific set of styles, and, just as importantly, gives the consumers their first clue as to whether or not they might be interested in the product. Genres and styles also act back upon culture creators. After particular genres are distinguished, creators must learn to produce materials that fit into those categories. Not fitting into *any* category may be a sign of great creativity, but it also means that the publicity machinery, various types of distributors, critics, and consumers, may be confused. For example, in the music industry, radio stations and music stores rely heavily on definitions of genre for developing formats and product placement. It is, in fact, possible for a particular recording not to fit easily into *any* established categories. An example of this is when singer–songwriters, such as the late Townes VanZandt, were at one time classified as "folk" and now are most often found in the "country" section of music stores. In the case of VanZandt, this is true even though his records are rarely if ever played on country music radio. Similarly, to make sense for marketing and consuming, books, screenplays, magazines, and other cultural products must fit into existent categories. Or, as happened with rap and alternative music, sufficient similar activity must take place to generate new categories.

Stylistic Confusion

Sometimes genres are strained by the inclusion of a wide range of styles, causing confusion in the industry and among fans. This is most likely to happen in the music industry where too many styles and the resultant confusion threaten brand integrity. If consumers do not know what to expect from a genre, then the category becomes meaningless. There has been some criticism of the current country music industry along these lines. As one commentator (Zimmerman 1997:5D) put it:

> *Nobody in Nashville seems to know which music is trendy and which is trite. And some of the genre's biggest stars are caught in the middle as the industry struggles through an identity crisis while trying to hold onto a huge, unwieldy audience spanning three generations.*

The importance of genre for marketing and consumption purposes differs by medium. Magazines, newspapers, and certain types of books (e.g., self-help) rely heavily on genre identification. For other media—fiction, popular music, motion pictures—genre is just part of the formula for attracting an audience. The music and book industries rely heavily on a "star" system as indicators of "brand quality." In television, designating genres may be enough to attract initial consumption, although the use of a star system and heavy promotional campaigns are employed there as well. What is this "star" system and how does it operate?

The Star System

How is it possible that a television network like NBC would be willing to offer (unsuccessfully) comedian Jerry Seinfeld $5 million an episode to continue performing in his hit show *Seinfeld*? Not just because of the show's ability to make money, although that is a major factor. It is also because Jerry Seinfeld is a "star" and, in cultural industries, stars are the closest thing to brand names. For audiences interested in a particular genre, stars carry with them a track record of success. Just as you may choose McDonald's over Burger King, to a certain degree, with a star you know what you are getting. Stars elevate particular products, and also help create an identity for an entire network or other culture-producing organization.

Star Creation

Particular creative artists have always risen to star status based on audience reaction, but corporations have increasingly been less willing to leave this to chance. In order to induce demand, they attempt to define stars for the public through advertising. Publicists attempt to create a unique identity for the artist, often woven out of both real and manufactured elements. In the music industry the identity of stars is particularly important. This is because musical performers *are* their music in ways that, for example, actors are not totally identified with particular roles. Just as cars and beers are "positioned" to sell something beyond their practical utility, so too are recording artists. They and their music are often intended to portray a certain lifestyle, a way of approaching life or worldview that fans identify with and aspire to. Some may be surrounded with the trappings of the moody, introspective, unconventional artist, some as "just plain folks," others as a fantasy love. And some appear to represent the group that identifies with them.

Consider the public outrage when, in 1992, Ice-T and the band Body Count released their rap/metal fusion song "Cop Killer" in which the singer describes his intention to kill some police officers with his 12-gauge shotgun. Then President George Bush, Vice-President Dan Quayle, and numerous media commentators condemned the song, and a boycott was launched against Time Warner. Eventually Ice-T pulled the song off the album and began shopping for another label. The media and much of the public seemed to be taking the position that the singer was advocating the killing of police officers (a contention Ice-T denied). Yet movies and television are filled with characters who injure or kill police officers and the actors are not considered to be advocates of violence. As Ice-T pointed out, Arnold Schwarzenegger has not been subjected to widespread condemnation for his role in *The Terminator*.

Overproduction

Mass media markets are crowded with performers and products. Considerable expense and effort must be made to make some stand out. However, a contradiction arises in that, sometimes, the more that mass media organizations push certain stars, the more quickly the public is likely to tire and go on to something else. This problem is compounded by the fact that where there is success, other producers will rush in to imitate those products, further accelerating the creation-to-burnout cycle. For example, the success of the "girl group" the Spice Girls has spawned numerous imitation acts. One commentator (Kroll 1997) describes the rush to sign similar groups:

> *As the new age begins with the cloning of sheep, the real sheep are the suits who man the Xerox machines of pop culture. Record moguls are hot for Girl Power. Polydor is readying a five-girl band called Chill. And Warner's WEA Records has signed a black three-girl group called Cleopatra. London Records has All Saints, a four-girl entry, and Virgin looks to sign Six Pack. Ireland has its first all-girl band, Fab, and Sony Music is launching a four-girl group (66).*

The rapid rise and fall of acts in the music industry has been a matter of some concern (Groebner 1997). In the early 1990s, the enormous success of the band Nirvana created an industry rush of imitations. This led to the boom of alternative rock. It also led to the wholesale signing of bands and an industry glut. Similarly, country music has attempted to capitalize on its success by greatly increasing the number of artists and releases. Increasingly, one hears that companies simply do not take the time to develop acts today. Acts are discovered, signed to short-term contracts, promoted heavily, and then disappear because they do not have the reservoir of material

The success of the Spice Girls has generated a search for similar acts.

and creative maturity to sustain a career. One act in country music is reported to have been promoted so rapidly that she did not have enough original material even to go on tour. Meanwhile, fans grow more cautious, less willing to purchase material from representatives of an undifferentiated mass of new artists.

A similar problem exists in the television, movie, and book publishing industries. The publishing industry is now churning out over 500 new novels each year, more than can reasonably be marketed effectively to consumers. Likewise, in 1997 the movie industry released over 40 films for the holiday season. Meanwhile, television networks are canceling and replacing series at an unprecedented rate. In part this is the problem of overproduction discussed in the previous chapter. However, it also a symptom of what we have been discussing here, the rush to imitate success and the resulting diluting of star power.

Summary
In this section we have examined some of the particular problems of marketing cultural products. We must remember that not only does the industry want to make money, consumers want these products. A central problem is differentiating a particular product from the abundance of similar products on the market. The task is to help consumers find what they want, and encourage them to want more. Cultural products do not carry "brand names" in the same way that many other manufactured products and services do. As a result, the industry has developed two main strategies for bringing the consumer and the product together. The first is the development of a classification system of cultural products, what we have earlier called "genres." Genres provide the distinct content for narrowcasting and for the development of general audience preferences. The second strategy is the "star" system. This promotional form alerts consumers to a few established performers and to "rising" stars. The star system injects personality into mass consumption and allows consumers to form what are sometimes deep emotional attachments. A "fan" is bonded to a star. In addition, they can have the special thrill of discovering "hot, new" performers. Genre and the star system are attempts to produce something analogous to brand names in cultural industries. There is, however, another aspect to the relationship between marketing and the mass media: the idea of market as an image of the mass media audience.

Images of the Audience

Marketing refers to efforts to attract an audience for particular products. **The market** for a product refers to the image that producers hold of who the likely consumers are. Producers develop beliefs about whether or not there is "a market" for a particular product and what the characteristics of that market are. In cultural industries these beliefs are based on such factors as market or audience research, experience, and, as

Gitlin (1983) notes, plain old "gut feelings." In the sections that follow we will examine this process of learning about the audience, and how producers' definitions of market affect the menu of cultural products available to consumers.

Measuring Sales

There are two measurement problems that mass media producers must solve: (1) tracking the amount of consumption, and (2) determining the characteristics of consumers. Each medium encounters its own particular problems in accomplishing these tasks.

Magazines and Newspapers

Magazines and newspapers can count subscribers easily, but sales in newsstands and stores are more complicated to follow because unsold merchandise can be returned. This is a much larger problem for book publishers due to the longer interval that lies between the ordering of the books by stores and the return of unsold copies. The large bookstore chains are particularly known for ordering more books than they can sell. Because of the large number of returns, publishers may not have a good picture of what is going until it is too late. The result may be costly overprintings and expensive but ineffective media campaigns. The music industry has a similar problem and, in recent years, has moved to limit returns. The downside of this strategy is that music outlets become more reluctant to purchase, or, at least purchase in quantity, products by unproven artists. As we shall see below, a new technology may help with these problems of tracking sales.

Motion Pictures

Motion pictures depend on ticket sales as the primary measure of how well their product is selling. This information has been coming more quickly and with greater precision through computerized systems. Vertical integration of producers and exhibitors makes this process simpler. The film industry also sells videos to the public through various retail outlets and to video rental stores.

Radio and Television

The media with the greatest problems measuring sales are broadcast radio and television, and nonsubscription cable television. In these media there is no "sale" in the sense of a consumer taking home a physical product. There is no checkout counter for a radio or television program. That fact makes simply counting who is watching and who is listening difficult. Even more difficult are the increasing demands from advertisers to know not only how many are consuming media products, but *who* is consuming.

We will now examine some attempts to deal with these problems of audience measurement and their impact on cultural products.

Measuring the Radio and Record Audience

In assessing overall audience, radio primarily relies on the Arbitron ratings. Arbitron is a private company that samples households and, if members are willing, distributes diaries to every member over the age of 12. The diaries provide data on age and gender and the listening preferences for particular radio stations at particular times of the day. In addition, Arbitron occasionally will add a section of 20 to 25 qualitative questions designed for analysis of a variety of consumer behaviors, from what type of beer the respondents drink to whether they plan to purchase a car in the upcoming year. In addition, the questions are conceived in such a way as to give radio broadcasters an indication of their listeners' use of television and newspapers as well as radio.

Response Rate and Accuracy

One difficulty with the diary method is the relatively low response rate in returning diaries. For example, in 1996, Arbitron sampled some 324,790 households. Depending on the particular market surveyed, response rates ranged from 38.8 percent to 43.4 percent. The overall response rate was 42.5 percent (Petrozello 1996). The question here, as with any survey, is whether those who refused to participate differ in significant ways from those that do participate. A second question is whether people are keeping their diaries accurately. Because the results are used to determine a station's position in its market, and, therefore, its importance to advertisers, these are important questions, and matters of much discussion within the industry.

The Charts

A different sort of data is critical to the radio industry as well. Because of the close relationship between the radio and music industries, radio programmers are interested in knowing the popularity of particular songs with consumers. There is a close interaction between sales and radio airplay. The cycle goes something like this: The more a recording sells, the more often radio stations will play it, and the more it is played the more it sells. In order to get a measure of sales, the radio industry relies primarily on weekly charts compiled by *Billboard* magazine. For most of their existence, these sales charts were dependent on reports from stores selling the recordings. The stores ranked the various releases in terms of sales, but did not provide actual sales figures. This method came under severe criticism when producers of certain genres argued that their sales were being underreported. The sales rankings were made particularly suspect by the fact that recording labels could manipulate the chart. The labels were able to do this by offering free goods to store personnel in return for giving a higher ranking to the labels' release.

Another problem with the system was that simply ranking records did not take into account that in one store the number one seller may have been only a few units ahead of number two, while in another store the difference might have been much greater. Another type of problem arose from classification. Stores tended to compartmentalize the music and the artists in reporting sales rankings. For example, even though a country or R&B artist might have the most sales overall, the store would not rank him or her number one on the "pop" charts (most popular songs overall) because, in the minds of the store personnel, these genres did not count as popular music.

Soundscan

In order to address this problem, in 1991 *Billboard* began phasing in a new "Soundscan" system, developed by Soundscan, Inc. The magazine pays Soundscan to collect sales data. Using this system, each CD or tape is labeled with a barcode and stores are paid by Soundscan, Inc. to record the data. At the time of purchase, the barcode is scanned, providing data on sales for that particular item.

The Soundscan database provides information on both local and national sales. These sales figures are then used to construct the *Billboard* charts at the end of each week. By using computerized sales data rather than store-ranking information, the charts are believed to be a more accurate reflection of sales. Soundscan is much less vulnerable to manipulation by the labels and to biases on the part of the reporting stores.

The first chart to use the new technology debuted in the May 25, 1991, issue of *Billboard* and the industry was temporarily thrown into turmoil. C. Miller (1991) describes some of the surprises under the new system: Michael Bolton knocked R. E. M. out of the number one spot on the pop charts, the soundtrack to the motion picture *Pretty Woman* shot up a startling 52 places, from number 127 to number 75, and country singer Garth Brooks placed two albums in the Top Thirty on the pop charts.

While country artists like Brooks, and middle-of-the-road artists like Bolton, showed the biggest gains, new and alternative acts showed some major losses. For example, the alternative group, Jesus Jones, fell from number 5 to number 29. The group Fishbone dropped an incredible 133 positions to number 182, and The Divinyls dropped from number 17 to number 40. Meanwhile, a new release from the rap group NWA went to number one on the charts with roughly the same kind of sales that left its previous album at number 37. Clearly, something was going on with the data.

Not surprisingly, given these dramatic changes in chart positions, Soundscan was quite controversial. Whether one was for it or against it depended on whether your artists had moved up or down the charts. Assuming that the data were accurate, the changes in chart position suggested that some of the problems with the old system were, in fact, real. One explanation for the change in results is that most record store workers are younger people less likely to be attracted to country and middle-of-the-road artists. This may account for the underreporting of sales of those genres. Likewise, new artists are most likely to be heavily promoted by recording labels in an attempt to achieve star status. Record companies may have been providing incentives for stores to rank these artists more highly, which would explain the overreporting of sales of new acts under the old system.

Soundscan has since been embraced by the industry, prompting one industry executive to remark: "Soundscan is the lifeblood of our industry. Without a doubt, these guys changed everything" (Sorkin 1997:C5). Now, not only do *Billboard* and the radio industry use the data, but the recording companies themselves use it to get a picture of what is going on with consumers.

Importance of Soundscan

The Soundscan story is important. It shows that the quality of market data can have important effects on the menu of available cultural products. It turns out that the picture of the audience presented by the old method was inaccurate. What this former method did was to allow greater manipulation of the system by music companies. By more accurately reflecting actual consumer buying habits, Soundscan may actually increase diversity in available products (Bowie 1997).

Bookscan

Soundscan has shown that mass media industry leaders do not always have an accurate image of the market for their products. When that image changes, careers can be made or lost, as with some of the acts noted above. Soundscan is now expanding into the book publishing industry with Bookscan (Turner 1997a). There is the potential that Bookscan will cause the same turmoil in publishing as it did in the music industry. Right now the *New York Times* best-seller list powers the publishing industry. Getting onto the list means that the large bookselling chains will discount the book (by as much as 30 percent) further driving up sales. The *Times* tracks sales at 4,000 bookstores and at wholesalers that serve another 50,000 retailers. But some believe that the list is inaccurate, favoring more literary works sold by independent bookstores. If Bookscan provides more accurate data, these literary works may drop off the list, hurting sales. On the other hand, with more accurate data publishers may be able to do a better job promoting their books. What is certain is that this new way of collecting data will have an impact on the way publishers do business and, ultimately, on the types of books available to the public.

Measuring the Television Audience

As noted earlier, one of the most difficult audiences to measure is the television audience. With most television programming, unlike with CDs, tapes, or videos, viewers are not purchasing anything. Thus, there is no point of sale to track.

In television the task of measuring the audience has been entrusted to the A. C. Nielsen Company (now Nielsen Media Research). This may represent one of the most unique commercial relationships in the economy, mirrored today by Arbitron and Soundscan: an entire industry contracting with a private company to tell the world how well they are doing. The Nielsen Company began measuring radio audiences in the 1940s, and then created a monopoly over television ratings. Larson (1992) has shown how Nielsen has patented and employed each new technology of audience measurement, and how each change has created a new view of the television audience. Nielsen's first innovation was to replace the conventional surveys with a mechanical meter that recorded which network a television was tuned to (diaries are currently used to measure local market viewing in all but the largest markets, where they are supplemented by household meters). Not only did this give at least the illusion of more scientific data, it was faster.

The process of collecting audience data has been controversial almost from the start and continues to be. In 1963–1964, Congress held an investigation of the ratings system and, through a set of Federal Trade Commission guidelines, warned of imperfections in the system. Criticism began to build again in the late 1970s and early 1980s when competition from cable led to a shrinking of the broadcast networks' viewership.

Ratings and Shares

Nielsen reports both a program's rating and its share. A **rating** is the percentage of America's total viewing audience—the roughly 98 million households with at least one TV—that are tuned to a particular program or network. However, not all television households have the TV turned on at a given moment in time. The **share** refers to the percentage of televisions that are actually turned on and are tuned to a particular program or network. In 1978–1979, the three major networks' share was 91 percent in prime time. By 1985, their combined share had fallen to 77 percent and, in 1996, had dropped to 42 percent and, in the third quarter of 1997, reached an all-time low of 37.5.

In order to place this decline in perspective, in 1964 a single episode of *The Beverly Hillbillies* drew a 65 percent share, far more than the three major networks combined today. Because of the struggle to grab and hold onto ever shrinking pieces of the viewership pie, accounting for viewers has become more and more important for television producers.

Pressure from Advertisers and Networks

Problems in measuring audience became even more severe as advertisers began to demand access to specific demographic and lifestyle groups. Nielsen's meters could tell when a set was turned on and to what program, but could not tell *who* in the household was watching, much less if they were paying attention. Data on the "who" question had thus far been answered through the use of diaries kept by Nielsen families. But with the explosion in the number of channels, confidence in the individuals' ability to remember viewing choices and record them accurately has declined. In 1987, Nielsen began using a new technology **the people meter,** intended to show not only what was being watched, but who was watching. Now there was more data and it even arrived overnight. The problem was, the news was not good for the networks: Audiences were even smaller than had been suggested by the old methodology. A new set of heated attacks on Nielsen's methodology began.

The Methodology

Because it is not economically feasible to wire every television household in the United States for data collection, Nielsen uses sampling to estimate audience data. About 5,000 families in the United States are "Nielsen Families" and their viewing habits are what determines the ratings. Larson (1992) describes how even a tenth of a point difference in these ratings can make or cost the networks millions of dollars. A single point can affect whether programs are kept or canceled. Yet, there are fundamental flaws in the sampling procedure that makes such precise use of the data ludicrous. Even under optimal conditions of true random sampling, in which each television household in the United States has an equal chance of being selected and there are no refusals to participate, there would be a certain amount of sampling error. That is, with any sample you cannot estimate with complete accuracy what is going on in the population (the larger group you're sampling from); there is always a degree of sampling error. With a sample the size of Nielsen's, you can be 99 percent sure that the numbers are accurate within about 2 percent in either direction. That's pretty good and relatively economical. To be 95 percent sure of being within 1 percent, you would need a sample of about 9,600, and to be 99 percent sure you would need a sample of 16,590. Without getting too much into the details, using a sample of 5000, you can be 99 percent sure that if a single episode of *Seinfeld* earns a rating of 30, the actual percent of television households tuned to the program nationally would be somewhere between 28 and 32. This is assuming a truly random sample.

But, because of sampling difficulties, estimates may really be more skewed than that. Sampling difficulties begin with the fact that Nielsen demands a lot of its families. Homes must be wired for the monitoring equipment and every TV, VCR, and satellite dish in the home must be equipped to send data. This process takes several hours. In addition, families must promise not to purchase or use any unmetered reception equipment. They are also told not to tell anyone of their participation. This is in order to keep unscrupulous television producers from trying to influence the household's viewing habits.

After following some careful sampling procedures, Nielsen narrows the population of all TV households to about 5,000 "basics," randomly chosen households. Families are paid, but just two dollars a month for each piece of reception equipment per month. All of this results in a high level of refusal to participate. Typically about 48 percent of the sample at any given time is made up of the basics, the households originally chosen at random to be in the sample (for technical reasons, the actual percentage of true basics is actually smaller than that).

With such a high refusal rate, the question arises, "Are Nielsen families truly representative of the U.S. television viewing population?" Or is there something different

---

BOX 10.1   Life in a Nielsen Family

In a 1997 article (Raymondo and Stipp 1997), sociologist James C. Raymondo, a member of a Nielsen family himself, describes the experience of being part of the Nielsen survey. In addition to the problems already mentioned, he points out some of the difficulties in using the Nielsen equipment. For example, when viewers in the household begin to watch television, each one must punch in a code number. Likewise, the viewer must push a button to let the meter know when they have stopped watching. Because people often forget to log off, it is also required that a special button be pushed every 70 minutes. Raymondo felt that the biggest annoyance was having to press the "OK" button every time someone changed a channel. Dedicated channel surfers will probably recognize what an annoyance this could be. In return for all of this, he received a one-time payment of $50, a monthly payment of $2 per unit hooked up, and every six months a small prize chosen from a catalog. Raymondo's catalog earnings were "a flashlight, clock, and small hatchet" (Raymondo and Stipp 1997:24).

---

about those who agree to take part? If there is, then the ratings will not accurately reflect the larger population's viewing habits. Another problem is that the data transmission technology itself is sometimes faulty. Data are transmitted daily from the households to Nielsen's central computer. For various reasons, about 10 percent of the data on any given day is defective, and the heavier the viewing in a particular household, the more likely this is to happen.

Statistical Significance

All of this suggests that measuring the audience for television is extremely difficult. Nevertheless, thanks to sophisticated methodological and statistical techniques, data that would be considered reasonably accurate for many purposes can be obtained. But "reasonably accurate" does not produce the precision in measurement that would make a tenth of a rating point meaningful. In Chapter 3, we mentioned the concept of "statistical significance." What this means is that it is possible, using statistics, to tell with some confidence whether the difference between two numbers is the result of chance or whether a real difference exists in a population. With Nielsen's sample, the difference between a rating of 16.2 and 16.4 is probably not significant. That is, its difference may be due to chance or error. If that is the case, advertisers and networks are making decisions involving millions of dollars on differences that are, in a statistical sense, meaningless.

As the battle for audience and advertising revenue heats up, the television producers have become increasingly concerned about the precision of the data. Cable and broadcasters accuse each other of misinterpreting audience numbers, elevating their own and minimizing those of their competitors. Broadcasters have threatened to switch to a rival company, Statistical Research, which claims to have a new meter system with the ability to provide more comprehensive and accurate surveys. The American Association of Advertising has been threatening to develop an entirely new system. Meanwhile, Nielsen and the networks themselves have been experimenting with new technologies in an attempt to address some of the criticisms.

Audience Testing

Not all television research occurs after the programs have aired. In the attempt to find out what will work with the audience, both the television and movie industries employ consulting firms. These research firms bring in test audiences to view programs before they are aired or released. Several types of methodologies are employed. Some may use focus groups, in which groups of participants discuss their reactions to programs. Some audiences are given a device that allows them to rate a program every few minutes. Some subjects may even be hooked up to galvanic skin response transmitters to measure their physiological reactions to a program. Depending on audience response, characters may be changed, new endings developed, and so on. For example, the film *Jerry McGuire* was given a new ending for its cable television debut after it was shown that the original ending did not test well with audiences. In television, "pilot" episodes will be aired to test programs before committing to a series. But even these methods are notoriously inaccurate. After test audiences panned the original *Seinfeld* pilot, NBC rejected the program. A revised version resulted in research reports advising NBC that *FM* and *Dear John* were stronger programs (Marin 1998).

Other Media

We have seen how mass media industries attempt to collect audience data on everything from the sale of books and recordings to radio listening and television viewing. As noted earlier, each medium presents its own particular problems of data collection. This is no less true for such new media as computer software and CD-ROMs, the Internet, and interactive television. If you can't measure the audience then you can't sell it to advertisers. Cable television faced this problem in the 1980s and bowed under to pressure from advertisers in accepting Nielsen's "People Meter" as a tool for measuring audience.

New measurement technologies are quickly being developed to measure the audience for new media. The result is that the Internet and other interactive media are rapidly being commercialized. The medium of greatest commercial interest is the Internet. It has been estimated that web advertising already amounts to several hundred million dollars per year, and is expected to reach $5 billion by the end of the decade (Darlin 1996). With its millions of users every day, the Internet is a lucrative source of income. The problem is that, for any given site, it is difficult to tell who has visited. Several companies, including Nielsen, are already providing data to advertisers, counting the number of hits at web sites and demographic data behind the hits. Once this is perfected, it is likely that commercialization of the Internet will increase dramatically.

The Noncommercial Media and Audience

We have seen that it is the link to advertising, the foundation of our commercial media system, that fuels the need to define an audience through audience research. We have also seen that mass media producers alter content to please advertisers. In contrast, public television and radio are lauded for their seeming immunity to commercial pressure. But our public broadcasting system has its own brand of pressure to contend with. Peterson (1993), in his study of the fate of classical music in radio, shows how the pursuit of financial support, in whatever form, can shape mass media content. In the early days of radio, classical music was heard on a wide variety of stations. The industry wanted to be perceived as elevating national culture, bringing high culture to those who did not have the opportunity or finances to attend. This was not a purely altruistic goal; the industry was desperately trying to avoid regulation, and, according to Peterson, the highbrow stance was intended to create an identification with a BBC-type system and curry favor with Congress.

After World War II, television began to steal away network radio's audience, advertisers, and prestige. Radio survived in the form of primarily independent stations acting as a jukebox for particular genres of music. Classical, which had been subsidized on the networks by popular music, nearly disappeared from the airwaves. However, the decision by the FCC to promote FM radio by setting aside a portion of the spectrum for public radio had an important effect. The educational stations, largely immune to financial pressure, and with a clear mission to protect high culture, created a haven for classical, semiclassical, and jazz music.

The Conservative Attack

Things continued that way until the legitimacy of the publicly funded system was attacked by conservative politicians in the 1980s. Now there was increased pressure for public television and radio to raise more money directly from listeners. The public system also felt pressure to justify its existence to Congress by increasing the size of its audience. Peterson points out that the audience for public radio had, in fact, been growing, but the new members were different from the traditional National Public Radio (NPR) audience. This new audience was more likely to tune to public radio for news than for classical music. Market studies showed that nearly half of NPR's 10 million weekly listeners were tuning in almost exclusively to its news programming. Once more, most of this new audience was not paying to help support programming. The task for public radio was clear: to hold onto this audience during nonnews programming, and to recruit these listeners as members.

Cume and AQH

Peterson outlines two different radio strategies for capturing an audience. For example, if the goal is to double the audience, one strategy would be to double the number of people who listen in on a particular day. This is known in industry language as increasing **the cume** (cumulative audience). The other way is to get people to listen twice as much, referred to as increasing the **AQH** (average time spent listening per quarter hour). Stations trying to increase the cume will play several different genres of music in block format, trying to attract different listeners for each block. Stations trying to increase the AQH stick to a single format and try to hold onto the same listeners for longer periods of the day.

Commercial radio primarily relies on a strategy of increasing the AQH as opposed to attracting the greatest number of listeners. Most employ one of six basic formats. This strategy attempts to deliver a particular type of audience rather than a broad spectrum of listeners to advertisers. A consulting firm hired by NPR recommended that the network use the AQH strategy in its attempt to attract and hold on to listeners. According to Peterson, the result has been a mostly subtle but significant change in NPR formats. In addition to a continued emphasis on news programming, many stations have evolved toward what Peterson calls "classical lite," relatively small portions of larger classical works accompanied with educational material. Other stations have evolved more toward a New Age format. One station in North Carolina (WNCW) plays an unusual mix of contemporary singer–songwriters, blues, and bluegrass. Thus, any time the mass media are forced to compete for audience, content is altered to reflect that competition. As in the case of classical music, the presence in the media of cultural forms with less commercial viability may well be threatened in the process.

Consequences of Market

The purpose of audience research is to gain information about how many and, ideally, what types of people are consuming cultural products. Based on research data, experience, and intuition, producers develop opinions about what will work with audiences and what will not.

Given the difficulty in measuring audiences and the subjectivity of experience and intuition, the producers' image of the audience is often inaccurate. There are many examples of producers being taken by surprise by consumer response, either positive or negative, to products. Well-known examples from the nonmedia world include the failure of the Edsel automobile in the 1950s and New Coke in the 1980s. However, perhaps more than any other area of the economy, the landscape of culture production is littered with failed products. Every canceled television program (and most are), every song that does not reach the charts, every movie that flops at the box office, every book that quickly ends up in the "bargain bin" is an example of a failed audience image. Likewise, many cultural creations disappear because industry decision makers decide that there is "no market" for that product. It is worth stopping to consider what "no market" means in the context of culture production. What it often does *not* mean is that no one wants that product. No market may mean that there are not sufficient numbers of people, or not enough people with the correct demographic or lifestyle characteristics, to satisfy the advertisers.

Audience Size

The requirements for audience size are dependent on the particular medium. Early in its first season the program *Saturday Night Live* was nearly canceled because it had an audience of *only* 8 million viewers. For its time slot at that time, an audience of 11 million was considered the measure of success. So, in this case, 8 million people nearly translated into "no one is interested in a late night comedy program." Similarly, in the fall of 1997, newspapers and news programs were abuzz over the low ratings of the baseball World Series between the Cleveland Indians and Florida Marlins. The first three games had drawn a 14 rating, the lowest ever. Commentators contended that this did not bode well for the future of the sport, and offered various reasons for the poor ratings, from fan dissatisfaction after the strike in 1995 to a failure to woo younger viewers to the size of the television markets of the two contenders. While the ratings were comparatively low, each rating point equals 980,000 households. Thus, a rating of 14 means that at least one person in each of 13,720,000 households was tuned to the series. And these numbers represent failure! On the other hand, a country song can be a hit with sales of a few hundred thousand, a book can reach the best-seller list with sales of less than 100,000, and all of these audiences are huge compared to the audience for most live performance.

Inaccurate Audience Images

Often the producers' image of the audience for a particular cultural product is just wrong. For example, the original *Cosby Show* was turned down by both ABC and CBS before being picked up by NBC in 1984 (Gold 1985). The show was produced by the then-fledgling company, Carsey-Werner, which at that time had produced only one previous show (it failed). The producers were widely advised not to take on the program. Conventional industry wisdom was that the sitcom was dead and that white Americans would not watch a program about an upper-middle-class African American family. In an interview with *Broadcasting* magazine (*Broadcasting* 1988: 60), cofounder of the company, Marcy Carsey, put it this way:

> *I can't tell you how many people told us how this will never pay off, the idea was not glitzy enough, that comedy was dead. You just have to put blinders on, and do what you have to do because you believe in the thing you're doing.*

The original *Cosby Show* was turned down by both ABC and CBS before being picked up by NBC.

The *Cosby Show* took NBC from last place to first place in the ratings, grossing $130 million in advertising revenue in one season alone. It went on to become one of the most successful television programs of all time and did so with a huge white audience. In a more recent example, the late Brandon Tartikoff has said that he believed that *Seinfeld* was too New York–oriented to be successful. He initially ordered only four shows to be made, the smallest number of shows ever ordered for a network sitcom.

There are many examples of flawed audience images from the music industry. The Beatles were turned down by several large record companies in England before being signed by EMI. Even after several of their songs had reached the charts in Britain, their U.S. subsidiary, Capital records, refused to release their records in America because the company felt there was no market for the music here (Chapple and Garofalo 1977). Only after U.S. radio stations imported copies on their own for broadcast did Capital relent. The group eventually accounted for half of all of Capital's sales revenue.

Another example is that of country music songwriter Don Schlitz. While working the nightshift at a university computer center in Nashville, Schlitz penned a song that was to be rejected over a three-year period by every major publisher and producer in Nashville. Legendary producer Chet Atkins is reported to have told Schlitz that the song was "too complicated for country listeners." Schlitz recorded the song himself on a small independent label and, when it began to receive some airplay, it came to the attention of singer Kenny Rogers' producer, Larry Butler. Rogers was not particularly interested in the song, but Butler had him record it after the rest of the songs for the session had been completed. That song, *The Gambler,* went on to become the "song of the year" in 1979, the biggest hit of Rogers' career, his signature song, and the basis for a television movie and 4 sequels.

Summary

In this chapter we saw how the marketing of mass media products poses special problems for their producing organizations. Audience reaction is difficult to predict and difficult to measure. There are no such things as "brand names," although media organizations try to approximate them through genres, styles, and the star system.

We have also learned that when it comes to mass media content, audience *does* matter. But not all audiences matter. Audiences are important if advertisers are interested in them. For example, in broadcast television, those with the most clout are between the ages of 18 and 49. The very young and older Americans are of not much interest to advertisers and therefore to the broadcast networks. Minority groups have traditionally not been of much interest either. Fortunately, new technologies have greatly expanded media outlets and narrowcasting has interested advertisers in providing content for a greater variety of groups.

We have also seen that culture producers form images of the audience based on research findings, intuition, and experience. Producers try to give the audience what it wants, but in the context created by the producers' needs and the needs of advertisers. More accurately, they are trying to give the audience what they *think* the audience wants, but often they are working from faulty or misleading data and assumptions. Even so, the content they do produce must take into account the constraints of law, technology, industry structure, organizational structure, market, and the career requirements of industry personnel discussed in earlier chapters.

Afterword: Change Is Now

In this book we have examined the role that the mass media play in society and in our personal lives. We have seen that the production of culture in the mass media is truly interwoven with all levels of our social system, from our legal, political and economic systems to the behavior of media organizations to the individual acts of audience members and culture creators. The mass media both reflect certain aspects of our society and are the creators of that society. Mass media products have meaning, but that meaning is not the same for everyone. And meaning can only come from those products available at any given point in time. That is why understanding the production process, from law to technology to industry and organizational structures to markets and to careers is so important. It is out of this process that the tools are produced for creating the large, complex, postindustrial society we live in and, to some extent, for constructing our very identities.

In the process of exploring the production and the meaning of the mass media, we have attempted to use as many industry examples as possible. But we have also made the point that this is a turbulent time for media industries. It seems as though each day brings news of new technological developments, new mergers and acquisitions, and new legislation affecting production. What is important is not so much these details of which company has the largest market share or the going rate for TV advertising, but the process through which such factors influence what we, as consumers, have available to us. Hang on, change is coming. We hope that this book has helped you to make sense of that change.

References

Adler, Lou. 1996. "Off the air," *Media Studies Journal* vol., no. (Spring/Summer), http://www.mediastudies.org/mediamergers/adler.html

Ahlkvist, Jarl A., and Robert Faulkner. 1997. "Putting records on the air: Programming methodologies in music radio," paper presented at the Annual Meeting of the American Sociological Association, Toronto, Canada, August.

Allen, Chadwick. 1996. "Hero with two faces: The Lone Ranger as treaty discourse," *American Literature: A Journal of Literary History, Criticism, and Bibliography,* September, 68:3, 609–38.

Ashkinaze, Carole. 1997. "'Nothing Sacred' loses four more sponsors," *USA Today,* September 30:3D.

Asia Watch. 1988. "Freedom of expression in the Republic of Korea," August:40–42.

Bach, Steven. 1985. *Final Cut.* New York: William Morrow.

Bagdikian, Ben H. 1985. "The U.S. media: Supermarket or assembly line?" *Journal of Communication* Summer: 97–110.

———. 1997. *The Media Monopoly,* 5th ed. Boston: Beacon Press.

Baker, Russ. 1997. "The squeeze," *Columbia Journalism Review,* September/October: 30–36.

Bandura, Albert. 1994. "Social cognitive theory of mass communication," pp. 61–90 in Jennings Bryant and Dolf Zillman (Eds.), *Media effects.* Hillsdale, NJ: Lawrence Erlbaum Associates.

Bandura, A., D. Ross, and S. Ross. 1963. "Vicarious reinforcement and imitative learning." *Journal of Abnormal and Social Psychology,* 66: 3–11.

Barcus, F. E. 1983. *Images of life on children's television: Sex roles, minorities, and families.* New York: Praeger.

Barr, Tony. 1982. *Acting for the camera.* New York: Harper & Row.

Basow, S. A. 1992. *Gender: Stereotypes and roles,* 3rd. ed. Pacific Grove, CA: Brooks/Cole.

Becker, Howard. 1982. *Art worlds.* Berkeley: University of California Press.

Bendix, Reinhard. 1962. *Max Weber: An intellectual portrait.* Garden City, NY: Anchor Books.

Bennett, William, Daniel Anderson, and Patricia Collins. 1988. *The impact on children's education: Television's influence on cognitive development.*

Berger, Peter L. 1979. *The heretical imperative.* Garden City, NY: Anchor Press.

Berger, Peter, Brigitte Berger, and Hansfried Kellner. 1973. *The homeless mind: Modernization and consciousness.* New York: Vintage Books.

Bielby, Denise D., and William T. Bielby. 1996. "Women and men in film: Gender inequality among writers in a culture industry," *Gender & Society* (June 10), 3:248.

Bielby, William T., and Denise D. Bielby. 1992. "Cumulative versus continuous disadvantage in an unstructured labor market: Gender differences in the careers of television writers," *Work and Occupations* (Nov. 19), 4:366.

Bloom, Allan. 1987. *The closing of the american mind.* New York: Simon and Schuster.

Bogart, Leo. 1995. *The media system and the public interest.* New York: Oxford University Press.

Bowie, James. 1997. "Soundscan: A technology's effect on the music industry," paper presented at the Annual Meeting of the American Sociological Association, Toronto, Canada, August.

Brainard, Tess. 1995. "Superstores zero in on City Lights in S. F. (venerable bookstore in San Francisco, CA, faces competition from nearby Borders and Barnes & Noble bookstores)," *Publishers Weekly* (Oct 16), 242, 42:15.

Brand, Stewart. 1987. *The media lab: Inventing the future at MIT.* New York. Penguin Books.

Broadcasting. 1988. "Carsey-Werner: The little programming engine that did," July 18, 1988 v115 n3 p60(2).

Brody, E. W. 1990. *Communication tomorrow; new audiences; new technologies; new media.* New York: Praeger.

Burgi, Michael. 1997. "Goodwill games: Time Warner to add all its muscle to troubled Turner event for '98," *Mediaweek* July 14 v7:28.

Burnett, Robert. 1992. "The implications of ownership changes on concentration and diversity in the phonogram industry," *Communication Research* 19:749–769.

Burstein, Daniel and David Kline. 1995. *Road warriors: Dreams and nightmares along the information highway.* New York: Dutton.

Center for Media and Public Affairs. 1998. "Number of stories about crime on ABC, CBS, and NBC evening news" (http//:www.cmpa.com/Factoid/Factindex.htm).

Centerwall, Brandon S. 1993. "Our cultural perplexities: television and violent crime," *The Public Interest* 111:56(16).

Chapman, Gabrielle L. 1994. "Attitudes of permissiveness toward premarital, extrmarital, and homosexual relations in the U.S. in the 1980's." Unpublished Thesis, Clemson University.

Chapple, Steve, and Reebee Garofalo. 1977. *Rock 'n' roll is here to pay.* Chicago: Nelson/Hall.

Christopher, Maura. 1985. "How profits shape news companies and the news," *Scholastic Update,* April 26:10.

Cole, Jeffrey. 1996. "The UCLA television violence report 1996." Los Angeles: UCLA Center for Communication Policy.

Coleman, Price. 1997. "Cable's $23 billion-plus year," *Broadcasting & Cable* Feb. 3, V127:20(1).

Comstock, G., and H. Paik. 1991. *Television and the American child.* New York: Academic Press.

Coulson, David C., and Stephen Lacy. 1996. "Journalists' perceptions of how newspaper and broadcast news competition affects newspaper content," *Journalism & Mass Communication Quarterly* 73:354–363.

Crane, Diana. 1987. *The transformation of the avant garde.* Chicago: University of Chicago Press.

Crowe, Bill. 1997. "Advertisers see big guys in little eyes," *Broadcasting & Cable,* July 28, v127 n31 p47(2)

Darlin, Damon. 1996. "Ratings game," *Forbes* v158 n13:226(1).

Davis, D. K., and T. Puckett. 1991. "Mass entertainment and community: Toward a culture-centered paradigm for mass communication research." In S. Deetz, Ed., *Communication Yearbook 15.* Newbury Park, CA: Sage.

De Sola Pool, Ithiel, et al. 1984. *Communications flows; A census in the United States and Japan.* North-Holland, Amsterdam: University of Tokyo Press.

Denisoff, R. Serge. 1986. *Tarnished gold: The record industry revisited.* New Brunswick, CT: Transaction Books.

Dimaggio, Paul, John Evans, and Bethany Bryson. 1996. "Have Americans' social attitudes become more polarized?" *The American Journal of Sociology* 102:690–756.

Downs, P. (1982). "Sex-role stereotyping on prime-time television," *Journal of Genetic Psychology* 138:253–258.

Duncan, Hugh Dalziel. 1968. *Symbols in Society.* New York: Oxford University Press.

Durkheim, Emile. 1965. *The elementary forms of the religious life.* New York: Free Press.

Dusenberry, Phil. 1997. "Today's issue: The challenges of managing creative people," *USA Today,* November 20:4B.

Duvignaud, Jean. 1970. *Change at Shebika.* New York: Pantheon.

Dyson, Esther. 1997. *Release 2.0: A design for living in the digital age.* New York: Broadway Books.

Editor & Publisher. 1997. "1996 daily newspaper sales," January 4:38–47.

Ellul, Jacques. 1970. *The technological society.* New York: Vintage Books.

Entman, Robert. 1989. *Democracy without citizens.* New York: Oxford University Press.

Eron, L. D., L. R. Huesmann, M. M. Lefkowitz, and L. O. Waller. 1972. "Does television cause aggression?" *American Psychologist* 32:237–244.

Ewen, Stuart. 1976. *Captains of consciousness.* New York: McGraw-Hill.

Ewen, Stuart, and Elizabeth Ewen. 1982. *Channels of desire.* New York: McGraw-Hill.

Farber, Jim. 1994. "Is the guitar solo dead?" *Greenville News,* April 22:D1.

Federal Communications Commission (FCC). 1974. *Children's Television Programs: Report and Policy Statement 39 Fed Reg. 39396.*

Felson, Richard B. 1996. "Mass media effects on violent behavior," *Annual Review of Sociology* 22:103–129.

Fine, Gary Alan, Sarah M. Corse, Lori J. Ducharme, Elizabeth West, Paul R. Spickard, Rowena Fong, Marylee C. Taylor, Christopher G. Ellison, Darren E. Sherkat, Robert Tillman, Henry Pontell, Brian Powell, Lala Carr Steelman, Jane D. McLeod, Kevan Edwards, Ellen M. Bradburn, Phyllis Moen, Donna Dempster-McClain, William T. Markham, and Charles Bonjean. 1995. "Nations and novels: Cultural politics and literary use," *Social Forces* v73 n4:1279–1309.

Fornatale, Peter, and Joshua E. Mills. 1980. *Radio in the information age.* Woodstock, NY: Overlook Press.

Freedman, J. L. 1984. "Effect of television violence on aggressiveness," *Psychological Bulletin* 96:227–246.

———. 1986. "Television violence and aggression: A rejoinder," *Psychological Bulletin* 100:372–378.

————. 1988. "Television violence and aggression: What the evidence shows." Pp 144–162 in S. Oskamp (Ed.), *Applied social psychology annual: Televsion as social issue,* Vol. 8. Newbury Park, CA: Sage.

Friedrich-Cofer, L., and A. C. Huston (1986). "Television violence and aggression: The debate continues," *Psychological Bulletin* 100:364–371.

Funkhouser, G. Ray. 1973. "The issues of the sixties: An exploratory study in the dynamics of public opinion," *Public Opinion Quarterly* 66: 942–948, 959.

Gerbner, G., L. Gross, M. Morgan, and N. Signorielli. 1980. "The 'mainstreaming' of America: Violence profile number 11. *Journal of Communication* 30:10–29.

————. 1986. "Television's mean world: Violence profile no. 14–15." Philadephia: The Annenberg School of Communications, University of Pennsylvania.

Giddens, Anthony. 1987. *Social theory and modern sociology.* Cambridge: Polity Press.

Giddens, A. 1989. "The Orthodox and the Emerging Synthesis." In B. Dervin, L. Grossberg, B. J. O'Keefe, and E. Wartella, Eds., *Rethinking communication: Volume 1, Paradigm Issues.* Newbury Park, CA: Sage.

Giles, Jeff, and Ray Sawhill. 1998. "A brand-new chapter," *Newsweek* April 6: 39.

Gitlin, Todd. 1980. *The whole world is watching.* Berkeley: University of California Press.

————. 1983. *Inside prime time.* New York: Pantheon.

Glaberson, W. 1995. " For newsday, cutback is still traumatic," *New York Times* October 2 D1, D12.

Gold, Todd. 1985. "Bill Cosby: The doctor is in." *Saturday Evening Post,* April v257 p42(4).

Goldberg, Morton D., and Jesse M. Feder. 1991. "China's intellectual property legislation," *The China Business Review,* Sept-Oct v18 n5 p8(4).

Griswold, Wendy. 1981. "American character and the American novel," *American Journal of Sociology* 86:740–765.

————. 1987. "The fabrication of meaning: Literary interpretation in the United States, Great Britain and the West Indies, *AJS* 92:1077–1117.

Groebner, Simon Peter. 1997. "Musical chairs," *City Pages* http://www.citypages.com/cp97/cover.cfm

Gubach, Thomas. 1987. "The evolution of the motion picture theater business in the 1980s," *Journal of Communications* Spring:60–77.

Gunther, Marc. 1995. "All in the family," *American Journalism Review,* Oct v17 n8 p36(6).

Hans, Valerie P., and Juliet Dee. 1991. "Media coverage of law," *American Behavioral Scientist* 35:136–149.

Haring, Bruce. 1997. "Digital distribution via Net is music's next wave." *USA Today* Oct 7:10D.

Harré, Rom, and Grant Gillett. 1994. *The Discursive Mind.* Thousand Oaks, CA: Sage.

Hay, J. 1989. "Advertising as a Cultural Text (*Rethinking Message Analysis in a Recombinant Culture*)." In B. Dervin, L. Grossberg, B. J. O'Keefe, and E. Wartella, Eds., *Rethinking Communication: Volume 2, Paradigm Exemplars.* Newbury Park, CA: Sage.

Herzstein, Robert E. 1978. *The war that Hitler won: The most infamous propaganda campaign in history.* New York: Putnam.

Hirsch, Paul. 1980. "The 'scary world' of the nonviewer and other anomalies: A reanalysis of Gerbner et al.'s findings on cultivation analysis," *Communication Research* 7:403–456.

————. 1981. "On not learning from one's mistakes: A reanalysis of Gerbner et al.'s findings on cultivation analysis part II," *Communication Research* 8:3–37.

Horovitz, Bruce. 1997. "Cashing in on kids," *USA Today* December 16:1A–2A.

Hovland, C. I., A. Lumsdaine, and F. Sheffield. 1949. *Experiments in mass communication.* Princeton, NJ: Princeton University Press.

Hubbard, Ruth, and Elijah Wald. 1993. *Exploding the gene myth.* Boston: Beacon.

Hughes, Michael. 1980. "The fruits of cultivation analysis: A reanalysis of some effects of television watching," *Public Opinion Quarterly* 44:287–302.

Jaquet, Janine. 1997a. "Cornering creativity," *The Nation Digital Edition* http://www.the-nation.com March 17.

———. 1997b. "Indies' reservations," *The Nation,* August 25/September 1:10.

Johnson, Peter. 1997a. "CBS's Heyward demotes news vet after Di lapse," *USA Today,* October 8:3D.

———. 1997b. "ABC angers DeGeneres with parental warning," *USA Today* October 9:3D.

———. 1997c. "Taking on TV news," *USA Today,* October 9:1D–2D.

Kapsis, Robert. 1987. "Hollywood Filmmaking and Audience Image." In Sandra Ball-Rokeach and Muriel Cantor, Eds. Media, audience, and social structure. Beverly Hills: Sage, pp. 161–73.

Katz, Richard. 1997. "More commercials than ever in prime, daytime," *Mediaweek,* March 24, v7 n12 p10(2).

Kelly, Kevin, and Paula Parisi. 1997. "Beyond Star Wars: What's next for George Lucas," *Wired Magazine* February:160–166 (210).

Kelly, Kevin. 1995. "Interview with the Luddite," *Wired Magazine* June: 166–168.

Klapper, J. T. 1960. *The effects of mass media research.* New York: Columbia University Bureau of Applied Social Research.

Kline, Stephen. 1995. "The play of the market: On the internationalization of children's culture." *Theory, Culture and Society* 12:103–129.

Kornbluth, Jesse. 1996. "{you make me feel like} A Virtual Woman," *Virtual City* Winter. 57.

Krattenmaker, Thomas G., and Lucas A. Powe, Jr., (1994). *Regulating Broadcast Programming* Cambridge, MA: MIT Press.

Kroll, Jack. 1997. "Wannabes," *Newsweek* July 14:64–66.

Kunkel, Dale. 1998. "Policy battles over defining children's educational television." *The Annals of the American Academy of Political and Social Science* 557:39–54.

Kunkel, Dale, and Julie Canepa. 1994. "Broadcasters' license renewal claims regarding children's educational programming." *Journal of Broadcasting and Electronic Media* 38:397–416.

Larson, Erik. 1992. "Watching Americans watch TV," *The Atlantic Monthly,* March: 66–80.

Lashley, Marilyn. 1992. "Even in public television, ownership changes matter," *Communication Research* 19:770–786.

Lazich, Robert S. (Ed.). 1997. *Market share reporter.* Detroit, MI: Gale Research.

Lerner, Daniel. 1958. *The passing of traditional society.* New York: Free Press.

Lichter, R. S., L. S. Lichter, and S. Rothman. 1991. *What television tells us about our lives.* New York: Prentice-Hall.

———, and D. Amundson. 1987. "Prime-time prejudice: TV's images of blacks and Hispanics," *Public Opinion:* 13–16.

Lieberman, David. 1997a. "Off target?" *USA Today,* December 8:1B, 2B.

———. 1997b. "Consumers to feed growing media appetite," *USA Today,* October 10:3B.

———. 1997c. "McClatchy deal draws criticism," *USA Today,* November 11:2B.

Liebes, Tamar, and Lihu Katz 1993. *The export of meaning: Cross-cultural readings of Dallas.* Cambridge, UK: Polity Press Liebes.

Lopes, Paul. 1992. "Innovation and diversity in the popular music industry, 1969 to 1990," *American Sociological Review* 57:56(16).

Lowery, Shearon A., and Melvin L. DeFleur. 1995. *Milestones in Mass Communications Research,* 3rd ed. White Plains, NY: Longman.

Maney, Kevin. 1995. *Megamedia shakeout: The inside story of the leaders and the losers in the exploding communications industry.* New York: John Wiley and Sons, Inc.

———. 1997. "Infant industry stirs passion and paranoia," *USA Today,* November 14:1B, 2B.

Margolis, Mac. 1996. "In the company of giants," *Media Studies Journal* Spring/Summer, http://www.mediastudies.org/mediamergers/margolis.html

Marin, Rick. 1998. "Jerry seins off," *Newsweek,* January 12:54–57.

Marx, Karl. 1964. *The economic and philosophic manuscripts of 1844.* Dirk J. Struik, Ed. New York: International Publishers.

———, and Friedrich Engels. 1970. *The german ideology,* Part 1. C. J. Arthur, Ed. New York: International Publishers.

Mast, Sharon. 1983. "Working for television: The social organization of TV drama," *Symbolic Interaction* 6:71–83.

Matthews, Martha. 1996. "How public ownership affects publisher autonomy," *Journalism & Mass Communication Quarterly* 73:342–353.

McConnell, Chris. 1995a. "License revocation sought over Stern remarks." *Broadcasting & Cable* Oct 2 125:23(2).

McConnell, Chris. 1995b. "Semantic battle over children's TV; Major differences as to what constitutes 'educational' programming" *Broadcasting & Cable* Oct 30, 125:22(2).

McKean, M., and V. Stone. 1991. "Why stations don't do news," RTNDA *Communicator,* June:22.

McLuhan, Marshall. 1962. *The Gutenberg galaxy.* Toronto: University of Toronto Press.

———. 1964. *Understanding media: The extensions of man.* New York: McGraw-Hill.

———. 1967. *The medium is the message.* New York: Bantam.

McManus, John H. 1995. *Market-driven journalism: Let the citizen beware?* Thousand Oaks, CA: Sage.

McQuail, Denia D. 1994. *Mass communication theory: An introduction.* Thousand Oaks, CA: Sage.

McQuire, William J. 1986. "The myth of massive media impact." Pp. 173–258 in George Comstock (Ed.), *Public communication and behavior, vol. 1.* Orlando, FL: Academic Press.

———. 1989. "Theoretical Foundations of Campaigns." Pp 43–65 in R. E. Rice and C. K. Atkin (Eds.), *Public communication campaigns,* 2nd ed. Newbury Park, CA: Sage.

Mead, George Herbert. 1962. *Mind, self & society.* Chicago: The University of Chicago Press.

Mediaweek, 1997. Sep 15, v7 n34 p8(1).

Meyrowitz, J. 1985. *No sense of place: The impact of the electronic media on social behavior.* New York: Oxford University Press.

Mifflin, Lawrie. 1998. "An increase is seen in the number of violent television programs." *The New York Times* April 17, v147:A14(N),A16(L)col 4.

Miller, Cyndee. 1991. "Mag's research strikes sour note with some singers," *Marketing News,* Sept 2, v25 n18 p11(2).

Miller, Mark Crispin. 1990. *Seeing Through the Movies.* New York: Pantheon.

———. 1997. "The crushing power of big publishing," *The Nation,* March 17:11(7).

Miller v. *California* 413 U.S. 15 (1973), 01

Mitchell, Arnold. 1983. *The nine American lifestyles.* New York: Macmillan.

Moeder, Michael-David. 1996. *A comparative analysis of narrative structure in the prime-time television situation comedy.* Dissertation-Abstracts-International, Ann Arbor, MI (DAI). Aug, 57:2, 498A DAI No.: DA9620222. Degree granting institution: U of Missouri, Columbia, 1994.

Molotch, Harvey. 1970. "Oil in Santa Barbara and power in America," *Sociological Inquiry* 40:131–144.

Morgan, Ted. 1974. "Sharks: The making of a best-seller," *New York Times Magazine,* April 21:8–13.

Motion Picture Association of America. 1997. Press release: "Number of pirate videos seized in 1996 reaches all-time high," February 19.

NBC v. *United States,* 319 U.S. 190 (1943)

Negroponte, Nicholas. 1995. *Being digital.* New York: Vintage Books.

Nisbet, Robert A. 1974. *The sociology of Emile Durkheim.* New York: Oxford University Press.

Norton, Kevin I., Timothy S. Olds, Scott Olive, and Stephen Dank. 1996. "Ken and Barbie at life size," *Sex Roles* 34:287–295.

Okerson, Ann. 1996. "Who owns digital works?" *Scientific American* July:80–84.

Paik, Haejung, and George Comstock. 1994. "The effects of television violence on antisocial behavior: A meta-analysis." *Communications Research* 21(4):516–546.

Pelles, Geraldine. 1963. *Art, artists and society.* Englewood Cliffs, NJ: Prentice-Hall.

Perrow, Charles. 1970. *Organizational analysis: A sociological view.* Monterey, CA: Brooks/Cole.

———. 1984. *Normal accidents.* New York: Basic Books.

Peterson, Richard A. (Ed.) 1976. *The production of culture.* Beverly Hills, CA: Sage.

———. 1993. "The battle for classical music on the air." Pp. 271–286 in Judith H. Balfe (Ed.), *Paying the piper: Causes and consequences of art patronage.* Chicago: University of Illinois Press.

———. 1997. *Creating country music: Fabricating authenticity.* Chicago: University of Chicago Press.

———, and David G. Berger. 1975. "Cycles in symbol production: the case of popular music." *American Sociological Review* 40:158–173.

———, and David G. Berger. 1996. "Measuring industry concentration, diversity and innovation in popular music." *American Sociological Review* 61: 175–179.

———, and John Ryan. 1983. "Success, failure, and anomie in arts and crafts work." Pp. 301–324 in Ida Harper Simpson and Richard L. Simpson (Eds.), *Research in the Sociology of Work,* vol. 2, Greenwich, CT: JAI Press.

———, and Howard G. White. 1979. "The simplex located in art worlds," *Urban Life* 7:411–439.

Petrozello, Donna. 1996. "Diaries going qualitative: Arbitron will include consumer behavior questions in select markets," *Broadcasting & Cable,* Nov 18, v126 n48 p46(1).

Piirto, Rebecca. 1991. "VALS the second time (Second Values and Lifestyles program)," *American Demographics,* July, v13 n7 p6(1).

Ploman, Edward, and L. Clark Hamilton. 1980. *Copyright: Intellectual property in the information age.* London: Routledge and Kegan Paul.

Powers, Stephen, David Rothman, and Stanley Rothman. 1996. *Hollywood's America: Social and political themes in motion pictures.* Boulder, CO: Westview Press.

Prindle, David F., and James W. Endersby. 1993. "Hollywood liberalism," *Social Science Quarterly* 74:136–149.

Puig, Claudia, and Andy Seiler. 1997. "'Amistad' suit just one of many ownership disputes," *USA Today,* December 9:1A,2A.

Rathbun, Elizabeth. 1997. "News/talk still leader," *Broadcasting and Cable* Sept. 8 127:46.

Raymondo, James C., and Horst Stipp. 1997. "Confessions of a Nielsen household," *American Demographics,* March v19 n3 p24(7).

Red Lion Broadcasting v. *FCC* U.S. 86 (1969).

Roberts, Johnnie L. 1997. "Can MGM roar again?" *Newsweek* November 24:53.

Robinson, John, and Geoffrey Godbey. 1997. *Time for life: The surprising ways Americans use their time.* State College, PA: Pennsylvania State University Press.

Rogers, Everett M. 1986. Communication technology: The new media in society. New York: Free Press.

Rojek, Cris. 1985. *Capitalism and leisure theory.* New York: Tavistock.

Rosenberg, Bernard, and Norris Fliegal. 1979. *The vanguard artist.* New York: Arno Press.

Rothenbuhler, Eric W. and John W. Dimmick. 1982. "Popular music: Concentration and diversity in the industry, 1974–1980," *Journal of Communication* 32:143–149.

Rushkoff, Douglas. 1994. *Media virus! Hidden agendas in popular culture.* New York: Ballantine.

Ryan, Bill. 1992. *Making capital from culture.* New York: Walter de Gruyter.

Ryan, John. 1985. *The production of culture in the music industry: The ASCAP-BMI controversy.* Lanham, MD: University Press of America.

———, Kevin Bales, and Michael Hughes. 1988. "Television and adolescent occupational aspirations," *Free Inquiry in Creative Sociology* 16:103–108.

———, Legare Calhoun, and William Wentworth. 1996. "Gender or genre? Emotion models in rap and country music," *Popular Music and Society* 202: 121–153.

———, and Richard A. Peterson. 1982. "The product image: The fate of creativity in country music songwriting." Pp 11–32 in James S. Ettema and D. Charles Whitney (Eds.), *Individuals in mass media organizations: Creativity and constraint.* Beverly Hills, CA: Sage.

———, and Richard A. Peterson. 1993. "Occupational and organizational consequences of the digital revolution in music making," *Current Research in Occupations and Professions* 8:173–201.

———, and Deborah A. Sim. 1990. "When art becomes news," *Social Forces,* 68 (1990):869–890.

———, William Wentworth and Gabrielle Chapman. 1994. "Models of emotions in therapeutic self-help books," *Sociological Sprectrum* 14:241–255.

Sandin, Jessica, and Harry A. Jessell. 1996. "Westinghouse/CBS tops in TV: Newly merged giant reaches the most homes with 14 stations; Tribune ranks second" *Broadcasting and Cable* July 8:12, 7,

Savan, Leslie. 1996. "Your show of shills," *Time,* April 1:70–71.

Schoemer, Karen. 1998. "The world according to Garth." *Newsweek* March 16:66, 68, 70.

Scott, Christina. 1996. "What does it taste like?" *Media Studies Journal,* Spring/Summer, http://www.mediastudies.org/mediamergers/scott.html

Seiler, Andy. 1997. "TV trendsetter Tartikoff dies," *USA Today,* August 28: D1, D2.

Shapiro, T. 1976. *Painters and politics.* New York: Elsevier.

Shaw, Donald L., and Maxwell E. McCombs. 1974. *The emergence of American political issues: The agenda-setting function of the press.* St. Paul, MN: West Publishing.

Shils, Edward. 1959. "Mass society and its culture." Pp. 1–27 in Norman Jacobs (Ed.), *Culture for the millions: Mass media in modern society.* Princeton, NJ: D. Van Nostrand.

Signorielli, N., L. Gross, and M. Morgan. 1982. "Violence in television programs: Ten years later." Pp. 158–173 in D. Pearl and L. Bouthilet and J. Lazar (Eds.), *Television and behavior: Ten years of scientific progress and implications for the eighties: Vol. 1, Technical Reviews.* Washington, DC: Government Printing Office.

Silverstone, Roger. (1994) *Television and everyday life.* London: Routledge.

———. 1995. "Television and everyday life," University of Sussex Professorial Lecture, Univ. of Sussex, May 25th. http://www.sussex.ac.uk/USIS/CULCOM/nexus/rog.htm

Sklar, Robert. 1975. *Movie made america.* New York: Random House.

Snider, Mike. 1997. "Fewer homes on line, study shows," *USA Today,* September 3: D1.

Soloman, Norman. 1997. "Buyout threat looms for public broadcasting," *The Real News Page* http//www.rain.org/~openmind/solomon.htm

Sorkin, Andrew Ross. 1997. "Soundscan makes business of counting hits," *New York Times,* August 11 v146:pC5(N) pD5(L) col 1 (28 col in).

Sorokin, Pitirim. 1957. *Social and cultural dynamics.* Boston: Extended Horizon Books.

Stack, Steven, and Jim Gundlach. 1992. "The effect of country music on suicide," *Social Forces* 71:195–210.

Steinem, Gloria. 1990. "Sex, lies and advertising," *Ms.* July/August :18–28.

Stossel, Scott. 1997. "The man who counts the killings," *Atlantic Monthly,* 279 (5) May:86–104.

Stroman, C. A. 1989. "To be young, male, and black on prime-time television," *Urban Research Review,* 12: 9–10.

The Greenville News. 1997a. "Barnes & Noble faces obscenity indictment." Nov. 24:2A.

The Greenville News. 1997b. "CBS cites hard-news focus for jump in the ratings," December 8: 8B.

The Toronto Star. 1997. "Ottawa must be firm on protecting culture," August 10:F2.

Thomas, Evan, and Peter Annin. 1997. " 'Baby Jessica grows up," *Newsweek,* October 27: 34, 35.

Thomas, Karen. 1997. "Minding kids in the electronic age," *USA Today,* November 20:1D, 2D.

Thompson, James D. 1967. *Organizations in action.* New York: McGraw-Hill.

Tuchman, Gaye, Arlene Kaplan Daniels, and James Benet (Eds). 1978. *Images of women in the mass media.* New York: Oxford University Press.

Tuchman, Maurice. 1965. *The New York School the first generation.* New York: Graphic Society Ltd.

Tucker, Robert C. (ed.). 1970. *The Marx-Engels Reader.* New York: Norton.

Turner, Richard. 1997a. "Of books and bar codes," *Newsweek,* November 24:75.

———. 1997b. "Selling a little net music," *Newsweek,* July 14: 54.

Turow, Joseph. 1997a. *Breaking up America.* Chicago: University of Chicago Press.

———. 1997b. *Media systems in society.* New York: Longman.

USA Today. 1997. "Fiction sells." Sept 3:1D.

U.S. Government. 1970. *Technical report of the commission on obscenity and pornography.* Washington, DC: U.S. Government Printing Office.

Vandewalker, Jim. 1996. "Netway," *Wired Magazine:* 128.

Vines, Stephen. 1996. "A very hard market," *Media Studies Journal,* Spring/Summer, http://www.mediastudies.org/mediamergers/vines.html

Walker, Chip. 1996. "Can TV save the planet?" *American Demographics Magazine,* May: 42–43, 46–48.

Waterman, David. 1991. "A new look at media chains and groups: 1977–1989," *Journal of Broadcasting & Electronic Media* 35:167–178.

Weber, Max. 1958. *From Max Weber: Essays in sociology.* Translated, edited, and with an introduction by H. H. Gerth and C. Wright Mills. New York: Galaxy.

Weiss, Michael J. 1988. *The clustering of America.* New York: Harper & Row.

Wells, Melanie. 1997. "Networks pay when viewers stay away," *USA Today,* October 10:1B–2B.

White, Armond. 1997. "On the charts, off the covers," *The Nation,* August 25/September 1:16–18.

Wiegman, O., M. Kuttschreuter, and B. Baarda. 1992. "A longitudinal study of the effects of television viewing on aggressive and antisocial behaviors," *British Journal of Psychology* 31:147–164.

Wired Magazine. 1997. "Your master's voice: A report from Common Cause," August:45–48, 164.

Wolzien, Tom. 1996. "The big-news business bargain," *Media Studies Journal* Spring/Summer, http://www.mediastudies.org/mediamergers/wolzien.html

Wood, Julia. T. 1993. *Who cares: Women, care and culture.* Carbondale, IL: Southern Illinois University Press.

———. 1994. *Gendered lives.* New York: Wadsworth.

Zimmerman, David. 1997. "In Nashville, a growing sense of struggle for its musical soul," *USA Today,* September 24:5D.

Index